EMERGING TRENDS IN ASSET RECOVERY

GRETTA FENNER ZINKERNAGEL
CHARLES MONTEITH &
PEDRO GOMES PEREIRA
BASEL INSTITUTE ON GOVERNANCE

EMERGING TRENDS IN ASSET RECOVERY

PETER LANG
Bern · Berlin · Bruxelles · Frankfurt am Main · New York · Oxford · Wien

Bibliographic information published by die Deutsche Nationalbibliothek
Die Deutsche Nationalbibliothek lists this publication in the Deutsche Nationalbibliografie; detailed bibliographic data is available on the Internet at ‹http://dnb.d-nb.de›.

British Library Cataloguing-in-Publication Data: A catalogue record for this book is available from The British Library, Great Britain

Library of Congress Cataloging-in-Publication Data

Emerging trends in asset recovery / Gretta Fenner Zinkernagel, Charles Monteith & Pedro Gomes Pereira; Basel Institute on Goverance.
pages cm
„Book was ready to be launched at the 5th Session of the Conference of the States Parties to the United Nations Convention against Corruption in Panama in November 2013" – Acknowledgments.
ISBN 978-3-03-431308-7
1. United Nations Convention against Corruption (2003) 2. Political corruption. 3. Forfeiture.
4. Reparation (Criminal justice) I. Zinkernagel, Gretta Fenner, 1975- editor of compilation.
II. Monteith, Charles, editor of compilation. III. Pereira, Pedro Gomes, editor of compilation.
IV. Basel Institute on Governance, sponsoring body.
K5261.E44 2013
345'.0773–dc23

2013036522

The opinions expressed are solely of the author and do not represent the view of the Basel Institute on Governance.

Cover Design: Eva Rolli, Peter Lang Bern

ISBN 978-3-0343-1308-7 ISBN 978-3-0351-0602-2 eBook

Printed in Hungary

Contents

Emerging trends, good practice

Part 1: Overarching themes

Returning stolen assets

MARK PIETH

Preface: Are we recovering any assets yet?

The publication date of this book marks the fifth anniversary of the ratification of the UN Convention against Corruption (UNCAC), which has put the recovery of stolen assets firmly on the international agenda. It is published seven years into the life of the Basel Institute on Governance's International Centre for Asset Recovery (ICAR), the first and – together with the World Bank / UN Office on Drugs and Crime's Stolen Asset Recovery (StAR) Initiative – still one of only two organisations exclusively dedicated to helping developing countries in recovering stolen assets. We have seen and supported several other international initiatives on asset recovery, including those by the G8 and the G20, the FATF, OECD and many other international players. Have all these laudable efforts made any difference?

It's easy to be pessimistic. Money continues to get stolen, and it gets stolen at a much faster pace than it is being recovered. Asset recovery practitioners still see hurdles more often than easy solutions. Poor people in particular are still suffering far too much under the impact of large-scale corruption, and their frustration has, if anything, grown in recent years.

Yet, I would like to paint a more optimistic picture, and indeed I am proud that with ICAR we could make a small contribution to what I see as a positive trend. Ten years ago, the topic of asset recovery was hardly on the radar. In fact, even the C-word has not been around for much longer than that. Today, as the above-mentioned initiatives illustrate, no serious international initiative or organisation can close its eyes to asset recovery. The fact that people are getting more and more frustrated about the lack of asset recovery is a good sign, as it shows that the pressure is increasing, demand is growing, and awareness raising activities of NGOs and international organisations have paid off.

To get here in so little time has taken the work and concerted efforts of many governments, international organisations, civil society groups and, first and foremost, courageous individuals, many of whom have written in this book and worked with ICAR over the last seven years to help us achieve our mission.

This being said, it is the sad truth that very little money has actually been returned in the last five years since UNCAC has been in place, with some notable exceptions as for example the recent return to Angola and Kazakhstan by the Swiss government or also the return effectuated by Lebanon to Tunisia. This book shows us why, and depicts what needs to be done, urgently, to translate the heightened awareness, the heightened understanding of the need to recover stolen assets, into true action. Here, I would just like to highlight what seem the most critical ones to me:

First, I notice the continuous apathy of some governments to take radical actions. Many hide behind the complexity of legislation, using law to slow down rather than to enable asset recovery, applying the lowest common denominator rather than being bold enough to take radical action, including by trying new legal avenues and introducing innovative new legislation. This ambiguity also applies to the international donor community. While many statements are made, only few developed countries actively support efforts to help developing countries recover stolen assets, despite the immediate and direct impact that asset recovery has on development and poverty.

Second, there are still massive problems with trust – trust between requesting and requested States and trust among concerned State actors, in particular in requesting States when they come out of political turmoil. To this is added the still considerable differences in experience and capacity in both requesting and requested States.

Letting these issues slow down or even bring to a standstill the recovery of stolen assets is scandalous, because the assets are so dearly needed in the concerned countries. I call upon all governments, be they requesting for the return of assets or requested to return these assets, be they in the position of recipient or donor of development aid, to overcome barriers to trust, barriers to political will and legal and financial barriers. Only with this will we be able to capitalise on the current international dynamics and transform it into action.

With ICAR, we remain committed to do our best to help make this happen.

Mark Pieth
President of the Board, Basel Institute on Governance
Professor for Criminal Law and Criminology, University of Basel
Chairman, OECD Working Group on Bribery

Basel July 2013

ANDREW DORNBIERER AND GRETTA FENNER ZINKERNAGEL

Introduction

Each year crime generates an unsettling amount of profit. It would seem that the old adage 'crime doesn't pay' is not always true, at least in a financial sense. A United Nations Office on Drugs and Crime report released in October 2011 estimated that:

> The total amount of criminal proceeds generated in 2009, excluding those derived from tax evasion, may have been approximately USD 2.1 trillion, or 3.6 per cent of [the global] GDP in that year.[1]

Corruption alone accounts for a sizeable chunk of this figure, as it continues to generate billions of dollars in earnings. The amount of public assets stolen from developing and transitional states each year is approximately USD 20-40 billion.[2]

As for the victims of corruption, the damages suffered can be catastrophic. This is particularly the case with corruption in the public sector, in which individuals in public office abuse their powers for their own benefit and at the detriment of the people they are supposed to serve. A frequent example is that of kickbacks paid by corporations to public officials or members of developing state governments in the context of obtaining mining concessions. Another example is the outright theft of public funds through embezzlement and fraud. It should also be noted however that corruption is not limited solely to developing countries, as these examples might at first reading seem to suggest. An estimated EUR 120 billion is stolen through corrupt acts each year throughout the 27 EU member states (with some studies suggest-

1 Available at: www.unodc.org/unodc/en/frontpage/2011/October/illicit-money_-how-much-is-out-there.html.

2 JP Brun, L Gray, C Scott, K Stephenson, Asset Recovery Handbook: A Guide for Practitioners, 2011, the World Bank, p.1

ing that as much as 20 to 25 percent of the value of public contracts is lost to corruption).[3]

Unfortunately, the figures surrounding the recovery of stolen assets barely pale in comparison to the above estimations of the total money stolen. Even if corruption is identified and exposed, victims rarely recover all the assets that have been lost. This is usually because of one simple reason: the assets cannot be found. To benefit from the profits gained through their corrupt activities, criminals will usually need to insert these assets into the international financial system. Consequently, offenders have become exceptionally skilled at laundering their criminally acquired assets through financial channels in order to disguise their original illegitimate origins. It is for this reason that states need to improve their ability to investigate, trace, identify and freeze corrupt assets. This is not only a matter of law enforcement but indeed of prevention, as through effective asset recovery states can deny corrupt individuals from reaping the benefits of their offences and further deter others from committing corrupt acts in the first place.

The aim of this publication is to provide an overview of the present environment of asset recovery. This year marks the 10th anniversary of the United Nations Convention against Corruption (UNCAC), and it is important that the international community takes stock of the developments that have been achieved in the field of asset recovery in the past decade. The predecessor to this publication, '*Recovering Stolen Assets*' (Mark Pieth [ed.], 2008), assessed the progress that was made during the first five years of UNCAC. To compliment this assessment, the current publication aims to provide an overview of the advancements made in the subsequent five years, as well as to discuss areas of asset recovery where challenges remain, and to present some good practices and useful tools developed in recent years by practitioners to help overcome these challenges.

3 Available at: http://euobserver.com/justice/119300.

Road to recovering stolen assets

The first section of the publication primarily discusses some of the most recent major cases and events relating to asset recovery, with a view to ascertaining some of the lessons that have been learnt in the past five years. The first chapters in this section focus chiefly on the so-called Arab Spring and the resulting effect that this shift in political environment has had on asset recovery issues in the region as well as the implications that may arise from it. The chapters note that even though the Arab Spring may have somewhat subsided, it has left a situation of political and judicial uncertainty in many Middle Eastern countries, particularly in Egypt, Syria (where civil war is ongoing at the time of print of this book), Libya, Tunisia and Yemen. The region has experienced a significant political shift, and many institutions in these countries are still far from stable (see: Hottinger). This has significant implications for the recover of stolen assets as cases are further politicised, domestic proceedings are slowed down by bureaucratic uncertainties, and attitudes towards international cooperation remain cautious.

Several significant cases of stolen assets have emerged from the Arab Spring. For instance, ex-Libyan leader Muammar Gaddafi is estimated to have looted between USD 30-80 billion from state coffers, while the former Tunisian president, Zine el-Abidine Ben Ali, is said to have stolen between USD 3-5 billion during his reign.[4] The estimates surrounding the extent of funds stolen by Hosni Mubarak of Egypt are even more uncertain, though no less unnerving, and experts place the amount at anywhere between USD 1-70 billion.

Conversely, the value of the assets frozen by foreign governments to date is disappointingly small, though some steady progress is being made in a few countries, particularly in Switzerland and the United Kingdom. Nonetheless, of the assets stolen by Ben Ali and Mubarak,

4 StAr, Asset Recovery Watch Database, available at: http://star.worldbank.org/corruption-cases/arwcases; The Economist, 'Making a Hash of Finding the Cash', Print Edition, 11 May 2013, available at: www.economist.com/news/international/21577368-why-have-arab-countries-recovered-so-little-money-thought-have-been-nabbed?frsc=dg|a.

less than USD 1 billion has currently been located. Consequently, the initial feeling of hope (specifically in the Egyptian case) that there would be a rapid repatriation of stolen assets following the revolutions has been worn down through consistently frustrating obstacles to asset recovery efforts (see: Saad, Feller, Frey, Shah and Welsh). This gap between (potentially excessive) expectations and the slow pace at which asset recovery, even in the best of cases, proceeds, leads to further political unrest and frustration. In some cases, it has led the concerned authorities to act rashly in an attempt to appease the public, with sometimes negative consequences inflicted on the asset recovery process. The Arab Spring cases demonstrate that there is a definite need for international-based strategies to be improved and utilised to better streamline and coordinate asset recovery processes.

The second set of chapters in this section touch on some of the frustrations faced in financial centres in recent asset recovery experiences. For instance, the Tommy Suharto-related case that has played out in Guernsey illustrates how difficult securing a favourable judgment in a financial hub can be. It particularly highlights the unfortunate existing situation in grand corruption cases whereby those alleged of grand corruption use the rule of law in financial centres (and will abuse prevailing vulnerabilities in legal procedures) to ruthlessly protect assets they stole specifically by ignoring the rule of law in their own countries in the first place (see: Raffray). However, while it is easy to lambast financial centre legal systems for not releasing stolen assets, it is also important to remember that it takes willingness on the part of both the country of origin and the destination financial centre to achieve successful confiscation. Many times the breakdown in the asset recovery process can also be pinpointed to a lack of willingness of countries of origin to supply financial centres with the necessary elements of proof required to commence legal proceedings to confiscate funds (see: Schnebli).

Major stumbling blocks

The second section of the publication discusses in more detail some of these challenges currently faced by asset recovery efforts. Asset recovery is generally an international process of engagement premised on mutual learning, expertise and constructive dialogue. Unfortunately, as it relies heavily on effective communication, even small breakdowns in accurately transferring information can delay, or ultimately undo, the entire process (see: Davies). To make things more complicated, technical hurdles can arise from the intricacies of different money laundering strategies and methods. For instance, the vast majority of grand corruption cases have involved the use of shell companies to disguise assets, and such corporate vehicles continue to substantially hinder the tracing of stolen assets (see: Sharman). In a similar vein, issues surrounding the lack of information regarding beneficial ownership continue to plague law enforcement officers in their efforts to trace assets. More needs to be done by the private sector to maintain accurate records of beneficial owners of assets so as to disempower money launderers (see: Schulz). Additionally, political immunity laws in some jurisdictions go beyond their necessary scope and only serve to facilitate corruption and prevent prosecution of criminal acts by public office holders (see: Marques). Finally, complications arising from the necessary use of mutual legal assistance mechanisms can cause further breakdowns in the asset recovery process, as many developed states still do not provide effective and efficient support to requesting states in democratic transition. They instead operate on an out-dated notion of a relationship based on passivity between requested and requesting states (see: Wyss).

Furthermore, recent experiences of several states have demonstrated how macro-level conflicts of interest can also hamper asset recovery efforts. For instance, questions were raised by civil society groups when the Swiss Financial Market Supervisory Authority (FINMA) failed to hold Swiss banks accountable for their relations with deposed groups and politically exposed persons (PEPs) in the Arab Spring – raising legitimate doubts regarding the level to which money laundering standards are applied to financial intermediaries when overarching political agendas and commercial considerations come into play (see: Longchamp and Herkenrath). Moreover, experiences in developing countries such as Kyrgyzstan (see: Mambetzhanov) and Cote d'Ivoire (see: Förster) have demonstrated how turbulent political histories can hamper current asset recovery efforts. Finally, the situation in Kenya over the past few decades has certainly highlighted the catch-22 situation faced by many African and other developing jurisdictions whereby the process of seeking the return of assets is invariably controlled by the government, and the members of that same government are also the people against whom the recoveries are sought (see: Wachanga).

Emerging trends, good practice

The third section in the publication examines major trends in practice and legislation that have evolved over the past five years regarding the different stages of asset recovery efforts. The first set of chapters in this section provides some general analysis of the overarching asset recovery developments. For instance, the past decade has seen an increase in policy discourse on asset recovery facilitated by UNCAC – and in particularly through the Conference of the States Parties to the Convention and its Open-ended Intergovernmental Working Group on Asset Recovery – and other international policy forums. Consequently, states are continuing to build up institutional and legislative frameworks to facilitate asset recovery processes (see: Vlassis, Gottwald, Won Park). For example, Switzerland is drafting new legislative instruments in an attempt to tackle some of the issues that arose in the context of the Arab Spring cases. This proposed new act on asset recovery would, amongst other things, allow for the proactive freezing of PEPs' funds as a preventative measure to money laundering (see: Adam and Zellweger).

States are also improving their ability to investigate cases of corruption. Law enforcement authorities are learning to draw on an ever-strengthening toolkit of investigative strategies and powers to successfully track and trace illicit funds (see: Monteith). Furthermore, donor agencies are beginning to take a two-way approach when tackling issues of corruption through aid money: rather than only funding (sometimes struggling) anti-corruption programs in developing countries, donor agencies are now starting to look inwards and are using some of their funds to support strategies to return stolen assets located in their own jurisdictions. For instance, the United Kingdom's Department for International Development (DFID) is funding the UK Proceeds of Corruption Unit (POCU). Since the beginning of this program, the POCU, which has required an 'investment' of GBP 5 million in operating costs, has successfully located and frozen over GBP 100 million in stolen assets (see: Mason).

The second set of chapters in this section discusses the emerging good practices regarding the actual tracing and freezing of illicit assets. For instance, financial intelligence units (FIUs) have now been established in a significant number of states and are playing an increasingly valuable role in tracing assets and investigating corruption offences by providing instrumental analysis of financial transactions and important channels for the rapid sharing of information between jurisdictions (see: Thelesklaf and Salihodzic). Additionally, law enforcement bodies are honing their skills to investigate crimes of corruption; in particular they are enhancing their ability to conduct thorough and effective financial investigations, sometimes helped by organisations such as the Basel Institute's International Centre for Asset Recovery (ICAR) or the World Bank / UNODC Stolen Asset Recovery Initiative (StAR). Furthermore, they are increasingly focusing on following the flow of the money, which is going a long way towards establishing links between the origins of the money, the beneficiaries and the underlying criminal activity. This strategy also greatly improves the chances of successful prosecution and eventual confiscation orders (see: Atkinson). Moreover, the increasingly effective implementation of financial disclosure laws is proving to be an important factor in both alerting enforcement authorities to sudden changes in the wealth of individual public office holders and in establishing the required level of evidence to secure corruption-related convictions (see: Messick).

The third set of chapters in this section discusses the freezing and confiscation of illicit assets. For instance, illicit enrichment laws are proving to be quite effective in reducing the potentially hindering procedural and evidential requirements associated with other corruption offences (see: Muzila, Berger, Mathias and Morales). Furthermore, non-conviction based forfeiture is another strategy enforcement authorities are increasingly taking to achieve asset recovery, particularly when it is difficult for prosecutors to establish the criminal offences which initially generated the proceeds of crime (see: Monteith). The same can be said for the use of negotiated resolution agreements (NRAs). The use of NRAs is likely to become a trend in complex cross border foreign bribery cases (see: Solorzano and Pereira). The concept of social damage is an equally new yet not fully explored concept in law enforcement practice, though increasingly nonstate actors and other concerned stakeholders request a comprehensive debate about this matter. The experience of Costa Rica presented in this book (see: Víquez Solís) will be useful to inform this dialogue. Finally, the creative involvement of civil society organisations (CSOs) can also be pivotal in achieving a result, and more CSOs are providing effective support to law enforcement and asset recovery efforts (see: Sanz and Sesé).

Returning stolen assets

The final section explores the developments and challenges in relation to the actual return of stolen assets. Establishing the ownership of funds in foreign jurisdictions can be an arduous task. For instance, Brazilian authorities in the case of Nicolau dos Santos were forced to adopt a 'double way' strategy and lodged both criminal and civil complaints in foreign jurisdictions before funds stolen by dos Santos were officially recognised as belonging to Brazil (see: Soares). Once ownership over funds in foreign jurisdictions is established, further (and somewhat contentious) issues arise surrounding the proper restitution of these funds to their country of origin. For instance, debates exist over the degree to which states in which stolen funds are located can determine the conditions under which money is returned to their state of origin, particularly with regards to ensuring that the returned money is used transparently. While some argue civil society can assist in the monitoring of stolen assets once they have been repatriated to their country of origin (see: Jimu), many states in which stolen funds are located would prefer to attach specific conditions to the restitution of assets to ensure that these funds are used for productive and developmental purposes. While there is no doubt that state sovereignty must be preserved, the proponents of a 'controlled asset return' are concerned about renewed misappropriation of funds and thus lobby for increased transparency in the use of confiscated funds. UNCAC only provides incomplete guidance in this area; however, the experience of Switzerland and some other countries in returning assets to Peru, Nigeria, Kazakhstan and Angola has demonstrated a practical and pragmatic approach to restitution that can be tailored to the specific needs of different cases (see: Fenner Zinkernagel and Attisso).

In conclusion

Overall, this publication presents a multitude of perspectives on the current asset recovery environment. It is hoped that the views of leading experts in this field, combined in this volume, will contribute to stimulating discussions on the best practices in asset recovery procedures and the most effective ways to streamline and improve efforts to return funds stolen through crime, and particularly corruption.

Enhancing efforts to recover stolen assets is the most effective way to curb corruption – it denies criminals the benefits of their acts and effectively removes any motivation for such criminal action in the future.

Due to the international nature of money laundering however, effective asset recovery will not occur without an underlying ethos of cooperation between the concerned authorities of all the states involved. A common metaphor compares an asset recovery case to a puzzle with different pieces in different jurisdictions. Ultimately, to form a complete picture and achieve a result, all the pieces will have to be collected and linked together in their proper place – and this cannot occur without communication and trust between all the relevant jurisdictions. It is hoped that this publication will assist in the movement towards an asset recovery environment based on such principles and encourage the major players in asset recovery to move forward together in combating corruption through effective cooperative strategies.

Contributors

RITA ADAM is Vice-Director of the Directorate of Public International Law (DPIL) at the Swiss Foreign Ministry. She studied law at the University of Berne and holds a degree as an attorney at law. Her previous postings abroad include South Africa and France.

KODJO ATTISSO is a lawyer by training with Bachelor's and Master's degrees in business law and civil law from the Université du Bénin (also known as Université de Lomé), and a Master's degree in Advanced Studies in Economic Crime Investigation from the Institute de Lutte contre la Criminalité Economique in Neuchâtel, Switzerland. He also completed a Certificate of Advanced Studies in Conflict Management from the School for Social Work in Basel, Switzerland. He joined the International Centre for Asset Recovery (ICAR) of the Basel Institute on Governance in 2009 as an Anti-Corruption and Asset Recovery Specialist.

MARCUS DAVIES is a lawyer in the Criminal, Security and Diplomatic Law Division at the Department of Foreign Affairs, Trade and Development Canada (DFATD). His work focuses on international corruption, transnational organised crime, asset recovery, international security and terrorism. Prior to joining DFATD in 2008, Davies worked for the Federal Department of Justice and the Federal Court in Canada, and he has worked abroad in India, Montenegro and Haiti. He holds common and civil law degrees from the University of Ottawa, a Master's degree in international affairs from the Norman Paterson School of International Affairs at Carleton University, and he is currently completing a Master of Laws with Concentration in International Humanitarian and Security Law from the University of Ottawa. Davies is a member of the Law Society of Upper Canada and the Canadian Council on International Law.

ANDREW DORNBIERER is a researcher for the Basel Institute on Governance. A qualified lawyer in Australia, Andrew predominantly works for the Legal & Case Consultancy team within the International

Centre for Asset Recovery (ICAR). Andrew graduated from the University of Western Australia and holds degrees in both law and international relations. He has completed internships at several international NGOs, including the United Nations Crime and Justice Research Institute in Turin, Italy.

URS FELLER is head of Prager Dreifuss' litigation & arbitration group. He acts for international and domestic clients in a variety of disputes before courts and administrative authorities in Switzerland as well as before international arbitration tribunals. He is a member of the executive committee of the International Bar Association's litigation section and also a member of STEP, the Society of Trust and Estate Practitioners.

GRETTA FENNER ZINKERNAGEL is the Managing Director of the Basel Institute on Governance and the Director of ICAR. She is a political scientist by training, and holds an MBA from Curtin University in Australia. From 2000 to 2005, Gretta worked at the Organisation for Economic Co-operation and Development (OECD) managing the ADB/OECD Anti-Corruption Initiative for Asia-Pacific. In the past and still today she advises governments, international organisations and multinational corporations in governance and anti-corruption related topics, development processes and policy design.

MARCEL FREY is a senior member of Prager Dreifuss' litigation and private client team. He represents local and foreign clients in court and arbitration proceedings. He also advises clients with regard to corporate law and enforcement matters. Marcel is regularly involved in mutual legal assistance matters and asset recovery. He is a member of the management committee of the Swiss South African Chamber of Commerce (SwissCham Southern Africa).

PEDRO GOMES PEREIRA is a Senior Asset Recovery Specialist at ICAR. He is a lawyer and a member of the Brazilian Bar Association. He has previously worked in the Brazilian central authority for international cooperation, where he assisted authorities worldwide in coordinating their international strategies to combat organised crime, money laundering and corruption cases. Pedro joined the ICAR in June 2009.

DOROTHEE GOTTWALD is a Crime Prevention and Criminal Justice Officer of the Corruption and Economic Crime Branch of the United Nations Office on Drugs and Crime (UNODC).

MARK HERKENRATH is a Programme Officer for Alliance Sud, the Swiss Coalition of Development Organisations. He holds a Ph.D. in sociology from the University of Zurich, at which he has served as a Senior Lecturer since 2010. He is also a member of the Swiss Federal Council's Advisory Committee on International Development Cooperation.

ARNOLD HOTTINGER is a Swiss journalist and publicist. From 1961 to 1991 he was the correspondent for the Neue Zürcher Zeitung in Beirut where he reported on the Middle East and the Islamic and Arab world. Later, he was a correspondent in Madrid and Nicosia. He worked for many radio stations and wrote for various journals. He has published numerous books on Islam, Arabia and the Middle East, some of which are considered standard literature in their fields.

IGNASIO MALIZANI JIMU received his PhD in social anthropology from the University of Basel. His dissertation focused on the everyday practices and relations in peri-urban land transactions in Malawi. During his doctoral studies, he worked part-time (October 2008–September 2009) as a research assistant at the International Centre for Asset Recovery (ICAR) of the Basel Institute on Governance (BIG). Currently, Ignasio is an associate professor of human geography at Mzuzu University in Malawi. His teaching and research interests are in the areas of economic and environmental geography and rural development studies.

MELIS MAMBETZHANOV is Chairman of the State Financial Intelligence Service of the Kyrgyz Republic.

OLIVIER LONGCHAMP has been Coordinator of the International Finances Program at Berne Declaration since 2009. He holds a PhD in history from the University of Lausanne (Switzerland).

SILVIO ANTONIO MARQUES is a State Prosecutor in São Paulo, Brazil. He holds a Master and a PhD in law from the Pontifícia Católica de São Paulo and is a PhD candidate in law from the Université Paris 1 Panthéon-Sorbonne, France. He is also a member of the Corruption Hunter Network of NORAD, Norway.

PHIL MASON is the Senior Anti-Corruption Adviser at the Department for International Development, the UK's aid agency. He began DFID's anti-corruption work in 2000, and he served on the UK delegation at the negotiations for the UN Convention against Corruption. Since 2010, he has been chair of the OECD Anti-Corruption Task Team.

MARIANNE MATHIAS has a law enforcement background in France (Customs and Financial Intelligence Unit) and she is specialized in financial investigations. She holds a Master Degree in Law from the University Pierre Mendes-France, Grenoble, France. She has worked 6 years with both the Financial Market Integrity Unit and the StAR Initiative at the World Bank before joining the Inter-American Development Bank as an anti-corruption investigator.

RICHARD E. MESSICK consults for development agencies and non-government organizations on rule of law and anti-corruption measures.

CHARLES MONTEITH is Head of Legal and Case Consultancy at the International Centre for Asset Recovery (ICAR). Prior to joining ICAR, he worked as Counsel for White and Case providing advice, strategy and training on corporate compliance and anti-bribery matters. He was also formally Head of Assurance at the UK Serious Fraud Office (SFO) where he was a key architect of the UK Bribery Act and, on the Law Commission's Bill Advisory Group, led the drafting of the Attorney General's guidelines. Charlie has many years' experience in prosecuting serious crime, including high-profile cases.

BONI DE MORAES SOARES is a State Attorney acting currently as the Director of the International Department of the Attorney General's Office of Brazil. From 2007 to 2010, Boni worked at the Department of Asset Recovery and International Legal Cooperation of the Ministry of Justice, in which he was appointed General Coordinator for International Legal Cooperation and later Director. In the past, he participated in several negotiations of bilateral agreements on mutual legal assistance, and today he conducts cases on a wide variety of matters, including international fraud and corruption. He holds a Master's degree in Law of International Relations from University Center of Brasilia.

JI WON PARK is a consultant to the Stolen Asset Recovery Initiative (StAR) of the World Bank and UNODC and the Financial Market Integrity Unit of the World Bank.

MARK PIETH is a professor of criminal law at the University of Basel and President of the Basel Institute on Governance. He has chaired the OECD Working Group on Bribery since 1990 and was appointed by the UN Secretary General to the Independent Inquiry Committee into the Iraq Oil-for-Food Program from 2003–2005. He is a board member of the World Economic Forum Partnering against Corruption Initiative. In autumn 2008, Prof. Pieth was made a member of the Integrity Advisory Board (IAB) of The World Bank Group where he advises the president of the bank and the audit committee on integrity issues. He regularly acts as an advisor to governments and multinational corporations on bribery and integrity matters.

FREDERIC RAFFRAY is a Barrister (England & Wales 1991) and Advocate (Guernsey 2003, Crown 2004). After spending several years in private practice at 17 Bedford Row London (common law with commercial / chancery bias) he joined St. James Chambers in 2000. Since 2007 he has been responsible for mutual legal assistance and international cooperation. In this role he has undertaken significant judicial review litigation (international economic crime and corruption) including appellate work as counsel. He sits on the principal local committees on law enforcement and AML/CFT. In addition he represents Guernsey internationally on criminal cooperation matters. With the Guernsey Border Agency he sits on the Camden Asset Recovery Inter-Agency Network steering group. He has also undertaken both technical assistance and expert roles with, and on behalf of StAR, the UNODC (under the UN Convention against Anti Corruption) and the World Bank. He has degrees in English and French Law from King's College, London and Paris 1 (Sorbonne – Pantheon).

COUNSELLOR AHMED SAAD is a member of the Illicit Gains Department and the Asset Recovery Judicial Committee in Egypt. Since the fall of the Mubarak regime, he has been aiding the efforts to recover the assets misappropriated by Mubarak, his family and other politicians. Counsellor Ahmed Saad has extensive experience in litigation and arbitration and has represented the Arab Republic of Egypt in numerous ICSID proceedings and in cases before the Cairo Regional Centre for International Commercial Arbitration.

AMAR SALIHODZIC is in charge of International Affairs with the Financial Intelligence Unit in Liechtenstein. As a permanent member of the Liechtenstein delegations to both Moneyval (Council of Europe) and the Egmont Group as well as the national AML/CFT Working Group, Mr. Salihodzic`s work focuses on implementing the international standard on AML/CFT domestically. Mr. Salihodzic holds a Master`s degree in International Affairs from the University of St. Gallen.

NURIA GARCÍA SANZ is a lawyer. She has worked for the Human Rights Association of Spain since 2007. Currently, she is working on cases involving corruption and money laundering. In 2006, she provided advice for the Legal Action Center for Human Rights in Guatemala, an organisation that works in the defence of victims of genocide. She has lectured on human rights violations, and she has participated in conducting research and writing articles in the field.

MARIA SCHNEBLI is a Federal Prosecutor and Head of the Competence Centre for International Mutual Legal Assistance at the Office of the Attorney General of Switzerland (OAG). Ms Schnebli graduated from the law studies programme at the University of Zurich in 1992 and obtained an LLM (Master of Law in International Economic Law) from the University of Zurich and the Institute for European Studies in 2002. She was admitted to the Bar of the Canton of Zurich in 1998. She is also a member of the Corruption Hunters Network.

MANUEL OLLÉ SESÉ is a professor of criminal law at the Rey Juan Carlos University in Madrid. He specialises in international criminal law and litigating in international courts. He also is the author of numerous articles and several monographs. He has participated in international missions related to the defence of human rights and the prosecution of international crimes. He was president of the Human Rights Association of Spain between 2004 and 2010.

KAMAL SHAH is the head of Stephenson Harwood's Africa and India Groups and has a leading reputation in relation to advising on disputes in Africa. His experience extends across a wide range of activities particularly on international matters for Governments and Government entities. He was listed in the UK Top 100 Lawyers, a list produced by The Lawyer publication and is cited in the Legal 500, Chambers & Partners and Global Arbitration Review directories in the context of his arbitration work in Africa and India.

JASON SHARMAN is a professor at the Centre for Governance and Public Policy at Griffith University, Australia. His research is focused in particular on the laundering of the proceeds of grand corruption and the beneficial ownership of shell companies. Sharman has earlier carried out consultancy work on these subjects for the FATF, the World Bank, Asian Development Bank and others.

RONALD VÍQUEZ SOLÍS is a lawyer specialised in Criminal Sciences and has over 30 years experience. He works as Prosecutor for Public Ethics in Costa Rica. He has taken over the claim pertaining to the compensation of social damages in criminal cases related to the fight against corruption. He has represented his country before the UN and the OAS as an expert in this matter. Ronald has published on other matters in Criminal Law.

DANIEL THELESKLAF, a lawyer by profession, is the Director of the Liechtenstein Financial Intelligence Unit and Deputy Chairman of Moneyval. After a career in the private sector at Swiss Life and Dresdner Bank, he joined the Swiss Federal Office of Police in 1998 to become the first Director of Switzerland's FIU. In 2002/2003, he led the Due Diligence Unit (the AML regulator) in Liechtenstein and, from 2003 to 2011, he has been a board member of Transparency International, Switzerland. He was engaged in various anti-money laundering, counter-terrorist financing and anti-corruption projects and technical assistance missions for the OECD, the UN, the Council of Europe, the OSCE and the IMF. From 2008 to 2011, he was Director of the Basel Institute on Governance.

DIMITRI VLASSIS is the Chief of the Corruption and Economic Crime Branch of the United Nations Office on Drugs and Crime (UNODC) and Secretary of the Conference of the States Parties to the United Nations Convention against Corruption (UNCAC).

JESSE MWANGI WACHANGA is a native Kenyan. He is working as Project Officer (Capacity Building) for anti-corruption at the UNODC Country Office in Abuja, Nigeria. Previously, he worked for over 10 years as Principal Attorney with the anti-corruption authorities in

Kenya. He holds a Bachelor's degree and a Master's degree of laws, both from the University of London's international programmes.

CHARLOTTE WELSH is an associate in Stephenson Harwood's commercial litigation department. She has acted on a broad range of commercial disputes and has experience in fraud and asset tracing, multi-jurisdictional contractual disputes and contentious financial regulatory work. She is part of Stephenson Harwood's Africa group and has worked on cases concerning disputes in Africa.

RUDOLF WYSS is a lawyer by training and is admitted to the Bar in Switzerland. He has 35 years of experience in Swiss Federal law enforcement, having served with the Federal Office for Police in matters of International Police Cooperation and later investigated cases of illegal dealing in drugs and arms at the Swiss Federal Prosecutor's Office. Before joining the International Centre for Asset Recovery, Rudolf was Head of Mutual Legal Assistance and Extradition in Switzerland and Deputy Director of the Swiss Federal Office of Justice (Federal Ministry of Justice and Police), where he worked from 1996 to his retirement from federal service at the end of 2011. During that time, he had lead responsibility for several historic asset recovery cases, most notably the Marcos case and the Abacha case. Rudolf has furthermore published widely on topics pertaining to international mutual legal assistance in criminal matters. He advises foreign jurisdictions on asset recovery cases, with a particular focus on the MENA region and mutual legal assistance.

VALENTIN ZELLWEGER is the Legal Adviser of the Swiss Foreign Ministry and Head of the Ministry's Directorate of Public International Law (DPIL). He holds a PhD in international law from the University of Basel. As a Swiss diplomat, he represented Switzerland in numerous international negotiations and served in different diplomatic posts abroad.

Basel Institute on Governance
International Centre for Asset Recovery (ICAR)

The Basel Institute on Governance is an independent non-for-profit competence centre specialised in corruption prevention, public and global governance, corporate governance and compliance, anti-money laundering, criminal law enforcement and the recovery of stolen assets. While based in Basel, Switzerland, the Institute's multidisciplinary and international team works around the world with public and private organisations towards its mission of tangibly improving the quality of governance globally.

In 2006, the Basel Institute established the International Centre for Asset Recovery (ICAR) as an in-house hub of expertise to support developing countries around the world in strengthening their capacities to recover stolen assets. For this purpose, ICAR experts train officials in financial investigation and asset tracing techniques, mutual legal assistance and international cooperation in relation to corruption and money laundering cases. ICAR further assists countries by facilitating mutual legal assistance and providing advice to concerned law enforcement authorities in handling specific asset recovery cases. ICAR also provides ICT advisory services and develops IT-based tools, including e-learning programmes, in support of financial investigations and asset recovery.

Basel Institute on Governance
International Centre for Asset Recovery
Steinenring 60, 4051 Basel, Switzerland
Phone +41 61 205 55 11
info@baselgovernance.org
www.baselgovernance.org

GRETTA FENNER ZINKERNAGEL, CHARLES MONTEITH, PEDRO GOMES PEREIRA

Acknowledgements

The Basel Institute and the editors would like to extend their deepest appreciation to all the authors who have contributed to this publication. It is only because of their dedication that this book was ready to be launched at the 5th Session of the Conference of the States Parties to the United Nations Convention against Corruption in Panama in November 2013. The authors in this book bring together rich expertise and unfailing commitment to the cause of recovering stolen assets, and we are grateful to have them as our partners in this endeavour.

Our heartfelt thanks also go to Nina Schild and Andrew Dornbierer from the Basel Institute on Governance, and to Amanda Dooley, freelance editor, for their dedicated work and invaluable support.

Finally, we wish to express our profound appreciation to the Government of Liechtenstein, the Swiss Agency for Development Cooperation (SDC) and the United Kingdom's Department for International Development (DFID). With their funding, the Basel Institute's International Centre for Asset Recovery (ICAR) can continue to support countries from around the world in their efforts to recover stolen assets. And through this, these three countries are making a unique contribution to this cause.

Abbreviations

AC	Anti-Corruption
ACC	Anti-Corruption Commission
AML	Anti-Money Laundering
APDHE	Asociación Pro Derechos Humanos de España
ARINSA	Asset Recovery Inter-Agency Network of Southern Africa
ARIS	Asset Recovery Intelligence System
AUCPCC	African Union Convention on Preventing and Combatting Corruption
BOTA	Kazakh Child and Youth Development Foundation
CARIN	Camden Assets Recovery Inter-Agency Network
CARP	Comprehensive Agrarian Reform Program
CBK	Central Bank of Kenya
CCT	Conditional Cash Transfer
CFT	Counter Terrorist Financing
COMJIB	Conference of Ministers of Justice of Ibero-American Countries
CPS	Crown Prosecution Service
CSOs	Civil Society Organisations
CTRs	Cash Transaction Reports
DFID	United Kingdom's Department for International Development
DLR	Department of Land Reform
DRC	Democratic Republic of Congo
ESW	Egmont Secure Web
EU	European Union
FACFOA	Freezing Assets of Corrupt Foreign Officials Act
FATF	Financial Action Task Force

FCC	Federal Criminal Court (Bellinzona, Switzerland)
FEDADOI	Special National Fund for the Administration of Forfeited Corruption Proceeds
FIS	Guernsey Financial Intelligence Service
FIUs	Financial Intelligence Units
FPO	Federal Prosecutors' Office
FT	Federal Tribunal
GAFISUD	Financial Action Task Force of South America
GDP	Gross Domestic Product
IACAC	Inter-American Convention against Corruption
IAD	Income and Asset Disclosure
ICAR	International Centre for Asset Recovery
ICIC	International Corruption Intelligence Cell
ICRC	International Committee of the Red Cross
IMAC	Swiss Federal Act on Mutual Assistance in Criminal Matters
IREX	International Research & Exchanges
KACA	Kenya Anti-Corruption Authority
KACC	Kenya Anti-Corruption Commission
KYC	Know Your Customer
LEAs	Law Enforcement Agencies
MDBs	Multilateral Development Banks
MDGs	Millennium Development Goals
MENA	Middle East and North Africa
MESICIC	Mechanism for Follow-Up on the Implementation of the Inter-American Convention against Corruption
MLA	Mutual Legal Assistance
MNE	Multinational Enterprises
MROS	Money Laundering Reporting Office Switzerland
NCB	Non-conviction based
NEEDS	Nigeria's National Economic Empowerment Development Strategy

NGO	Non-governmental Organisation
NNSA	Nigerian Network on Stolen Assets
NRA	Negotiated Resolutions Agreements
OACU	Overseas Anti-Corruption Unit
OAS	Organization of American States
ODA	Official Development Assistance
OECD	Organisation for Economic Co-operation and Development
OPM	Oxford Policy Management
PEMFAR	Public Expenditure Management and Financial Accountability Review
PEP	Politically Exposed Person
PFO	Property Freezing Order
POCU	Proceeds of Corruption Unit
RIAA	Restitution of Illicit Assets Act
RRAG	Network for Asset Recovery of the GAFISUD countries
SAG	Swiss Attorney General
SAR	Suspicious Activity Reports
SBA	Swiss Bankers Association
SCC	Swiss Criminal Code
SCCP	Swiss Code of Criminal Procedure
SDC	Swiss Agency for Development and Cooperation
SEPBLAC	Servicio de Prevención de Blanqueo de Capitales
SFO	Serious Fraud Office
SOCA	Serious Organised Crime Agency
SOEs	State-Controlled Enterprises
SPO	Summary Punishment Order
SPOC	Single Point of Contact
SSP	Social Services Program
StAR	Stolen Asset Recovery Initiative
STRs	Suspicious Transaction Reports
TAP	Tuition Assistance Program
TRACK	Tools and Resources for Anti-Corruption Knowledge

UN	United Nations
UNCAC	United Nations Convention against Corruption
UNODC	United Nations Office on Drugs and Crime

Road to recovering stolen assets

Part 1: The Arab spring

ARNOLD HOTTINGER

Two years later: The Arab revolutions in transition

To date the Arab revolutions that swept over Tunisia, Egypt, Yemen, Bahrain, Libya and Syria at the beginning of 2011 have not achieved their goal of a transition from paternalistic, authoritarian state structures to new participatory regimes. The years following 2011 have shown that the transition will take years, at best, and that the possibilities of failure are real.

Since the revolutions the ruling patriarch was ousted in Tunisia, Egypt, Libya and Yemen. In Bahrain the leader has managed to stifle the revolution, at least temporarily. In Syria a civil war has developed, and in Yemen it is a distinct danger. In Libya a foreign intervention derailed an imminent civil war and transformed the conflict into a relatively short, foreign assisted inter-Libyan war.

Much has remained

Even in countries where the ruling patriarchs were removed the building blocks of their power structures remain. The armies, the bureaucracies, the police apparatus, the judiciary, the state media and significant parts of the economic structures, both private and state owned, persist post-revolution. In Tunisia, Egypt and Libya – where elections have been held – new ruling powers have come to the fore. However, it cannot be said that participatory structures (i.e. democratic structures) have been definitely established. Rather, potential new strongmen attempt to found their own authoritarian regimes.

This development is not surprising. The surviving building blocks of the decapitated regimes are structured so that they require an ultimate authority to function. For instance, when the new authorities were elected – albeit legitimately – they needed a strong police apparatus to keep order and to maintain their newly acquired power, especially in the new climate of street contestation. The only police apparatus available was the one leftover from the previous ruler. Although the police force should have been reformed, it was needed immediately, which did not allow time for reorganisation. The police force withheld intervention until it was desperately needed, and thus achieved the goal of retaining the pre-revolution hierarchy of police officers and police generals. Additionally, the judiciary – which was also of the old regime and resistant to reform – helped to protect the police apparatus. Together the police apparatus and the judiciary had collaborated for decades in order to suppress the individuals and powers that were now the newly elected regime.

As a consequence of the prevailing alliance between the police and the judiciary, the personnel of the old police machines remain in place as well as their methods. The police routinely torture confessions out of people with impunity and use these 'confessions' for their own aims. In these instances, the collaboration between the police force and the judiciary is clear, and it serves to illustrate the long-standing link between the two institutions.

Since the Arab Spring it has become evident that the transition of society from authoritarian rule to participatory government will be, at best, a long and difficult process. To be successful, the process will require both the reorganisation of all political and economic structures and a change in the mentality of the rulers, especially in regards to their administrative tools.

It has become apparent also that changes in the political and economic structures and changes in the rulers' mentalities are interdependent. Unreformed political, administrative, judicial, military and economic structures exert pressure on the newly elected heads of the state to conform to the authoritarian, paternalistic model. Likewise, unreformed mentalities of the new rulers tend to confirm and strengthen the instruments of rule inherited from their predecessors. Processes of this kind have been observed in Tunisia and, especially, in Egypt.

Libya, conversely, has been a different story. There the whole state, however idiosyncratic in form under Gaddafi, was toppled. But ironically the process of fighting the old power monolith galvanised new micro-structures that emerged in the form of a myriad of armed fighting groups each ruled by their own paternalistic leaders. The competing factions have now become the main obstacle to building the participatory state structure desired by the overwhelming majority of Libyans.

From demonstrations to civil war

In Syria the youth revolution ended in civil war, and in Yemen the revolution came close to resulting in civil war. These outcomes were the result of splits in the armies that were provoked by the massive street demonstrations, which were meant to be peaceful.

In Syria the army split horizontally. The mostly Sunni soldiers tended to desert when they were ordered by their mostly Alawite superiors and controllers to shoot at the Sunni population.

In Yemen the splits were vertical, between generals and their sections of the armed forces. Each group of soldiers sided with their tribal allies. They adhered to family loyalties to commanders and roused old grudges against one another. Under the pressure of the street demonstrations and the violent suppression by the security men of Ali Abdullah Saleh, the pre-existing fissures in the army split definitely. The ultimate disintegration came after 52 unarmed demonstrators were shot and about 400 wounded by security men stationed on rooftops in Sanaa on 18 March 2011. Similar massacres took place in several provincial capitals.

In both Syria and Yemen the armed forces were under the direct control of the pre-revolution, authoritarian rulers. In Syria, Alawite officers controlled the army and the security services, because the ruling family was a part of the same Alawite minority. In Yemen the son and two nephews of the authoritarian ruler commanded the best-armed army units – the presidential guard and the security apparatus. When the rulers were contested by a wide section of the population, it was the tight association to the person of the president that caused the armed services to split. Libya followed a similar pattern when Benghazi rose against Gaddafi in the second half of February 2011.

Egypt and Tunisia avoided army splits and therefore civil wars, because the armies were not as closely tied to the person of the ruler. In Tunisia the soldiers were distant from Ben Ali, who used the police force as his main tool for control and suppression. In Egypt the army was closer to former President Mubarak than the Tunisian army was to Ben Ali. However, the leading Egyptian officers – albeit after some days of hesitation – opted to drop Mubarak to avoid the risk of splitting the army between the lower ranks who sympathised with the protesting population and their commanders who may have remained loyal to the contested patriarch.

An army owning much of the country

In Egypt the army has strong special interests, because it owns a considerable part of the national economy. The army budget is secret, so the exact amount is unknown. According to some estimates the army could own as much as 40 per cent of the gross national product.

Once President Mubarak fell, the chief interest of the army commanders was to preserve their social and economic privileges and the privileges of the army. With this in mind, the army commanders assumed the management of the transition to 'democracy' once the president was removed. The army also would not sanction a new authority unless he guaranteed the army its privileges. With the help of the judges of the Supreme Constitutional Court, the army managed to dissolve the first parliament, because the majority party, the Muslim Brotherhood, had not agreed to protect the army's privileges or to keep the elected president powerless until he agreed to do the same.

To reach an agreement between the army and the new ruling power, it became necessary to depose of the old leadership of the armed forces. On 12 August 2012, new leading officers were nominated under the auspices of the new commander-in-chief and defence minister, Abdul Fatah Said Hussain Khalil Al-Sissi.

Under the rule of the officers

The struggle between the army and the newly elected Muslim Brotherhood overshadowed the first year of the Egyptian transition to democracy. For this reason, the Brotherhood felt it was urgent to cement their power without associating with other political currents or parties. The Brotherhood feared that their organisation would be marginalised and outlawed – as it had been for most of its 84 years of previous existence – by competing politicians or political entities which might manage to secure the backing of the army. Ironically, rivals of the Brotherhood suspected them of secretly plotting with the army officers and accused them of this offense.

As was the case under Nasser, Sadat and Mubarak, the faction that could obtain the backing of the army would come to dominate civilian politics. This fact undermined the transition to a functioning democracy. A civilian power in collaboration with the absolute power of the army would be expected to subvert democratic change by ignoring or falsifying voting results, which had taken place under the previous regimes.

The role of the street

These were not the only dynamics at play. There had been unprecedented street demonstrations, and they proved capable of effecting real change in the political system. Pressure from the street continued after the falls of Mubarak and Ben Ali. This pressure in itself was a new phenomenon. There had been bread riots in Egypt and Tunisia before, but they died down as soon as bread was made available again. The bread riots were short-lived and apolitical. There had been revolutions against the colonial powers, and in Egypt against a corrupt royal oligarchy, but these revolutions occurred under the direction of the leaders Zaghloul and Nasser. This time the masses where the protagonists. For the first time, the masses revolted against the patriarch without the leadership of another patriarch.

The masses knew they did not want patriarchal regimes, but they did not know how to build the participatory government they desired. There was a belief that elections would bring about democracy. When this did not happen the people claimed that the revolution had been stolen from them. At first, these accusations were directed at the army, because it reigned supreme. Later, the accusations were levelled against President Morsi, 'the new Mubarak', who in August 2012 seized civilian power by allying with the new army leadership.

Pressure from the masses is likely to remain. Segments of Arab society – in particular the growing youth population – seem unwilling to obey the patriarchs. This does not mean that a patriarch will not come back into power; nevertheless, it is unlikely that a patriarch will remain in power for life, as was previously the case.

If this proves to be true, further turbulence must be expected, and perhaps for quite a long time. Thus, the Arab revolutions that started in 2011 can indeed count as a revolution, but not as 'a spring'. The urban Arab youth are unlikely to accept and follow patriarchal leadership and ideological indoctrination as earlier generations have done.

The Brotherhood, patriarchs as well?

And what about the Brotherhood? They won the elections in Egypt and their cousins, the Ennahda Movement, won in Tunisia. The organisations have patriarchs and authoritarian internal organisations and ideologies, but they have promised also to deliver 'democracy and Islam' and 'Islamic democracy'.

There are two considerations regarding their future. The first is that it is highly uncertain that the Brotherhood will win the next elections – if they take place – in Egypt and Tunisia. The Brotherhood's solid organisational structures have allowed them to reach power after a long period of opposition, but their success comes at a time of economic turmoil and social upheaval, neither of which will be resolved easily. Now that the Brotherhood carries the responsibility for what happens in Egypt and Tunisia they are bound to disappoint a wide spectrum of their previous sympathisers and supporters. Even if they can keep intact their core organisations they will probably lose the vote of wide circles of their more occasional partisans.

The second consideration is that inside the Brotherhood and the Ennahda Movement there are young men who want to think for themselves. These men will either change their organisation and its politics, or they will leave it.

The deep split in Arab societies

Will there be further elections and will they be honest? The enemies and opponents of the present day Islamist ruling parties do not trust them. The opposition refuses to believe that the Muslim Brotherhood and the Ennahda Movement will return to the verdict of the urns, except if they intend to falsify the vote in their favour.

But a parallel mistrust exists on the Islamist side. The Islamist ruling parties point to the years of persecution and semi-legality they suffered and also to the fact that the instruments that served to repress them are still present in the economy, the bureaucracy, the police, the judiciary and even the army. If the forces of the old regimes regain power, what would happen to the Islamic parties and their project of 'Islamic democracy'? Without trust that all parties will follow the established rules (except perhaps a few criminals who can be isolated), it is indeed difficult to build a democratic government.

The flags of Islam and of secularism

The difficulty is compounded by the fact that both sides in this contest of mutually distrusting political fronts have amassed themselves behind two flags of great emotional power: Islam and secularism. The secularists are Muslims as well, but they want a modern state that is religiously neutral or nearly so. Meanwhile the Islamists want to merge, to a considerable degree, their version of Islam with the state.

The idea of an Islamic state ignites fears that are mobilised by the secularist front. Large portions of the populations of Tunisia and Egypt see the 'Islamisation' of the state as the beginning of something that will end like the Taliban rule of Afghanistan. However, there are even larger portions of their populations that view Islam as a positive force. Given the fact that the states are in dire need of reform, why not incorporate Islamic law?

Both sides have their ideologues who seek to spread their beliefs. The consequence is that the power struggle between the two rival political fronts has acquired ideological overtones of deep emotionality: Islamists against secularists and their contrasting ideas about the kind of state they desire.

Divisive dynamics

This struggle has a divisive quality. It forces both sides into opposite camps, and it strengthens the extreme factions of these camps. Building a viable democracy, however, requires the opposite condition. It requires the strengthening of the moderate wings of both parties, because these are the forces that can build a collaborative system based on a minimum of shared ground – thus is the indispensable principle of a working democracy.

The deep split between these two opposing factions presents another challenge to the transition to democracy. The rift tends to join all groups in opposition to the new Islamist rule into one secular front. This combines, to a substantial degree, the surviving powers of the previous regime, *les ci-devants*, and the revolutionaries who rose against them. These players tend to become one amalgamation reinforced by street thugs, who remain on the payroll of the old, wealthy ruling classes, and by the more-or-less hidden sympathies of the police officers and their friends in the secret services and the judiciary. In Egypt the football fans also belong to this amalgamation. All of them have turned against Morsi, 'the new Mubarak', under the banner of secularism.

Islamic militias?

The Islamists have been tempted to use their partisans as a militia defending their views on the streets, because the police – theoretically at their command – continues to sympathise with their enemies. The alleged use of Islamic militias has led to the activities of the 'committees for the defence of the revolution' in Tunisia. In Egypt it led to fights between Brotherhood strong-men and anti-Morsi demonstrators. The Islamic militia allegedly captured and tortured some of the secularist anti-Morsi demonstrators. And in Tunisia enemies of the Islamists blame them for the assassination of the politician and human rights lawyer Chokri Belaid.

In both countries mobilisations of irregulars by the Islamist ruling powers has greatly increased indignation and fear among the 'secularist' opposition. The use of militias by the Islamist parties is seen as reinforcing the secularist's worst expectations.

The judiciary and the Islamists

The judges and President Morsi clashed several times and their fight is ongoing. At first Morsi tried to depose of the Prosecutor General, who was nominated by Mubarak, in order to nominate his own candidate. But the judges declared Morsi had no power to do so, and they called a judicial strike against him. Morsi was forced to back down and re-admit the previous Prosecutor General. But later the president managed to impose his will by using a heavy-handed maneuver that cost him a great deal of political support. In a surprise move on 22 November 2012 Morsi declared himself superior to the Supreme Constitutional Court, at least for a period of time. Despite protests by the judges and violent denunciations by his enemies, Morsi used this power to re-impose his own candidate for Prosecutor General and to guarantee that the court could not dissolve the constitutional assembly, where the Brethren had a majority. Morsi's high-handed action of doubtful legality rendered the split between him and his secular enemies, including many of the judges, definite and insuperable.

Later, Morsi used the Brotherhood majority in the constitutional assembly to include a paragraph in the new constitution that reduced the number of judges of the Supreme Constitutional Court. In this way, Morsi forced some of his bitterest enemies to quit their positions. The Court, however, had their revenge when they dealt Morsi a crushing blow by stopping the planned election for a second parliament. They declared the new and emended election law under which the election was to take place unconstitutional.

To Morsi this came as a stunning setback. His strategy was based wholly on obtaining a quick election victory, a functioning parliament and the consequent consolidation of the ruling position of the Brethren. The suspension of the elections hinders Morsi's effort to fulfill, at least in part, his electoral promises. The longer the elections are delayed the worse are Morsi's chances of an electoral victory for his party. Egypt's economy is sinking fast and the people will see the president and his government as responsible for their suffering.

At present, Morsi is engaged in another round with the judges. He has prompted the Egyptian Senate, which acts provisionally in place of the dissolved parliament and is dominated by the Brotherhood and their allies, to formulate a new law ordering the tribunals. This reduces the age of retirement of the judges to 60 years. If it is enacted many of the most outstanding enemies of the Brotherhood in the tribunals will be forced to retire. The judges, however, have declared that the Senate in its current provisional capacity can only promulgate laws of immediate urgency. The judges argue that the proposed law concerning the tribunals is not urgent. Here the matter rests for the time being.

Throughout these contestations the high judges of the Supreme Constitutional Court proved themselves, at least in the eyes of the Brotherhood, to be the clear enemies of their political prosperity. Apart from the questions of sharia and man-made law, the judges have to fear that the Brotherhood will try to replace them with their own people – if ever they obtain the power to do so.

Even if the judiciary appears to be independent and uninvolved in state affairs, it is doubtful that the relationship between the president and the highest judges of Egypt can be repaired. This hostile relationship might well have an influence on the questions of recovering and repatriating supposedly illicit gains procured by dignitaries of the previous regime – the regime to which the judges used to belong and which has been superseded, though only partially and provisionally, by their previous victims and enemies.

Appendix, 19 August 2013

On 30 June, the Egyptian revolution took a new turn. The army decided that it would no longer continue to co-exist with President Morsi. The commanding officer, General as-Sissi, deposed the president and imprisoned him in an unknown location. The officers took advantage of the growing unpopularity of Morsi. He was accused by ever widening circles of 'secularists' in the Egyptian population of governing only in the interest of the Muslim Brethren, not in the interest of the country as a whole. His enemies feared that his party would ignore future election results or falsify them in their favour.

In the months before 30 June, the one-year anniversary of Morsi's rule, a group calling itself *tamarrod*, meaning rebellion, had begun collecting signatures for a mass petition postulating an immediate plebiscite for or against Morsi. Their declared aim was to obtain 15 million signatures by 30 June. When they had collected about 2 million signatures the army officers, as well as the Copts, influential bureaucrats and rich enemies of the Brethren, began taking an interest in the initiative and helped them achieve their goal. The group claimed that by 30 June they had obtained 22 million signatures for their petition. The enemies of Morsi organised a large demonstration on Tahrir Square on 30 June and the army officers claimed that the demonstration was a mandate by the people to depose the elected president. They gave Morsi 24 hours to come to an agreement with his enemies. He refused, and they deposed him on 3 July. The officers abolished the constitution, which had been ratified under Morsi but was strongly disliked by the 'secular' opposition, deposed the government and installed a new civilian government under the economist Hazem Beblawi. They nominated a new interim president, Adli Mansour, who was a previous president of the Supreme Constitutional Court. General as-Sissi, the commander of the army, became minister of defence and vice-prime minister of the new government. They proposed a new 'road map' towards democracy with a revised constitution and elections for a new parliament and presidency within six months.

In response, the Muslim Brotherhood mobilised their mass support to resist the new order. They built large protest camps on two squares in Cairo and protested all over the country. They vowed to continue protesting, without violence, they said, until Morsi was reinstated. The army officers and their government tolerated these protests at first. Attempts were made to reconcile with the Brethren. International intermediaries also stepped in; but all was to no avail. Finally, on 14 August, the officers and their government decided to clear the protest sites. The sites were cleared, but at the expense of much bloodshed. The numbers are unclear, but officials have admitted to over 600 dead on that day alone. The Brethren claim the death toll to be at least 2000. The Brethren continued their protest in the following days, and the police backed by the army killed more people every day. Some factions from the Brethren also used fire-arms against the police, which endured 43 mortal casualties. In southern Egypt, the Copts became victims of the indignant Brethren. They were accused of conspiring with the army against Morsi's regime and many of their churches were burned. The new regime declared a state of emergency and a nightly curfew. The hated and feared Mubarak-era political police, which had been abolished by the revolution, was reintroduced. General As-Sissi became the hero of the Egyptian 'secularists'.

The split that divided Egyptian society since the election of Morsi grew deeper. There were manifestations of bitter hatred on both sides of the population, but the 'secularist' portion proved to be more numerous than the 'Islamist' portion. However, the growing 'secularist' segment of the population was to a great extent the result of the worsening economic situation. Price increases, a shortage of petrol and cooking gas, and a lack of jobs during the Morsi months caused many people to support his enemies. Despite these hardships, however, the Brethren maintained the loyalty of considerable masses of dedicated followers and activists willing to sacrifice their lives for their convictions and ideology.

One can expect that the economy will play a leading role in the unfolding of events in medium-term future. In the short-term future, the military, the police and the bureaucracy of the Mubarak period will probably dominate, because these factions have the means of coercion. Most likely there will be even more bloodshed. A campaign to arrest the leaders of the Brethren is on its way.

But if the economy cannot be turned around, the masses that came out against Morsi will turn against any government, be it elected or nominated by the army. The new regime has managed to obtain large sums of cash from Saudi Arabia, Kuwait and the Emirates. These counties feared the Brethren, and they welcomed the coup against them. However, their billions of dollars of aid (said to total USD 11 or 12 billion) cannot last for more than six months. The economy cannot return to growth if there is turmoil in Egypt. Under such circumstances, the state will not be able to maintain the heavy subsidies for bread, petrol and gas that it still pays today. This could well mean hunger and hunger riots in many parts of the country. The Egyptians have learned to protest in the streets, and they will use this instrument again when their economic situation grows desperate.

In Tunisia, the split between Islamists and secularists has led to a blockage as well. But the army has not intervened and imposed its own solution. For this reason, in Tunisia, the two opposing camps continue to negotiate, albeit with increasing bitterness, but also without coming to a compromise.

It was the second of two political murders committed against 'secularist' politician Mohamed Brahmi on 26 July that brought things to a crisis. (The preceding assassination of Chokri Belaid on 6 February 2013 had already led to a political crisis that was eventually resolved by the dissolution of the government and the formation of a succeeding one.) The numerous opposing parties from the centre and the left joined together for the common cause of demanding the dissolution not only of the government but also of the elected National Constitutional Assembly, which acted as the government and as a provisional parliament. The opposition forces also had the help of the powerful union UGTT. The reason the opposition gave for its demand to dissolve the elected assembly was that the assembly had been elected for only one year but had stayed in session for over two years, because the elaboration of the new constitution had made slow progress. The constitution is still not complete, because of the opposing positions of the Islamist majority and the secularist minority in the assembly. Decisions have to be taken with a two-third majority, and the Islamists can rarely muster sufficient numbers to impose their will.

While the Islamists were willing to recompose the government, they refused to dissolve the assembly. The secularist liberal and left alliance decided to boycott the assembly by refusing to participate. If they had retired from the assembly, they would have been replaced. Gradually, 62 deputies demonstrated in front of the assembly instead of participating in its labours. There were counter-demonstrations on the part of the friends of Ennahda. Notwithstanding the demonstrations in front of the building where the sessions took place, the Ennahda majority could have finished the constitutional proposal according to its wishes, but it wisely hesitated to continue imposing its partial views on the project. One of the coalition parties, the Congress for the Republic, did not leave the assembly, but they declared that in the absence of an opposition it could not continue to work. In the end, the assembly was closed provisionally until the two opposing sides can agree on the next steps. So far, they remain blocked over the question of the dissolution of the assembly.

The Tunisian population is losing patience with its politicians. It wants the politicians to take practical steps towards improving the economy and creating jobs. Instead, what the population sees is an assembly in permanent strife over doctrinal issues and positions of power. The population suspects the politicians of prolonging their meaningless activities for the sake of their attractive salaries, which they voted on themselves. As it was in Egypt in the case of the Bretheren, it is the ruling party, Ennahda, in Tunisia that receives most of the blame for the lack of economic progress. Ennahda is also blamed for the two political murders and for the general insecurity in the streets. The enemies of Ennahda say that even if they did not encourage the murders, they have not persecuted them with sufficient force. The events in Egypt have encouraged the secularist opposition in Tunisia. There is even a *tamarrod* movement that was founded in imitation of of the Egyptian one.

Counsellor Ahmed Saad[1], Urs Feller and Marcel Frey[2], Kamal Shah and Charlotte Welsh[3]

Recovering stolen assets: The Egyptian perspective

Background*

Following the upheaval of early 2011, the Egyptian people began the challenging task of breaking with the past and choosing new national leaders. State institutions, already challenged in their daily efforts, were faced with their hardest test yet.

In 2012, Egypt completed its first free election in the nation's history. Until it was declared a republic, Egypt was a monarchy from 1805–1953. Before the election of President Mohamed Morsi in 2012, Egypt had four other presidents: Muhammad Najib, Gamal Abdel Nasser, Anwar Sadat and Hosni Mubarak. The elections during their presidencies cannot be considered free. Therefore, the election procedure in Egypt, which is in a state of transition, was one of the first steps in recognising and respecting the rule of law and democracy.

The elections in Egypt in 2012 took place a year after the revolution and were an important move towards furthering democracy. Despite reports that the parliamentary elections in 2012 were overturned by the judiciary because of formal reasons, two important elements were demonstrated: i) the election procedure was perceived by the media and the political parties as fair and transparent, which was a significant achievement and ii) the judiciary was functioning inde-

* The manuscript of this chapter was completed in May 2013 and therefore only reflects events in Egypt up until then.

1 Member of the Illicit Gains Department and the Asset Recovery Judicial Committee (Arab Republic of Egypt).

2 Prager Dreifuss Ltd (Switzerland).

3 Stephenson Harwood LLP (United Kingdom).

pendently of political pressures. The independence of the judiciary remains a cornerstone in Egyptian society, and the commitment of the Egyptian people to have free parliamentary elections repeated is unimpaired.

In December 2012, a further step in Egypt's road to democracy was taken with the approval of a new draft constitution by an overwhelming 64 percent of voters. The new constitution goes further than the old constitution in several areas by protecting the rights and freedoms of the Egyptian people.

Whilst looking to the future with hopeful eyes, the Egyptian people also expect former members of the ruling elite to account for their behaviour, particularly for gains they made illegally thanks to their position of power and proximity to the former president, Hosni Mubarak. Assets obtained illegally and frozen by foreign jurisdictions need to be returned to Egypt for the benefit of the Egyptian people.

Assets frozen

Broad feelings of disappointment and anger towards the ruling elite whose wealth seemed to have been amassed at the expense of the electorate ignited the Arab Spring. The revolution in the streets of Tunisia, and shortly thereafter in Egypt, had major consequences abroad.

After the uprising in Egypt, a worldwide effort to trace and recover assets misappropriated by Hosni Mubarak, his family and prominent politicians and businessmen began in earnest. Currently, this asset tracing investigation is one of the largest ever, and it requires the dedication and cooperation of many institutions and authorities at the political, judicial, legal, technical and intelligence levels. Unravelling over 30 years of looting by prominent Egyptians is a mammoth task.

In early February 2011, the Swiss Federal Council led the way for the international community by freezing the assets of the former president and persons close to him within hours of Hosni Mubarak stepping down. This action set the platform for the process of asset recovery that was to follow. Shortly after freezing the assets, the Swiss government confirmed that approximately CHF 410 million (approximately USD 420 million) was frozen in Switzerland. At a later stage, the published amount increased to approximately CHF 700 million (approximately USD 720 million) based on further investigations. Approximately USD 1 billion worth of assets have been frozen globally.

On 21 March 2011, the European Union showed its support for Egypt and implemented legislation to freeze the assets of 19 Egyptian individuals by way of EU Council Decision 2011/172/CFSP of 21 March 2011 (the 'Decision') and EU Council Regulation (EU) No 270/2011 of 21 March 2011 (the 'Regulation'). The Decision was extended twice and is currently due to expire on 22 March 2014. The United Kingdom implemented the Regulation by passing the Egypt (Asset-Freezing) Regulations 2011 on 22 March 2011. In total, the United Kingdom has frozen GBP 85 million (approximately USD 130 million).

Similar legislation to freeze assets was implemented in a number of other countries and territories, including Liechtenstein, Canada, the British Overseas Territories, Jersey, Guernsey and the Isle of Man. Egypt's efforts to freeze and ultimately repatriate stolen assets back to its people have extended to other countries, including France, Spain, Liechtenstein, Cyprus, Hong Kong and the British Virgin Islands. Additionally, efforts are underway in other countries, which for confidentiality reasons cannot be disclosed.

Steps undertaken

The rest of this chapter focuses mainly on Switzerland's efforts to recover the stolen Egyptian assets, because Switzerland is the jurisdiction where the majority of assets are currently located.

In Switzerland, it is understood that the Money Laundering Reporting Office Switzerland (MROS) receives notifications of suspicious activity reports from Swiss financial institutions. In the event that these reports appear to be linked to money laundering activities, MROS forwards the reports to law enforcement agencies in Switzerland so they can review the matter.

In the case of Egypt, suspicious activity reports attracted the attention of the Swiss authorities, which led the Swiss Attorney General to begin criminal investigations into a number of key Egyptian individuals. Considering that the former president of Egypt comes from a humble background and bearing in mind that his official state salary as head of state amounted to less than USD 2,000 per month, and seeing that the ministers earned less than the former president, it was clear that these large sums of money could not have been accumulated legitimately.

Shortly after the upheaval in February 2011, Egypt issued a number of requests for mutual legal assistance addressed to various countries, including Switzerland. Some of the initial requests did not comply fully with local requirements and formalities. These requests were subsequently improved. In other cases, new requests for mutual legal assistance were issued following new findings and evidence in Egypt, and it seems likely that further requests from Egypt will follow.

Furthermore, Egypt applied to become a party in the criminal investigations in Switzerland on the basis that the State could have been harmed by the suspected crimes committed by the accused since crimes of corruption are usually to the detriment of the State and its public funds. The Swiss Attorney General approved Egypt's application, but the decision was appealed by a number of undisclosed respondents who are under investigation in Switzerland. The Federal Criminal Court eventually rejected the appeals, and the status of Egypt as a criminal complainant was confirmed.

Access to the criminal file is usually one of the rights accorded to a criminal complainant enjoying party status in proceedings. However, in December 2012 the Swiss Federal Criminal Court temporarily suspended Egypt's request for access to the criminal investigation file until more stability within the Egyptian institutions could be achieved.

In Egypt, as the investigations into illicit gains and other criminal activities progressed, they revealed that there was a close-knit group of individuals surrounding the former president and his family. As a result of these revelations, officials suspected and found evidence that these individuals had also obtained illicit gains. Based on these findings, Egypt applied for an extension of the Federal Council's freezing ordinance. Originally, the list of names of persons affected by the executive order to freeze all assets in Switzerland was first passed in February 2011 and contained 14 names. On 4 September 2012, the executive order was extended to include an additional 17 individuals. Some of the added individuals were already mentioned on a comparable list compiled by the EU Council, which included 19 individuals.

Repatriation of illicit gains as a joint endeavour between countries

The task of repatriating illicit gains has presented the Egyptian authorities with many new challenges, both nationally and internationally. The complexities of both the efforts to repatriate the assets and the various local laws and statutory requirements in a number of jurisdictions have become more apparent since the asset tracing investigations began after the revolution in 2011. A barrage of legal obstacles confronts the Egyptian authorities and hinders the return of assets worth millions of US dollars that are frozen around the world.

The Egyptian Public Prosecutors working on the ground often find it difficult to lead investigations against accused individuals who have enormous reserves of money in sophisticated off-shore financial structures and who have the resources to instruct highly paid legal counsel and other advisors.

In addition to the Egyptian Public Prosecution Department, there are many other Egyptian authorities dealing with the asset recovery process, including the Illicit Gains Department, the Egyptian courts and judiciary, the Asset Recovery Judicial Committee, the Department for International Cooperation at the Ministry of Justice, the Ministry of Foreign Affairs and the Egyptian Financial Intelligence Unit. All of these authorities require the continued support of the international community to recover assets misappropriated by the former regime.

Unequal arms

According to the Swiss Federal Council's freezing ordinance all financial intermediaries holding assets belonging to the persons in the schedule of the ordinance are required to inform a special branch of the Swiss government about the assets. This information, including for example the owners of the assets and the location of these assets, was submitted to the Swiss government and remains undisclosed. As of this time, the information is not available to the Egyptian authorities or their counsel. A similar situation exists in the United Kingdom where little is known about the assets that have been frozen.

The European Council took the same approach when implementing the freeze of assets pursuant to the Regulation. However, the European Council has since realised that merely freezing the assets is of little benefit to the requesting State, because it delays or even avoids an investigation into the source of the funds. Rather, the standard route to obtaining evidence of the origin of assets is by means of requests for mutual legal assistance. This is a cumbersome and slow path. It requires, for example, detailed knowledge of the accused's foreign bank account details. This knowledge is not easily obtained in a country like Egypt that is in a state of transition and where authorities sometimes struggle to maintain law and order in the streets. It is clear that in these situations sophisticated means of investigation are not always available.

The EU Council has thus amended the Regulation. It now permits EU Member States to introduce legislation that entitles them to share information on frozen assets with the Egyptian authorities and other Member States 'where necessary for the purpose of assisting the recovery of misappropriated assets'.[4] To date a similar step has not been undertaken by Switzerland. It remains to be seen how useful the amendment to the Regulation will be in the exchange of information between Egyptian authorities and EU Member States, because little concrete information is known about which assets belonging to the 19 individuals that are subject to the EU freezing order have been frozen.

4 Council Regulation (EU) No 1099/2012 of 26 November 2012 amending Regulation (EU) No 270/2011.

To allow for a speedy and effective investigation into the legitimacy of the funds' source a proactive approach and the disclosure of information pertaining to the assets under the freezing ordinances are needed. No party involved, neither the former members of the regime nor Egypt, has any interest in delaying a thorough investigation to establish the origin of the frozen assets.

As a first step, disclosing information obtained under the various national freezing orders to the competent Egyptian authorities would allow the authorities to prepare meaningful requests for mutual legal assistance and also allow them to embark on the question of whether the frozen assets were obtained legitimately. Disclosing this information would enable the prosecuting authorities, in many cases, to bring to trial upon well-founded suspicions former regime members. In cases in which suspicions cannot be confirmed, the authorities could release the frozen funds in so far as they concern the particular individual.

Interaction between criminal proceedings and mutual legal assistance requests

In Switzerland, the courts have ruled that when local Swiss criminal investigations are pending at the same time as a requesting State has submitted requests for mutual legal assistance the two parallel proceedings need to be treated with care and coordination. Granting file access to a requesting State in the criminal investigation could potentially interfere with the purpose of obtaining evidence in the mutual legal assistance proceedings.

So as not to prejudice the outcome of the pending proceedings regarding mutual legal assistance in criminal matters, a requesting State that has applied to take part in the national criminal investigation is, in practical terms, hindered to a great degree from enjoying its rights as a party to that investigation.

When access to the criminal file is granted, the Swiss Criminal Court requires that the requesting State copy by hand information from the Attorney General's investigation files. In addition, the requesting State may only use this information in other foreign jurisdictions and not in any proceedings – be they criminal, private or administrative – in the actual requesting State. Subsequently, in order for the requesting State to obtain the necessary evidence via official route, the information must be introduced into formal requests for mutual legal assistance addressed to Switzerland.

In its judgment of December 2012 the Federal Criminal Court found that because of the unstable nature of some aspects of Egyptian politics, the representatives from Egypt would not be permitted to access the Attorney General's prosecution file despite the fact that the Egyptian State guaranteed in writing to uphold all the requirements established in earlier cases.

It is obvious that a State like Egypt that is in a transitional phrase is faced with a number of obstacles and challenges associated with tracing, freezing and recovering misappropriated assets. In other cases, such as Tunisia, there may be developments in different directions. The recent turmoil in Tunisia that led to the murder of the opposition leader Mr Chokri Belaid on 6 February 2013 is by no means less dramatic than the events in Egypt. Additionally, in the cases of States undergoing transition, it would be fair and reasonable to not give too much credit to certain incidents used by politicians to further their own agenda. Rather it would be more beneficial to look at the broader picture of development in the country. States that are undertaking reconstruction, such as Egypt, should not be barred access to the criminal file. Instead, like Tunisia, they should be granted access.

Solutions to current problems

Forming an international task force aimed at assisting the countries affected by and suffering from the corruption of their former heads of state could be a solution to the challenges Egypt faces in its attempts to repatriate stolen assets. This proposal would require the conclusion of an international treaty that would facilitate a task force with well-equipped and sophisticated teams available to secure the financial evidence in a state of turmoil. At the approval of the requesting State such a team would work with and alongside local police, prosecutors and financial institutions. Often time today countries undergoing transition, such as Egypt, can only slowly build-up such know-how and resources. However, the passing of time poses a serious threat to the chances of securing convictions against parties accused of having misappropriated State funds. Money once siphoned from the State can quickly dissipate, and national borders are no longer barriers in today's connected international financial markets.

In addition, the sharing of intelligence between different agencies in a more transparent manner would assist the Egyptian authorities, and the authorities from other States in transition, to pursue investigations to recover misappropriated assets more effectively. The amendment to the EU Regulation is also a step in the right direction, because it encourages the sharing of information about frozen assets between the Egyptian authorities and EU Member States. However, more needs to be done to ensure that this legislation is effective so that information is shared more freely.

Furthermore, the introduction of additional legislation could assist the asset recovery process. In Switzerland, a new bill has recently been proposed by the Federal Council, which would enact the previous practice of recovering assets. The proposal also provides for new instruments to assist the concerned jurisdictions in the asset recovery process.

The most effective way to secure the return of assets to Egypt is by using a combination of legal means, intelligence sharing between various countries' financial intelligence units, diplomatic means and the passing of information between governments by way of requests for mutual legal assistance.

Conclusion

After the wave of enthusiasm and positive expectation that stolen money would soon be transferred back to the Egyptian people, there is now increased awareness of the various obstacles and challenges to the asset recovery process.

Investigations in various jurisdictions against accused individuals are proceeding and progress is being made. The political will and the commitment of the Public Prosecutors in Egypt to the promise of returning illicit gains to the country's people are unshaken. The Egyptian authorities and representatives intend to intensify their collaboration with other countries, and they welcome assistance offered in this regard.

Road to recovering stolen assets

Part 2: Practice in financial centres

FREDERIC RAFFRAY

The rule of law and 'Tommy Suharto' – son of (former) President Suharto

Introduction

> In July 2001, Judge Syafiuddin Kartasasmita, who had sentenced Hutomo Mandala Putra (known as TS) to 18 months in prison [for corruption] and fined him, IDR 30.6 billion on 22 September 2000[1] was shot dead in broad daylight in central Jakarta as he drove to work whilst TS was on the run following the conviction.
> On 20 November 2001, barely 3 months after the murder of Judge, the Supreme Court verdict of corruption against TS was quashed.
> At the opening of the murder trial the prosecution alleged that TS had paid two men USD 10,000 to carry out the killing and had personally given them the weapons…
> Prosecutors also said TS had initially planned to carry out the murder himself but had changed his mind.
> Prosecutors alleged that TS visited Judge Kartasasmita in November 2000 and asked why he had been convicted. [It was also alleged by the Judge's wife that before the trial for corruption TS had attempted to bribe the Judge].
> According to the prosecution charge sheet, which was read out in court, Kartasasmita told TS to seek a pardon from then-president Abdurrahman Wahid. TS is then alleged to have told the judge: 'Sir, if someone is nice to me, I can be nice to him in return but if he is mean I can do worse than what he does to me.'
> 'Our correspondent in Jakarta says the atmosphere was electric. No-one had ever imagined this case would come before the courts, such is the continuing power and wealth of the Suharto family'[2].

In July 2002, TS was convicted of murder of the Judge and sentenced to 15 years imprisonment, reduced to 10 years on appeal. In October 2006, after 4 years in prison, he was conditionally released. Since the

1 The Supreme Court of Indonesia in what was known as the 'Goro' case.

2 The BBC's correspondent in Jakarta, Richard Galpin, Thursday 21st March, 2002, 11.55 GMT BBC ONLINE

conviction for corruption was quashed, TS has not faced criminal proceedings for corruption or related charges in Indonesia or elsewhere.

Some 9 years later, in May 2011, Indonesia's court system awarded the convicted murderer IDR 12.5 billion (approximately USD 1.46 million) from a magazine that called him a convicted murderer.[3] From a layman's perspective that decision was remarkable – as he had not been acquitted of murder on appeal and had served a prison sentence for the crime.

The fates of the Bailiwick of Guernsey[4] and the Republic of Indonesia ('Indonesia') had also already become inextricably intertwined as of May 2011 in both civil private law (commenced in 2006) and public law proceedings (commenced in October 2009) involving Garnet (BVI) Limited ('Garnet'). TS accepted this company was (i) beneficially owned by him; (ii) the recipient of the proceeds of the sale of his shares in Lamborghini SA in 1998; and (iii) held those proceeds in its bank account with BNP Paribas in Guernsey (also opened in 1998).

In the context of the public law proceedings the Privy Council[5],

3 Asia Sentinel 25th May 2011.

4 The Bailiwick of Guernsey comprises of the Islands of Guernsey, Alderney and Sark. The UK is responsible for the Bailiwick's defence and representation in relation to foreign affairs, but otherwise the Islands are independent jurisdictions, governed by their own 'Parliaments', the States of Deliberation (for Guernsey), which legislate for all internal matters (through the Queen in Council), including taxation. Generally, UK statutes do not apply unless the Bailiwick jurisdictions agree to extension. The islands have their own individual court systems; whilst appeal can lie from the Alderney and Sark Court to the Royal Court in Guernsey, the final appellate court is Her Majesty's Privy Council in London.

The Bailiwick is not a member of the EU, but has a special relationship with the EU pursuant to Protocol 3 to the Act of Accession of the UK to the EU. Whilst being inside the EU's common external tariff wall, the Bailiwick is not required to adopt EU fiscal policies, nor is it required to implement EU directives on such matters as movement of capital, company law or rules regarding insurance, investment and banking business. For a definitive account of Guernsey's status as a Crown Dependency: see Ogier The Government and Law of Guernsey 2nd Edition Chapter 6 pages 205 – 207.

5 The Chief of Guernsey Customs and Excise was represented by the author (Law Officers of the Crown) in the Royal Court of Guernsey and by the author supported by Khawar Qureshi QC before the Court of Appeal and Privy Council. Garnet was represented by Advocate Christopher Edwards (Mourant Ozannes) supported by Andrew Mitchell QC in the Royal Court and Court of Appeal. In addition Ali Malek QC was instructed by Garnet to

found in November 2012 against Garnet's application for judicial review to declare a decision by the Guernsey Financial Intelligence Service (FIS), not to consent to BNP to pay away monies (out of the jurisdiction) at the instruction of Garnet, unlawful.

Garnet had argued in these proceedings that the refusal of consent[6] was unlawful and amounted to an improper informal restraint of Garnet's assets by the FIS. The FIS maintained that they could not within the legislative framework grant a consent to transact in the face of a subsisting suspicion that the Garnet funds were proceeds of crime; the FIS further argued that there was no informal freeze imposed by the FIS through a refusal to consent. The monies held by Garnet are sums which may be the proceeds of grand corruption[7] which should be susceptible to recovery within procedures consistent with the rule of law.

This chapter seeks to explore some of the complex issues which exist in this area based not only on the public law proceedings, but also on the civil proceedings. At the heart of the issues is the tension caused by the (proper) reliance on the rule of law by those accused of grand corruption to protect assets systematically acquired (and laundered) through their own (apparent) lack of respect for the rule of

lead in the Privy Council. Only Advocates of the Royal Court of Guernsey have rights of audience before the Royal Court and Court of Appeal of Guernsey.

6 Consent regimes operate on the premise that, but for the consent, an individual or business will commit a criminal offence if they do not seek consent about the transaction of which they have a concern.
A consent regime may or may not be subject to a time based moratorium period. The UK has operated a moratorium time based consent regime since the Proceeds of Crime Act 2002. It operates for a period of 31 days. Guernsey, Jersey and Hong Kong do not have such a system and operate unlimited (time) consent regimes where a no consent can theoretically be maintained for an indefinite period of time where there is a subjective subsisting suspicion about a transaction.
Persons and businesses may obtain a defence against money laundering charges by seeking, via suspicious activity regime ('SARs Regime'), the consent of an administrative or law enforcement body (normally an FIU) to conduct or undertake financial activity about which they have concerns.

7 'Grand corruption consists of acts committed at a high level of government that distort policies or the central functioning of the state, enabling leaders to benefit at the expense of the public good.' Transparency International, available at: www.transparency.org/whoweare/organisation/faqs_on_corruption.

law.[8]

In an attempt to move the debate on in this area, this chapter will also seek to explore whether the problems lie not so much in the (proper) reliance on the rule of law by such individuals but the manner in which they will ruthlessly (ab)use vulnerabilities in legal procedures (in any jurisdiction) to advance their interests.

The Suharto Presidency, 'graft' and 'poverty' grand corruption

President Suharto held the office of President between 1967 and 1998 and it was alleged that his family in that time had acquired assets of USD 70 billion. By the time he was deposed, Time magazine[9] estimated that the family controlled assets worth USD 15 billion. Of those, it was estimated that TS (the president's favourite son) controlled nearly USD 1 billion. By contrast, in 1990, 37 million people in Indonesia were still living in abject poverty, surviving on less than a dollar a day.

The Cars, the Company and the Isle of Guernsey

In July 1998 (barely a month after President Suharto's fall from power[10]) TS transferred the proceeds of sale of his 60% shareholding in Lamborghini (originally acquired in 1994 through V Power Ltd) to Audi AG. This transaction, dated from 13 March 1998, totalled USD 48 million and was done through an account held at BNP Paribas in

8 See Abacha, Montesinos, Marcos, Duvalier, Chiluba et al.

9 1999 Time magazine article. Available at: http://star.worldbank.org/corruption-cases/node/18647. Suharto Inc May 24 1999.

10 Coincidentally also the month in which President Sani Abacha of Nigeria died.

Guernsey, in the name of Garnet Limited, a company incorporated in the British Virgin Islands, a British Overseas Territory[11].

In August 1998, GBP 2 million said to originate from TS's personal account with Aspinalls in Mayfair, London, was transferred to the Garnet accounts with BNP. In September 1998, a further GBP 6 million was transferred from a company called Latona Limited, allegedly being the proceeds of a property transaction. Furthermore, in 1999, a company called Motorbike International Limited ('Motorbike') transferred approximately USD 12 million to Garnet as the result of the sale of an interest in the business of Superbike International Limited.

At the time of acquisition of the Lamborghini shares TS, who was well known for his love of fast cars, was still in his twenties and his father had been the President of Indonesia for 27 years.

Garnet's Instruction(s) to BNP Guernsey between 2002–2009: the Guernsey Proceedings[12]

In October 2002, some 3 months after TS's conviction for murder, Garnet issued instructions to BNP directing it to transfer funds totalling approximately EUR 36.46 million from the accounts. BNP refused to comply with these instructions and on 1 November 2002 BNP notified the Guernsey FIS of those instructions. The FIS refused to consent to BNP acting on the instructions.

On 28 February 2003 Garnet issued a new instruction to BNP to pay the balance of the BNP accounts, bar USD 1 million, to an account in Singapore. BNP refused to comply with this instruction. However in June 2004 following inquiries made in Indonesia by BNP, BNP notified the FIS that it was no longer suspicious of the source of the funds transferred by Motorbike and in due course transferred the

11 An Overseas Territory differs from a Crown Dependency in that the Queen is Head of State of an Overseas Territory as Queen of the United Kingdom whereas the Guernsey (and other Crown Dependencies) are self-governing possessions of the British Crown.

12 Facts as set out in this section are taken from Judgment with minor adaptation.

Motorbike funds on the instructions of Garnet, notwithstanding the existence of the no consent.

On 3 March 2006 Garnet issued proceedings in Guernsey against BNP ('the mandate proceedings') in connection with its failure to comply with the instructions given in relation to the funds from V Power connected with the Lamborghini transaction (the Lamborghini funds). The proceedings were intended to bring into the open the extent of any FIS involvement in BNP's refusal to transfer. On 10 March 2006 BNP, in the face of the proceedings, again sought consent from FIS to pay away the Lamborghini funds. On 14 March 2006, the FIS refused to consent to this.

BNP then proceeded to a defence in the mandate proceedings that pleaded, amongst other things, that it was an implied term of the banking contract with Garnet that the accounts would be operated in accordance with the provisions of the Guernsey Proceeds of Crime Law (POCL)[13] and that BNP could refuse to operate the accounts in any way if to do so might expose the Bank or its employees to the commission of a criminal offence. As part of its defence, in an affidavit sworn by the Director of the FIS in May 2006, BNP revealed that it had made disclosures under the Guernsey POCL to the FIS and that it had sought and been refused consent to act on the instructions given. On 30 October 2006 TS was afforded conditional release in Indonesia.[14]

In 2007 Indonesia joined the mandate proceedings as a party since an issue was raised by the Bailiff of Guernsey in those proceedings as to whether the funds held by BNP might be subject to a constructive trust in favour of Indonesia.

Indonesia sought and obtained a civil freezing order in the mandate action respect of the Garnet accounts on 22 January 2007. This order was in the event discharged on appeal in January 2009 by the Court of Appeal[15] in Guernsey. Guernsey appealed to the Privy Council.

13 Ante footnote 14.

14 BBC online Monday, 30 October 2006, 10:23 GMT.

15 See Garnet Investments Limited v. BNP Paribas (Suisse) S.A. and Government of Republic of Indonesia, Rowland, Bailiff, Vos and Montgomery, JJ.A.), [2009–10] GLR 1.

In February 2009, whilst the appeal in the mandate action was pending before the Privy Council, Garnet issued fresh instructions to BNP to transfer part of the Lamborghini funds to an account in Indonesia. In March 2009, Garnet through its legal representatives a law firm, wrote to the FIS explaining why the FIS should consent to BNP making this transfer. In June 2009 the FIS replied informing that BNP 'has been refused consent to make payments requested by Garnet Investments from its account at the Bank' ('The consent decision'). The FIS later confirmed, in July 2009, that the consent decision would be maintained, notwithstanding the dismissal of an application for special leave to appeal the discharge of civil freezing order in the mandate proceedings.[16]

In October 2009 Garnet made its application for judicial review[17] of the consent decision and on 14 February 2010 the Royal Court of Guernsey gave judgment in favour of Garnet, holding that the decision of the FIS was irrational and disproportionate, constituting an excessive interference with Garnet's property rights and a breach of Article 1 of Protocol 1 to the European Convention on Human Rights ('A1P1').

An analysis of the factual matrix at the commencement of the public law proceedings

In October 2009, Garnet instituted public law proceedings in the Royal Court of Guernsey. At the commencement of the public proceedings, the following information had been established:

Garnet/TS was able to assert the following incontrovertible facts:

16 A decision described as representing a 'remarkable degree of independence by the FIS' by the authors of Corruption and Misuse of Public Office 2nd Ed para 8.174 (Nicholls QC, Daniel, Bacarese and Hatchard).

17 A court's power to examine an administrative, executive or legislative act and to invalidate that act if it is contrary to the law, a superior law or constitutional principles. Guernsey Judicial review is based on English common law principles but is less well developed.

- No criminal investigation/proceedings for corruption had been instituted in Indonesia against TS after his release from jail in October 2006.
- No civil proceedings had been instituted by the Indonesian Government in any other jurisdiction in the world.
- There were no investigations or proceedings for corruption open against him anywhere in the world and none of his assets had been restrained anywhere in the world on grounds that they were believed to be the proceeds of criminality.
- It had been accepted by the Indonesian Authorities in the civil proceedings in Guernsey that TS had significant assets within Indonesia against which any domestic civil order could (presumably) be enforced;
- The Indonesian Government had failed to establish any basis for claiming the monies in civil proceedings in Guernsey, which monies (in any event) represented a small fraction of his alleged assets.

The Guernsey FIS was possessed of the following information:

- BNP had previously effected a transaction from the Garnet Account in the face of a no consent from the FIS where it had received a representation from the Indonesian Government which enabled BNP to satisfy itself as to the provenance of those Funds;
- BNP had received no such representation from the Indonesian Government as to the Lamborghini funds but was continuing to submit requests for consent at the instigation of Garnet;
- Whilst representations were repeatedly made by the Indonesian Authorities that a Letter of Request would come from Indonesia – none had been received;
- At the time the consent decision was made the Guernsey authorities were still engaged in confidential exchanges with the Indonesian Authorities;
- the person with intimate knowledge of the provenance of the monies was TS himself who maintained that there were no longer any records in V power to explain the origins of the funds.

Garnet and BNP Guernsey between 2009–2012: Summary of the public law proceedings:

- The clear purpose of the application by Garnet was to compel the FIS to consent to the transaction thereby legitimising the funds[18] and rendering the BNP defence in the mandate action redundant.
- Garnet contended that the FIS's refusal of consent amounted to an unlawful freeze/restraint of the Garnet funds which could not reasonably be justified

18 There was a live issue, left unresolved at first instance, whether the Court could order the FIS to grant consent through a mandatory order. The FIS maintained that whilst the Court could find the FIS to have acted unlawfully, it could not make a mandatory order.

as the Indonesian Government had failed to make out any civil claim to the monies. Further, and in any event, there had been no mutual legal assistance request to Guernsey from Indonesia to secure a restraint of monies and the Guernsey authorities had not opened any investigation of its own.

- Garnet contended that not only was the decision not to consent unlawful, it was also a breach of Garnet's human rights in that it amounted to a breach of A1P1[19].
- The FIS maintained that it had the requisite suspicion to refuse consent, the refusal of consent did not amount to a de facto or de jure restraint and there could be no breach of A1P1 because Garnet had not been deprived of its right of action in the mandate action which was in any event the proper legal recourse to pursue[20].
- At first instance the Royal Court found that the decision by the FIS was unlawful, irrational and disproportionate and in breach of Garnet's human rights.
- In the face of what the FIS believed to be compelling evidence that it had appropriate grounds to hold the requisite suspicion as to the provenance of funds the Court concluded that the inactivity of the Indonesian authorities should in fact have driven the FIS to conclude that consent should be granted holding, 'it is not the function of the FIS to arbitrate extra judicially on Garnet's rights to the funds in BNP's accounts'.[21] The Court of Appeal was later to hold that the refusal of consent by the FIS, 'was not only rational but almost inevitable on the facts'[22]. In November 2012 the Privy Council refused Garnet's application for permission to appeal.

Analysis

The proceedings before the Royal Court, Court of Appeal and Privy Council in the civil and public law, places in sharp relief the complexities and legal tensions that this PEP grand corruption matrix yielded (and still yields) in the domestic civil, regulatory, criminal and public law fields operating in an international context.

19 Human Rights (Bailiwick of Guernsey) Law, 2000.

20 The legal recourse would actually yield an evidential determination of the question as to whether the monies were the proceeds of crime.

21 Paragraph 42 B Royal Court Judgment.

22 Para 62 Court of Appeal Judgment.

It is important to explore the tensions at play not least because it casts light on the debate as to who should be responsible for the recovery of stolen in a grand corruption case.

The civil / public law context in the Royal Court

In the context of the civil proceedings in the Royal Court, the issue was Indonesia's ability to establish a claim over the Garnet monies. However, Indonesia's case rested solely on its ability to secure domestic civil judgments in Indonesia against TS which were proving problematic. This meant it could not establish a basis for a proprietary claim over the monies in Guernsey.

This problem was compounded in that Indonesia only took steps to bring civil actions against TS in Indonesia after the Royal Court had invited it to intervene in the civil proceedings and extracted an undertaking that Indonesia should commence proceedings at home. The following excerpts from the judgment of the Court of Appeal reflect the difficulties they were encountering in dealing with the factual matrix.

> 'It is no exaggeration to say that this case is puzzling and somewhat troubling. It is a case in which I was left after argument, with the clear impression that neither side had been able or felt able to be entirely frank or open with the court'.
>
> 'My conclusion is that the Government's proceedings against Mr. Putra have been largely, if not wholly, inspired by the Guernsey court's invitation in September 2006 to state whether the Government wished to assert any claim the moneys in the accounts. This aspect seems to have troubled Carey, Lieut. Bailiff as well, when he said in his May 23rd, 2007 judgment (2007–08 GLR 73, at para. 45):
>
> 'It is not appropriate for the Government to give the appearance of trying to use this small jurisdiction as the lead forum for taking proceedings against Mr. Putra'.
>
> (Later in the Judgment)
> 'I can only conclude that there is much that the Government has been unwilling to tell both us and the Royal Court about the difficulties in bringing proceedings in Indonesia against the Soeharto family, and that the truth may well be rather different from the picture that Mr. Sabda has painted. I cannot and will not speculate about where that truth may lie, but it seems at least possible that there is

> limited political will to take steps in Indonesia in relation to the alleged corruption, and that the substantive claims may be more difficult to conclude favourably for the Government than is presently being admitted.
>
> This possibility is given some foundation by what happened before Carey, Lieut. Bailiff, when Advocate Strappini was acting for the Government on the original application for the injunction on January 22nd, 2007. The Lieutenant Bailiff's May 23rd, 2007 judgment described (2007–08 GLR 73, at para. 44) how Mr. Strappini had made the revealing comment that 'the problem facing the Government was that the Soeharto family by virtue of the fact that they had a lot of money still in their possession, had great influence in Indonesia.'[23]

Further, even if Indonesia could succeed in a civil claim against TS at home, they were obliged to accept in the Guernsey proceedings that TS had more than enough assets in Indonesia to satisfy any judgment that might be awarded against him.

Equally, as correctly stated in the civil proceedings[24] at no time did the Bank or Indonesia seek an injunction 'to support the bank's plea that the moneys were the proceeds of criminal conduct'.

In the civil context Indonesia succeeded at first instance, but Garnet succeeded in the appeals to the Court of Appeal and Privy Council. On the other hand, in the public law field Garnet succeeded at first instance in challenging the lawfulness of the FIS's decision to refuse consent to transact only to lose in the Court of Appeal and the Privy Council.

The criminal law / international cooperation context

Turning to the criminal arena, the only realistic basis upon which Guernsey could open a domestic investigation and/or seek a domestic restraint rested on receipt of a letter of request from Indonesia outlining predicate offending by TS in Indonesia. The alternative was a

23 At paragraphs 60 and 61.

24 Paragraph 85.

letter of request seeking a restraint in support of proceedings and a restraint in Indonesia[25].

In no small measure this reflected the traditional approach to mutual legal assistance. The traditional approach, absent a domestic investigation, was firmly rooted on a request being received before action could be undertaken on behalf of a foreign jurisdiction,[26] whether or not the letter of request was also used as a basis for opening up a domestic investigation.

The traditional approach was equally characterised in grand corruption cases by the belief that the failure to make a request was more often to be characterised as an absence of political will in the requesting jurisdiction and used as justification (in some quarters) for an inability to act in aid of cooperation.

Against this backdrop one can perhaps understand how the Royal Court in the public law case could form a view that the, 'FIS was actually arbitrating extra judicially on Garnet's rights to the funds in BNP's accounts,' in continuing to refuse consent to transact.

The regulatory context

However, the regulatory framework in the AML field had been undergoing profound changes. Leaving to one side the fight against the proceeds of drug trafficking, organised crime and 9/11, the FATF 40+9 recommendations, published in 2004, were starting to take root in domestic legislation in a number of countries.

By 2011 the Crown Dependencies of Guernsey and Jersey had been independently assessed by the IMF, as having the highest FATF

25 Indonesia became a designated country on the coming into force of the Criminal Justice (Proceeds of Crime) (Bailiwick of Guernsey) (Enforcement of Overseas Confiscation Orders) (Amendments) Ordinance 2009.

26 Many civil law jurisdictions and some common law jurisdictions had however already adopted a practice of opening domestic money laundering investigations (upon receipt of a letter of request identifying money laundering) which enabled them to use domestic provisions to impose a freeze or restraint of monies.

compliance ratings in the world. Both jurisdictions were members of Egmont and were among the founding members of CARIN[27] in 2004.

The information financial institutions or regulated entities were obliged to hold about their clients (including the obligation to satisfy themselves as to beneficial ownership of structures combined with disclosure obligations) was altering the quality of the raw intelligence/ information available to law enforcement and the regulators.

Exchange of information and co-operation

The manner in which financial information was being transmitted across international boundaries for investigatory and tracing investigations was also undergoing transformation (e.g., Egmont and IOSCO[28]), whilst the rules governing the admissibility of such information for use in restraint and in cross border criminal cases remained governed by the established (albeit still developing) rules relating to mutual legal assistance. An integral part of the changing tide at operational level was a move away from reactionary cooperation (no information disseminated unless requested) towards proactive cooperation through the voluntary dissemination of information.

Information now had to be classified according to whether it was open or closed source as domestic disclosure regimes started to take effect and international transmission between FIS' services or Regulators became more effective. Classic mutual legal assistance was increasingly being recognised for what it was in fact – the exchange of information in an admissible format for trial or restraint purposes.

In practice this meant the mere existence of certain types information of information (whether closed or open source) could alter the nature of a relationship between a regulated financial institution and

27 Camden Asset Recovery Inter Agency Network.

28 The Egmont Group of Financial Intelligence Units (international and domestic exchange of financial intelligence) and the International Organization of Securities Commissions Multilateral Memorandum of Understanding Concerning Consultation and Cooperation and the Exchange of Information ('MMOU') international information exchange/cooperation in securities and derivatives enforcement activity.

its client (and or the complexion of a case) because information (once in the hands of a financial institution) necessarily imposed (regulatory) obligations on the financial institution to enquire of its client. Correspondingly law enforcement could also come under obligations when possessed of open or closed information whether or not received through a suspicious transaction report.

In the Guernsey context, therefore, it was unsurprising that the FIS had refused consent (and was continuing to refuse) for the Garnet transaction on the grounds that, on the information before it, it had cogent grounds for suspicion.

The ambit and impact of available information in the Garnet case

By the time of the public law action, all information (apart from confidential exchanges between the Indonesian and Guernsey authorities) was public or open source and it was tolerably clear after the judgment at first instance that Guernsey was unlikely to receive a letter of request from Indonesia.

The practical effect of this was as follows: the Bank was (seemingly) unable to take the matter any further with Garnet but had sufficient suspicion to warrant a refusal to pay away absent a consent providing it with a defence to a money laundering offence in Guernsey. In deciding to take a neutral stance, BNP (who did not appear) in the public law proceedings, resolved to let the FIS and TS 'fight it out'.

Furthermore, Indonesia was apparently unable to take matters further with TS (whether in Indonesia or Guernsey), and the Guernsey Authorities themselves had nothing more than a coherent well justified suspicion as to the provenance of the Lamborghini funds, based on (i) allegations of grand corruption against the Suharto regime, and (ii) TS's own (lack of) explanation as to why the provenance of the funds could not be explained. Crucially, however, Guernsey had no basis upon which to advance a domestic criminal case without assistance from Indonesia identifying predicate offending in Indonesia.

On the available evidence in the Garnet context, the individual with all the relevant knowledge was TS himself. His affidavit evidence (in both the civil and public law judicial review proceedings) explicitly stated that V Power no longer held the documentation to explain where the monies came from to purchase Lamborghini, but did not include an explicit statement that he could not remember where the monies had come from[29]. The affidavit evidence was therefore left to convey, without explicitly stating it, that he could not remember. In the same way that a criminal trial cannot be an objective search for the truth because rules as to the admissibility of evidence can preclude evidence from being placed before Court, so too the manner in which civil/public litigation is brought with its impact on burdens of proof (legal and evidential) as well as the nature of the

29 In his Affidavit of 29 September 2009, Mr. Hutomo depones that the funds in question arose 'from the sale by me of other assets which I already held'. Among those assets were shares in Lamborghini, sold in about 1999 and held at that time by a company, V Power Limited, which had been incorporated in order that it could acquire that shareholding. Mr. Hutomo also depones that he was at all material times the beneficial owner of V Power Limited. However, notwithstanding the concerns being expressed that there might be other claims to those funds, all that Mr. Hutomo depones as to the provenance of the funds to purchase the Lamborghini shares is as follows „Because of the period of time which has passed, V Power no longer has records which would permit me to provide any further information in relation to the purchase by V Power of the Lamborghini (sic) shares'.
It is not surprising that this statement failed to allay the suspicions held by the bank. The transaction for the purchase of the Lamborghini shares by Mr. Hutomo must have been a singular event, and it would be surprising if Mr. Hutomo, still in the prime of life, would not remember such an acquisition at the very maymorn of youth. But he does not say that he has no recollection. Nor does he give any reason why V Power – which, it is assumed from the terms of the affidavit, is still in existence – no longer has relevant records. Nor is there any indication that the directors or other officers of V Power, at the time of the Lamborghini acquisition, are no longer available. Had the funds used for the purchase of the shares come from Mr. Hutomo's own assets it is surprising in the extreme that, assuming him to be sound in mind and body, he has no recollection of the provenance. Equally, if the funds had been a gift from family or friend, it is only reasonable to assume, at first sight, that some information would be available to Mr. Hutomo from other sources.'

relief sought can (and will) impact, in common law based systems, on the outcome of cases.

The advantage of pursuing the public law judicial review case in Guernsey from TS's perspective was the reality that he was highly unlikely to be compelled to give live evidence before the Royal Court. The judicial review case necessarily turned on the lawfulness of the FIS decision to refuse consent, and the basis upon which the decision was taken was not in dispute.

As a matter of course, judicial review cases are resolved on affidavit evidence (only), as the basis upon which administrative decisions are taken are rarely in dispute. It is, therefore, only in exceptional cases that cross examination (or live evidence) will be permitted[30].

The issue for the FIS, on the other hand, was that it could not act in a way that would be seen as legitimising the funds without a determination of fact addressing their entirely justifiable suspicions. It had furthermore no legal powers to determine whether monies suspected to be the proceeds of crime were in fact the proceeds of crime.

By contrast, in a private law civil action (such as the existing mandate action) there will usually be a trial based on oral evidence. Therefore, in a civil trial situation, as well as different issues there are also different legal and evidential burdens at play to those being determined in the public law proceedings. The civil mandate action in the Garnet case involves the determination of whether BNP could make good its defence as to a breach of an implied term. The civil Court of Appeal case set it out as follows:

> 'Garnet's claims were brought to force the bank to comply with its mandate, and allow the funds in the accounts to be moved at the direction of Garnet. The *défenses* of the bank plead in essence as follows:
>
> (a) The bank considered that compliance with Garnet's instructions might expose it to the commission of a criminal offence under s.39 of the Criminal Justice (Proceeds of Crime) (Bailiwick of Guernsey) Law 1999, as amended ('POCL').
>
> (b) The bank had grounds for suspecting that Mr. Putra had been involved in criminal conduct, and that the moneys held in the account might represent the proceeds of criminal conduct.

30 As of this date no judicial review in Guernsey has involved oral evidence or cross examination on an affidavit submitted.

(c) The FIS has never given its consent to the bank's compliance with the instruction[31]'

This issue compels a person with actual knowledge of the facts who is seeking the transfer to advance their (oral) evidence. The evidence will be tested under cross examination. The Court then proceeds to render a judgment based on a determination of actual fact, based on that oral evidence (as tested). In short, the evidence relied upon to support a mandate action can be tested and the findings made by the Court (on credibility) and these form an integral part of the judgment of the Court.

There can be no better elucidation of the materiality of this distinction (between the judicial review and the civil mandate action) than the following: Garnet's prospects of success in securing the transfer of the funds out of Guernsey may now rest on whether TS is prepared to give oral evidence (and have it tested under cross examination) in the mandate action before the Royal Court of Guernsey.

TS' 'evidence' and the issue of political will

Political will is often cited as the make or break of international asset recovery cases involving grand corruption. This is, broadly speaking, correct. However, at a technical level it is the impact that political will has on the collation and transmission of admissible evidence (across international boundaries) from the victim country which is usually the fundamental key in recovering stolen assets in accordance with the rule of law. In the present cases, TS has shown no willingness to subject himself to cross examination outside Indonesia nor has there been any willingness, more generally, to transmit evidence out of Indonesia.

The Garnet case exemplifies the following (unfortunately not unusual) international asset recovery grand corruption matrix: often where the collation and transmission of evidence is proving impossible there is also cogent (if not compelling) 'evidence' of (egregious)

31 Paragraph 84.

grand corruption which is being independently identified by civil society or the press[32] (as evidenced here).

On the facts, as known through the media, civil society and this case, the absence of political will in Indonesia may not be all that surprising given the length of the Suharto presidency and the willingness of TS to murder the one judge who had in fact found him guilty of corruption. Where the ramifications of grand corruption are not being (or cannot be) addressed in the victim country, the common sense question must be asked what alternative remedies (compatible with the rule of law) are there available in other jurisdictions (which hold the money or assets) to recover allegedly stolen monies or assist in their recovery. The reality ought to be that the absence of political will in the victim jurisdiction should not be fatal to asset recovery in grand corruption cases because, if it were otherwise, it is unlikely that the real victims (the citizens) would ever be able to obtain redress for the theft of the 'patrimoine' of their country.

However, this case proves that situations continue to arise (and will continue to arise) where the absence of political may prove to be a fundamental impediment to asset recovery. It is well recognised that grand corruption cases are resource intensive and time consuming even where there is political will. In reality, the absence of political will in the victim country simply prolongs the time and expense. The Duvalier proceedings, in Switzerland, dragged on for 25 years. Garnet's (unsuccessful) complaint in the public law proceedings was that its funds had been unlawfully restrained by the Guernsey authorities for nearly 10 years.

It cannot (and should not) be ignored that the delay in substantively addressing these issues may necessarily be commensurate with the time it can take to obtain admissible evidence of illicit conduct which can then sustain an action for redress (in accordance with the rule of law). However, legal systems are not (unsurprisingly) finely tuned to address the acute issues presented by grand corruption cases. Domestic legal procedures and court rules (in developed, transit or recipient jurisdictions) are not naturally designed to address the (ex-

32 It is to be noted that it rarely in the interests of government to draw attention to such abuse.

treme) issues presented by these cases. It is therefore not unsurprising that highly paid lawyers will rely on these systemic vulnerabilities (in the name of the rule of law) whilst representing their clients.

Increasingly alternative solutions consistent with the rule of law are being found by practitioners, policy makers and civil society to address the difficulties presented by egregious grand corruption and a lack of political will/capacity in the victim country.[33]

However, despite those efforts/endeavours, grand corruption cases (such as Garnet) inexorably point to the need to resolve one international policy question: is it not time that an international framework be put in place enabling accountability for grand corruption where cases cannot be advanced in the victim country or in the country holding the funds or assets (acquired with the proceeds of grand corruption)?

Returning to the present international regime and the Garnet case/funds, the moot points (at this time) are what can properly be inferred the longer: (i) Garnet takes no step to prosecute the mandate action which has stood adjourned since the Privy Council refused permission to appeal in November 2012; and (ii) BNP takes no step to apply to dismiss the mandate action for want of prosecution.

Against this backdrop and moving onto current issues, it is unrealistic, even with the UNCAC umbrella and advances in practice, to think that the asset recovery problems presented by the Arab Spring will be resolved in a short time frame. In a very real way Dan Claman[34] was right to say we have one generation to thank as the architects of the UNCAC, it is now the obligation of our generation to find the tools to make it work.

33 See Attorney General of Zambia for and on behalf of the Republic of Zambia (Claimant) – and – Meer Care & Desai (a firm) & Ors [2007] EWHC 952; the Swiss Duvalier law 2011 (where it is said that the law will be used 'where a request for mutual legal assistance cannot succeed in the requesting state due to the failure of its judicial system); Sherpa (France) and Transparency International (France) Teodorin Obiang Equitorial Guniea 2011/12 and civil forfeiture action freeze in the USA US DOJ (AFMLS) 2011.

34 Head of the Kleptocracy Unit US DOJ AFMILS.

Postscript 2012 – Investigation by the Serious Fraud Office (SFO) of the UK, Rolls Royce and TS

In December 2012 the SFO opened an investigation into Rolls Royce over allegations that include the payment of a USD 20m (GBP 12.5m) bribe to TS in 1990 (who was then even younger than when he bought Lamborghini) to secure an aircraft engine order for Rolls Royce with the Indonesian national airline Garuda.

Jigsaw puzzles have many pieces. In the field of international asset recovery, as with any puzzle, one needs to have enough pieces to see the full picture to be able to recover assets in accordance with the rule of law.

In his book 'The Rule of Law' Tom (Lord) Bingham[35] made the following observation about the rule of law:

> 'The concept of the rule of law is not fixed for all time. Some countries do not subscribe to it fully, and some subscribe only in name, if that. Even those that do subscribe to it find it difficult to apply all its precepts quite all the time. But in a world divided by differences of nationality, race, colour, religion and wealth it is one of the greatest unifying factors, perhaps the greatest, the nearest we are likely to approach to a universal secular religion. It remains an ideal, but an ideal worth striving for in the interests of good government, and peace at home and in the world at large.'

Not unsurprisingly elsewhere in his work he had previously stated (with typical lucidity): 'Cross border problems call for cross border solutions'.[36]

The recovery of stolen assets in accordance with the rule of law is intrinsically a cross border problem calling for cross border solutions.

The simplicity of the proposition belies the complexity of the issues involved in the practical recovery of stolen assets even allowing for the innovations contained within the UNCAC framework and the considerable steps being taken to implement it.

The experiences acquired in cases such as Garnet suggest that the UNCAC framework, at this stage of its implementation, cannot without more address the acute issues presented to secure international

35 Epilogue, Page 174.
36 Page 98, albeit in a slightly different context.

recovery in grand corruption cases in accordance with the rule of law where there is significant residual influence being exerted in the victim jurisdiction which is precluding effective relief within the jurisdiction and or dissemination of the evidence out of it to secure recovery in a recipient jurisdiction.

MARIA SCHNEBLI

Lessons learned from the past: Today's response from requested countries

Introduction: Taking stock

Asset recovery has been in the limelight for a number of years now as a key issue of international cooperation. The legislative toolbox has considerably changed in the last years, on an international level as well as in the national legislation of several countries. The United Nations Convention against Corruption (UNCAC) has given various incentives that have been adopted by many countries before or after ratification by adapting their internal legislation accordingly. Other countries, however, blissfully ratified the Convention and immediately proceeded to send out mutual legal assistance (MLA) requests referring to UNCAC while neglecting to adjust their internal legislation to comply with the terms of the Convention. The circuit of experts active in asset recovery is growing steadily, and specialists and representatives from experienced as well as newly founded authorities from countries all over the world frequent international conferences dedicated to the subject. All of those working in the field of asset recovery are eager to exchange ideas and learn more about repatriating stolen assets. Study visits are taking place in various places, training seminars are being held and technical assistance is being sought and obtained.

However, the limits of the current system are basically unchanged and assets held in financial centres worldwide are still accumulating interests. Meanwhile the countries of origin to which these funds belong must continue to work with very limited resources and under dire financial constraints. Furthermore, there is the stress on governments as a result of recent political developments, for example in the so-called 'Arab Spring' countries. Revolutions took place and governments changed in countries previously ruled for several decades by dictators and their cronies. In some cases, newly constituted authorities are facing the challenge of entering the arena of international cooperation by attempting to obtain mutual assistance to recover the assets looted from their countries by the previous rulers.

From a Swiss perspective, the challenges associated with recent asset recovery cases, and particularly MLA requests, were not a result of the law failing but rather the inability, and sometimes the unwillingness, of the requesting States and their authorities to provide Switzerland with the necessary elements of proof to allow a refund within the framework of MLA or to open criminal proceedings in order to confiscate the amounts.[1] While this is certainly true for some drawn-out cases, it cannot be invoked for all the challenging scenarios, particularly with regard to post-revolutionary States.

In post-revolutionary States problems of cooperation can arise also from the lack of exposure to MLA, the lack of established and trustworthy contacts with foreign authorities or the lack of know-how relating to investigative strategies, to name just a few key issues.[2] Yet another issue is failing or failed States seeking MLA or being requested to provide MLA to other countries. Failing or failed States often lack the institutional stability required to carry out swift and successful MLA procedures. How countries can compensate for a lack of institutional stability 'on the go' with time running out is an open and crucial question. It is well known that the prospect of maintaining a freeze on assets decreases with the passage of time, both for legal and practical reasons.[3] Financial centres, such as Switzerland, are in difficult positions, because they are frequently asked to provide MLA while at the same time expected to remain focused on national money

1 Pierre-Yves Morier, in: Mark Pieth (Ed.): Recovering Stolen Assets, Bern 2008 p. 277, also Pieth, ibid. p. 389 concerning the requirement of financial centres towards victim States (countries of origin of assets) to provide a 'ready made conviction' even if it is a failing State.

2 Daniel Claman, in: Mark Pieth (Ed.): Recovering Stolen Assets, Bern 2008 p. 344 and p. 351, ibid.

3 Jean-Bernard Schmid, in: Mark Pieth (Ed.): Recovering Stolen Assets, Bern p. 235.

laundering investigations with predicate offences committed abroad and suspects frequently residing outside national territory.

Switzerland recognized a long time ago that financial centres today can no longer simply ceremoniously receive MLA requests in diplomatic pouches and either flatly refuse assistance or reluctantly produce bank documents and only after some time in order to preserve their interests and protect their financial institutions. On the contrary, the only way to address money laundering is with a proactive approach. The old familiar picture of 'victim countries' on one side and 'financial centres' on the other is no longer valid. Financial centres are expected to clean up their acts and investigate money laundering committed in their territory. In order to do this, financial centres must reach out to the countries of origin of the laundered funds. These countries in turn are expected, by their own citizens and by the international community, to investigate the predicate offenses committed in their territory with the aim to repatriate the stolen assets. To this end, victim countries must be able to request and provide mutual assistance in cooperation with the countries of destination of the stolen assets. Even after obtaining evidence of corruption, it is still a long process to get the money back. The existing and visible barriers to asset recovery can only be overcome if there is political will and continuity of efforts from all parties involved.

Lessons learned 101: Making full use of what you have

Roles and perspectives between countries of origin and countries of destination, i.e. financial centres, of stolen assets are not cast in stone and they can and must be changed. To cite the example of grand corruption cases, the scope of discussion should not be limited to the bilateral relations between so-called 'developed' countries and 'victim countries', which are often thought to be the countries where corrupt officials live and carry out their crimes. Complex cases of corruption affect various countries, including countries whose financial services are used to transfer, divert and hide illegal assets. These countries will consequently be responsible for investigations of money laundering connected to the corrupt offences. As a result, countries with large financial centres have an active interest in prosecuting the offences committed in their territory. If funds related to these offences can be seized and confiscated, the country of destination will seek to repatriate the assets to the country of origin where the underlying corruption occurred.

Long-term strategic and coordinated planning before, throughout and after the conclusion of MLA cooperation between the countries of origin of stolen assets and countries of their destination is essential, but so far surprisingly scarce in reality.

Making use of the full potential of national criminal proceedings

Criminal proceedings intended to recover stolen assets are not limited to the country where a prosecution for the predicate offence is or should be on going, rather the criminal proceedings also extend to the countries where related offences, i.e. money laundering, embezzlement and other crimes, are to be prosecuted.

Consequently, the countries where financial intermediaries and consulting companies are located must be able to prosecute the money-laundering and other offences related to the predicate offence in question in order to freeze the assets in their banks. If prosecution of such related offences is difficult or impossible because of the absence of a coordinated approach by all countries involved, it will have far-reaching consequences that ultimately only benefit the party who laundered the stolen funds to bank accounts abroad.

The importance of national proceedings in the countries receiving stolen assets has been clearly established. In order to puzzle together evidence and successfully recover stolen assets, authorities must build a transnational case.[4] To do this, all interested parties need to assemble at one table, preferably at the outset of the connected criminal investigations. This process can be greatly facilitated if each side identifies a single point of contact (SPOC), who is in charge of the investigation

4 See the Stolen Asset Recovery Initiative (StAR) Study, "The Puppet Masters", Washington 2011, p. 9.

and who makes and maintains contacts with the other SPOCs, so together they can build a relationship of trust. Continuity of people in key positions is a critical element to success in this context. Coordination is another key element.

The importance of careful and continuous coordination between the States involved in an asset recovery case is widely recognised. There are therefore platforms and organizations that offer support for coordinating transnational investigations.[5] Eurojust, a body of the European Union, is one such organisation. Its mission is 'to support and strengthen coordination and cooperation between national investigating and prosecuting authorities in relation to serious crime affecting two or more Member States'.[6] Eurojust can also be called upon by non-EU Member States, some of which have stationed Liaison Magistrates with Eurojust, including the US, Croatia and Norway. Eurojust has a valuable network of contact points all over the world and organises on a regular basis case-related coordination meetings, in which prosecutors and police officers from all countries working on a related investigation can discuss and coordinate their investigations and mutual cooperation issues.

In this context, the spontaneous transmission of information has repeatedly been cited as a criterion for the success of Chapter V UNCAC.[7] Financial centres which initiate criminal investigations for money laundering following the receipt of a suspicious transaction report (STR) issued by their financial intelligence unit (FIU) will often come across information related to the predicate offense. This information can be of key importance to the country of origin of the laundered assets. Often information from the destination country can enable the country of origin to initiate domestic criminal proceedings – if it has not already done so. It also allows the country of origin to send a MLA request to the country of destination, which requests the evidence necessary to obtain a confiscation sentence and therefore pursue the recovery of the assets stashed abroad. The UNCAC explicitly

5 It is strongly recommended to call upon also StAR with the World Bank and the Institute on Asset Recovery (ICAR) for technical assistance and facilitation of contacts between prosecuting authorities.

6 See Eurojust website available at: www.eurojust.europa.eu.

7 Claman, ibid. p. 352.

mentions the spontaneous transmission of information in article 46 paragraph 4. Other multilateral conventions, such as the Council of Europe's Convention on Laundering, Search, Seizure and Confiscation on Tracing, Seizing and Confiscating of the Proceeds from Crime article 10, also refer to the tool of spontaneous transmission of information.

Article 67a of the Swiss Federal Law on Mutual Assistance in Criminal Matters gives Swiss prosecuting authorities the possibility for spontaneous transmission of information resulting from evidence protected by secrecy. This means that a Swiss prosecutor cannot spontaneously send bank documents abroad, but he can alert foreign authorities to the existence of such records by submitting information relating to their content and importance. This method of information sharing is done on a regular basis. The main intention behind this method is to initiate what is informally called among Swiss prosecutors and police investigators 'mirror proceedings', i.e. on going criminal investigations in both the country of origin of stolen assets and the country of their destination. This gives maximum flexibility to both countries in coordinating their investigations and defining their respective needs for cooperation. As such, countries of destination are not limited by the scope of a specific MLA request. A spontaneous transmission of information, however, does not entail any kind of obligation for the victim country to respond. It does not substitute either the necessity for the victim country to build its own case and ask for the spontaneously offered evidence with a substantiated MLA request. On the other hand, engaging in the spontaneous transmission of information means that the country in possession of relevant information must be willing to share it with other countries, thereby considerably enlarging the scope and horizon of its own investigation and thus creating more work for itself. In practice, the process of spontaneously transmitting information can create considerable obstacles. From the Swiss perspective, only a relatively small amount of spontaneously transmitted information is successfully followed-up on by the countries receiving the information, and to this day very few financial centres actively use this option on a regular basis.

Making use of the full potential of MLA requests

Requested as well as requesting States need to take a more proactive approach to MLA.[8]

Expectations of obtaining assistance and recovering assets from other jurisdictions continue to be very low in many requesting States – both in countries of origin of stolen assets and in financial centres. UNCAC's provisions remain only a promise.[9] It should be admitted that when one lowers one's expectations of jurisdictions abroad, one also feels less inclined to meet high expectations. This can and should change.

Incoming MLA requests can and should be seen – insofar as national legislation provides for this possibility – as vehicles carrying precious information that not only enables the requesting State to provide useful assistance but which also can trigger national investigations in the requested State. Indications from the requesting State enable the requested State to hone its search for assets that then can be frozen. Other indications can provide the necessary elements for sufficient initial suspicions regarding offenses committed in the territory of the requested State.

In Switzerland and other countries, banks have adopted this attitude towards requests for information. When a bank receives orders to produce documents by a prosecutor charged with executing a MLA request, the bank reviews the information provided in the MLA request and proceeds not only to deliver the requested documents but also to submit a suspicious transaction report (STR).

8 See also recommendation n° 6 of the StAR Study "Barriers to Asset Recovery", Washington 2008: Allow for rapid tracing and temporary freezing or seizing of assets before receiving a formal MLA request (freeze before assets disperse). On the controversial issue regarding the hiring of local lawyers, see StAR Study on Barriers to Asset Recovery, Washington 2011, Barrier 29 and Antenor Madruga, in: Mark Pieth (Ed.): Recovering Stolen Assets, Bern 2008, p. 383.

9 Antenor Madruga, ibid.p. 375.

New approaches towards the outside of the box (thinking out of…)

The requesting State as 'partie civile'

According to Swiss law and court practice, a requesting State does not have party rights in the proceedings relating to the execution of its MLA request.[10] The requesting State must wait until its MLA request is executed. The requesting State has no right to appeal, for example, against a court decision rendered in the requested State in which assistance is denied. If the requested State opens a national criminal investigation related to the incoming MLA request it can be expected that the evidence resulting from this investigation will be of interest to the requesting State and will regularly coincide, at least partially, with the evidence requested by that State. Should this situation arise, the logical next step for the requesting State whose assets have been looted is to consider constituting itself as victim party in the investigation conducted in the requested State. As victim party it is possible for the country of origin to actively participate in the proceedings instead of waiting without any legal rights for its MLA request to be executed. While this scenario seems convincing in theory, there have not been many cases in which it has been done successfully. The reasons for which are manifold. Looking back on Swiss jurisprudence, the Abacha case was the first case in which the requesting country constituted itself as '*partie civile*' in the Swiss national criminal investigation. In appeal proceedings concerning the Republic of Nigeria's right to access the case file, the Swiss Federal Supreme Court identified the risk of the '*partie civile* circumventing MLA procedure, which could potentially cause irreparable prejudice against the parties targeted by the MLA request.[11]

10 Robert Zimmermann, La coopération judiciaire internationale en matière pénale, Bern 2009, N. 286 p. 265.

11 Zimmermann, ibid. n° 279 p. 261 about the Federal Supreme Court decision with reference BGE 127 II 198. Available at: www.bger.ch.

However, things have changed since the Abacha case. The recently introduced unified Swiss Code of Criminal Procedure allows in article 118 the victim country to constitute itself '*partie civile*' and declare its intention to participate in an on going criminal procedure. Since its introduction, this has been done in several cases with varying results. In regards to the Arab Spring cases, the Swiss Federal Penal Court up to this point has come to diverging conclusions. In the case of Tunisia, the Court ruled on 20 March 2012 that the country could be admitted as '*partie civile*' to the criminal proceedings conducted by the Office of the Attorney General of Switzerland. In this decision, however, the Court defined precise conditions to avoid the premature transmission and use of evidence that could only be obtained by Tunisia as a requesting State after the formal conclusion of related MLA proceedings. In particular, the Court stated that the legal representative from Tunisia could consult the Swiss criminal investigation file but could not make copies. Instead, he had to take notes of the file by hand and submit them to the Swiss Central Authority for MLA matters.[12] Regarding Egypt, however, the same Court ruled on 12 December 2012 that the country could not participate as '*partie civile*' in the related criminal proceedings conducted by the Office of the Attorney General of Switzerland.[13] Considering the political and institutional instability in Egypt at the time of decision as well as the risk of possible human rights violations, the Court concluded that Egypt could not provide sufficient assurances that no irreparable prejudice would be caused by allowing the country access to the Swiss case file.

There is another provision in the Swiss Penal Code that allows victims to regain stolen assets. Article 53 SPC states that criminal prosecution may be waived if the public interest and the interest of the victim in prosecuting the defendant are insignificant and if the defendant has compensated for damages or has made all reasonable efforts to compensate for damages. This can include, in particular, voluntary

12 Decision of the Federal Penal Court, reference BB.2011.130 consid.3.4.p. 16. Available at: www.bstger.ch.

13 Decision of the Federal Penal Court, reference BB.2012.122. Available at: www.bstger.ch.

restitution of assets as part of an agreement between the defendant and the victim.

The new kids on the block: NGOs as representatives of civil society and as active stakeholders in the prosecution of transnational criminal cases

Active interventions from civil society have become a an increasingly dynamic and important way to initiate and accompany criminal proceedings by focusing on the restitution of stolen assets to countries of origin and calling upon financial centres to investigate the related money laundering offenses. A prominent example is the French investigation into the ill-gotten gains of African leaders and the role of Transparency International in the investigation.[14]

In Switzerland, at least for now, the situation presents itself differently. In a recent decision concerning a criminal investigation for money laundering opened by the Office of the Attorney General of Switzerland in which a NGO had requested on behalf of the Penan and other indigenous people in Eastern Malaysia to be accepted as '*partie civile*' the Federal Supreme Court ruled on 12 December 2012 that 'the possible inadequacy of foreign jurisdictions regarding prosecution of offenses under national competence cannot lead to an expansion or enlargement of the legitimation of an association representing individual interests in a Swiss criminal investigation'.[15] According to jurisprudence in Switzerland today, no legitimation to constitute itself a '*partie civile*' is therefore accepted for NGOs on behalf of individual victims. The right to bring charges remains the only possibility according to Article 301 of the Swiss Code of Criminal Procedure (SCCP).[16]

14 Available at: http://archive.transparency.org/news_room/latest_news/press_releases_nc/2010/ 2010_11_9_paris.

15 Decision of the Swiss Federal Penal Court, reference BB 2012.174-177. Available at: www.bstger.ch.

16 Available at: www.admin.ch.

A word on plea-bargaining and settlements: Can justice be negotiated?

Settlements can reasonably be envisioned as part of international asset recovery cases, because they could save prosecutorial resources, provide certainty as to the outcome of a case and reduce case-processing time – all of which would benefit those involved in corruption cases.[17] Nevertheless, one must consider whether settlements could become obstacles to MLA from the perspective of other countries. Experience has shown that when investigative and prosecutorial resources are scarce, authorities are typically more likely to expend resources rapidly to resolve the matter in their own jurisdiction, which could include reaching a settlement to recuperate assets, than they are to divert resources to provide MLA to other countries. It seems therefore important to draw attention to the terms of a settlement. The terms of a settlement must include a clause that obligates the offender entering into the settlement, under the direction of the settling jurisdiction, to cooperate with other countries investigating related matters. In a settlement, the right of the prosecuting country or countries to conduct further investigations in the event that they receive MLA requests from other countries must be specifically mentioned. Settlement agreements and statements of facts must be made public so that other affected countries can quickly and easily determine what corrupt conduct led to the settlement and decide if they want to pursue the case further.[18]

17 '[…] a pragmatic end to a long-running and wide-ranging investigation' (former SFO Head R. Alderman in the press release of 5 February 2010 regarding the British Aerospace (BAE) case. Available at the SFO website: www.sfo.co.uk.

18 Once more, in practice not all of this is as clear-cut. In a recent case, the Office of the Attorney General of Switzerland issued an order of summary punishment against a multinational company that had accepted a fine for corrupt behaviour concerning in particular the bribing of foreign officials, thereby settling the criminal proceedings conducted by the OAG against it. The OAG published the order of summary punishment on the Internet. Subsequently, a lawyer representing the foreign officials submitted a complaint against the responsible federal prosecutors on grounds of bias which was granted by the Federal Penal Court with decision dated 14 February 2012, references BB.2011.135 und BB.2011.136. Available at: www.bstger.ch.

What to do when all hope seems lost?

Failing or failed States as partners in MLA

It is obvious that the UNCAC system – and the general MLA legal framework, for that matter – is not adequate for failing or dysfunctional States. However, such States can and do try to obtain mutual legal assistance, and they have a legitimate claim to do so. The question therefore is how to deal with failed or failing States without compromising the rule of law.[19]

Based on article 184 paragraph 3 of the Swiss Constitution, the Swiss Federal Government can intervene and issue asset-freezing orders. The purpose of this provision is to secure assets until they can be confiscated, either by way of national criminal proceedings or repatriation via MLA. However, freezing assets is only a temporary solution based on functioning MLA relations between Switzerland and other countries. This method is therefore not helpful when dealing with failing or failed States.

On 1 February 2011, Switzerland introduced a new Federal Law called the Restitution of Illicit Assets Act (RIAA), which was based in particular on past experiences involving high profile cases, such as the Mobutu case and the Duvalier case. In article 2 RIAA, the definition for failing or failed states is as follows: 'If the country [...] is unable to satisfy the requirements of legal assistance proceedings owing to the total or substantial collapse or unavailability of its national judicial system (failure of state structures)'. Whether a country meets these requirements must be determined on a case-by-case basis. The RIAA focuses on assets belonging to politically exposed persons (PEPs) and

19 No compromises can be made, under any circumstances, regarding the rule of law. This is made more challenging by circumstances of actual cases, in particular concerning long lasting regimes, cf. Bernard Bertossa, in: Mark Pieth (Ed.): Recovering Stolen Assets, Bern 2008 p. 25: 'Return [of assets] of any kind will have to be refused on even stronger grounds, where the public officials implicated in the criminal activities uncovered are still in position and act under the orders of a requesting State, where they control all the institutions, including the courts and the prosecution services.' See also Claman, ibid. p. 343.

their close associates, and it provides a definition for PEPs in article 2. A key feature of the RIAA is article 6, which contains the presumption of unlawful origin of assets at the disposal of a PEP or his associates with the consequence of reversal of the burden of proof. The RIAA is clearly designed as a fall back solution in regards to 'normal' MLA. In article 2 paragraph 4 RIAA, the possibility for MLA proceedings to resume is specifically mentioned. According to RIAA if MLA proceedings should resume, forfeiture proceedings shall be suspended immediately. The RIAA hopefully can provide a solution for very exceptional cases, which would in all likelihood be applied very rarely. Switzerland has recognized its responsibility to address the issue of failing and failed States, and it has been met with great interest by other countries worldwide. Canada, for example, has followed the Swiss example in its Freezing Assets of Corrupt Foreign Officials Act.[20]

The final step: Confiscation and restitution

'To some extent, international asset recovery is law in the making and cannot be conducted in a legal vacuum'.[21]

Switzerland has developed a multi-pronged approach to asset recovery, which includes a coordinated distribution of tasks between different authorities, the adaptation of the existing internal legislation and the introduction of a new law (the RIAA) that focuses on the restitution of illicit assets. It would be presumptuous to call the Swiss approach a solution to all asset recovery problems, and only time will tell if it yields the good results that are expected. Switzerland's active involvement in asset recovery regularly lands the country in the international limelight. This invariably reinforces long held and still harboured suspicions held by some that Switzerland, with its famous numbered bank accounts, continues to be a safe haven for crooks'

20 Available at: http://laws-lois.justice.gc.ca/eng/acts/F-31.6/FullText.html.

21 Paul Gully Hart, in: Mark Pieth (Ed.): Recovering Stolen Assets, Bern 2008, p. 185.

assets. The opposite, however, is true, and the international community has recognised this for some time now.[22]

22 As Bertolt Brecht so aptly expressed it in his Ballad of Mackie Messer: 'There are some who are in darkness And the others are in light And you see the ones in brightness Those in darkness drop from sight.'

Major stumbling blocks

Part 1: Technical

Jason Sharman

Shell companies and asset recovery: Piercing the corporate veil

One of the most common obstacles to tracing and recovering the proceeds of large-scale corruption is the use of so-called shell companies to obscure the link between criminals and the money they have stolen. This chapter briefly reviews the nature and uses of shell companies in serious international corruption crimes and then makes some suggestions as how to respond to this challenge. It is important to emphasise that while this chapter looks at the illicit uses of shell companies, the large majority of shell companies are used for legal and legitimate purposes.

What are shell companies?

How is a shell company different from any other kind of company? First, these are privately owned companies, rather than being publicly listed on a stock exchange. More importantly, shell companies are not engaged in the production of any good or service. A partial exception is that the shell company may ostensibly be involved in the provision of some hard-to-verify service, like consultancy or marketing services, as an alibi to explain the receipt of corruption proceeds. But the main function of the shell company is its separate legal personality, as such companies are generally used to hold assets or bank accounts in a corporate name. In doing so, they obscure the name of the real person or people in control, referred to as the 'beneficial owner'. When it comes to stolen wealth, the shell company is thus interposed to separate, screen and conceal the beneficial owner from those pursuing the stolen wealth.

Aside from the company itself and the beneficial owner (in this chapter assumed to be a corrupt official), the third important actor is the Corporate Service Provider. The latter is a firm, commonly a law or accounting firm, that does the paperwork, lodges the necessary forms and pays the government fee required to have the shell company created and maintained on behalf of the owner. Aside from being a matter of convenience, this provider may also play a key role in enhancing the secrecy of the shell company arrangement. The provider can do so by standing in as a placeholder or frontman in the capacity of a nominee director or nominee shareholder. Under such an arrangement, any public information in the national company registry relating to directors and shareholders gives the details of the provider acting on the instructions of the beneficial owner, not the actual owner in control of the company.

Shell companies are cheap, usually costing between one and a few thousand dollars, and can be set-up quickly almost entirely online. Simple web searches reveal the multitude of options available from providers' websites. Importantly, there is no necessary link between the location of the owner, the location of the service provider and the jurisdiction of incorporation. Very commonly, each of these three parties may be located in different countries, thus greatly complicating the task of investigators. Because such companies are so cheap to form, they are largely expendable, so there is little point in the authorities trying to fine or prosecute the company for any criminal activities. Shell companies are not the only kind of corporate entity that may be used by corrupt officials to obscure the true ownership and origins of their stolen wealth. Trusts, foundations, partnerships and other forms may also play the same role. Yet a study for the Stolen Asset Recovery Initiative (a joint product of the World Bank and the United Nations Office on Drugs and Crime) found that the vast majority of corporate entities used in grand corruption cases were in fact shell companies.[1]

1 World Bank/United Nations Office on Drugs and Crime. 2011.The Puppet Masters: How the Corrupt Use Legal Structures to Hide their Stolen Assets and What to do About It. Washington DC.

Challenges to investigating shell companies

The central challenge for those looking to investigate shell company-enabled financial crime is to pierce the corporate veil and find the real person in control of the company in question. Otherwise, the trail runs cold with the shell company, which serves to hide and shield the criminal. There are potentially two main ways to achieve this goal.

The first and seemingly most obvious is to seek out the real owner through the relevant jurisdiction's company registry. Every company must file at least some information on such a registry in order to exist. Very rarely, however, is there a requirement that the identity of the beneficial owner be included in this information. Corrupt officials are of course more likely than most to take precautions to conceal their identity, for example by using their Corporate Service Provider as a front in supplying the company's mailing address and acting as a nominee director and nominee shareholder. Furthermore, even in many developed country settings the information contained in company registries is often out of date or incomplete, as registries fulfil more of a passive archiving function rather than actively verifying the information they receive. In the developing world, these gaps and errors are even more common.

Understanding shell companies: The Magnitsky case

An example of the problems that shell companies can create is the case of Russian whistle-blower Sergei Magnitsky. Magnitsky uncovered a massive case of corruption among senior members of the Russian tax administration who had obtained a fraudulent tax refund of USD 230 million. Instead of investigating the corrupt tax officials, the Russian government chose to arrest Magnitsky in November 2008. Magnitsky died after almost a year in prison due to severe mistreatment. In 2012, the Russian government announced it would posthumously prosecute Magnitsky himself for the crime he had uncovered.

The USD 230 million was taken out of Russia shortly after the original fraudulent refund was paid out on Christmas Eve 2007. Much of the money was transferred to shell companies, which held accounts with Credit Suisse in Zurich. One such company was Aikate Properties, incorporated in the UK overseas territory of the British Virgin Islands, with the relevant Corporate Service Provider being Commonwealth Trust Services. In line with local law, the provider collected information on the beneficial owner, the husband of one of the corrupt tax officials. Later this information was made public, allowing the tracing and freezing of the funds in Switzerland. Commonwealth Trust Services had its British Virgin Islands company formation licence revoked for customer due diligence failures in 2011 (well before many of its business records were made public by the International Consortium of Investigative Journalists in April 2013).

Among the other shell companies used to transfer the money from Russia to Switzerland was Bristoll Exports, a New Zealand company set-up by New Zealand Corporate Service Provider GT Group. The GT Group gained some notoriety for also forming shell companies used by the Mexican Sinaloa drug cartel to launder their profits and North Korea to break arms sanctions. Under New Zealand law, however, GT Group had no legal obligation to conduct any due diligence on their customers or even establish their true identity. As such, Geoffrey Taylor, the owner, and his employees successfully argued that they had acted within the law. Although GT Group ceased trading, it has since been re-established under a new name.

Countering the misuse of shell companies

One solution to the problem of untraceable shell companies used to conceal financial crime being advocated for from several quarters is to establish a new global standard mandating that all registries contain the identity of all beneficial owners and that this information be publicly accessible to all. Such an ambitious new regulation would in principle go a long way to solve the problem of the misuse of shell companies. Not only would it be easier for the authorities to check up on suspicious activities involving companies, but journalists and NGOs, who often do most to uncover financial crime, could also scrutinize such activities if ownership information was in the public domain.

The potential drawback of imposing a requirement on all registries to hold and make public beneficial ownership information is the challenge of implementation. As noted, currently registries function as an archive, so this major expansion of their responsibilities would require significantly more funds. Relatedly, given that registries in many countries already struggle to meet their formal responsibilities in terms of keeping existing information correct and up to date, it is an open question as to how they would practically cope with the much more demanding responsibility of maintaining an accurate record of beneficial ownership.

An alternative to better regulating beneficial ownership focuses on the Corporate Service Providers. Here the solution is to require these private firms to collect identity documents from the beneficial owner when companies are formed. These documents are then held on file by the provider and made available to the authorities, but not the public, on request. The advantage here is that the costs are borne by the private sector rather than the public and that this system has been shown to be a practically effective solution in many countries.[2] The disadvantage is that some providers are willing to collude with criminal clients, and that because ownership information is not public, there is not the same scope for broader scrutiny and accountability.

Does the unusually detailed evidence available on how shell companies were used in laundering the proceeds of corruption in the Russian tax scandal offer more support for the solution of public registries of beneficial ownership, or for regulating Corporate Service Providers? This case illustrates that the misuse of shell companies is not just a problem that exists in exotic offshore financial centres like the British Virgin Islands. Apart from New Zealand, additional shell companies involved in this affair were registered in the UK, Moldova and Cyprus. Critics of relying on the regulation of company providers might note that Commonwealth Trust Services had failed to follow

2 Findley, Michael G., Daniel L. Nielsen and J.C. Sharman. 2013. *Global Shell Games: Experiments in Transnational Relations*. Cambridge: Cambridge University Press.

proper due diligence procedures and thereby abetted a serious crime. Proponents would note that there was much more information available on the real owner of the British Virgin Islands company than there was on the New Zealand company and that authorities had taken action against the former provider in a way that New Zealand law did not allow. Those arguing that only a public registry of company owners is sufficient to address the misuse of shell companies would maintain that many of the unknowns that still surround the money stolen by the senior tax officials (who the Russian government has declined to prosecute or investigate) would be resolved by such a policy solution.

Putting this basic dispute to one side, there are more incremental but nevertheless important changes that could and should be made to mitigate the misuse of shell companies in large-scale corruption and other related financial crime. The first is that jurisdictions that have failed to regulate their service providers while also leaving their company registries as passive archives pose a major point of vulnerability. Foremost among such jurisdictions is the United States, in which around 2 million companies are formed every year.[3] Rather than just a theoretical obstacle to asset recovery, the ready availability of anonymous or untraceable US shell companies has greatly facilitated many cases of serious corruption. Thus the Stolen Asset Recovery Initiative study referenced above found that US shell companies are used more often in laundering the proceeds of grand corruption than those of any other country.[4] At time of writing, proposed legislation to ameliorate this problem in the form of the Incorporation Transparency and Law Enforcement Assistance Act looks to be moribund in the US Congress, thanks to the opposition of powerful corporate lobbies and the state of Delaware.

Second is more rigorous enforcement of the laws that do exist in other countries with regards to regulating Corporate Service Providers. Thus although the UK is covered by the EU Third Money Laundering Directive, which specifies that providers must hold on file

3 Permanent Subcommittee on Investigations. 2010. *Keeping Foreign Corruption out of the United States: Four Case Histories*. US Senate, Washington D.C.

4 World Bank/United Nations Office on Drugs and Crime. 2011. *The Puppet Masters: How the Corrupt Use Legal Structures to Hide their Stolen Assets and What to do About It*. Washington DC.

identification documents for beneficial owners, according to a 2012 report by Global Witness not a single audit had been conducted to make sure that providers were actually following the law.[5] It seems unlikely that Britain is the only European Union country with weak enforcement of this directive. Although offshore financial centres generally regulate their providers and make some effort to actually enforce these laws, a series of journalistic exposés has illustrated that compliance is far from perfect.

The third measure once again relates to better enforcement of existing laws, this time with reference to banks. According to international standards and the national laws of most countries, banks must collect identity documents on the beneficial owner of any corporate vehicle holding an account with that bank. Here banks can act as backstop when authorities cannot obtain beneficial ownership information from either a registry or a Corporate Service Provider. Once again, though, a series of whistle-blowers, media stories, investigations by NGOs and the US Senate Permanent Subcommittee on Investigations reports have revealed serious compliance failures by banks and a pronounced complacency among those public agencies that are supposedly regulating the banks in this manner.[6,7,8]

Conclusion

In conclusion, shell companies are one of the most commonly used devices in laundering the proceeds of grand corruption. Shell compa-

5 Global Witness. 2012. *Grave Secrecy: How a Dead Man can Own a UK Company and other Hair-Raising Stories about Hidden Company Ownership from Kyrgyzstan and Beyond*. London.

6 Global Witness. 2009. *Undue Diligence: How Banks do Business with Corrupt Regime. London.*

7 Financial Services Authority. 2011. *Banks' Management of High Money Laundering Risk Situations*. London.

8 Permanent Subcommittee on Investigations. 2012. *US Vulnerability to Money Laundering, Drugs, and Terrorist Financing: The HSBC Case History*. US Senate, Washington DC.

nies that cannot be linked back to the real person in control, the beneficial owner, are one of the greatest obstacles to recovering stolen assets. Solutions include regulating service providers so as to require them to hold beneficial ownership information or, more ambitiously, imposing a blanket requirement on company registries to hold and make public beneficial ownership information for all companies. In many cases, however, addressing this problem is not a question of passing new laws but rather better enforcing those we already have.

MARKUS E. SCHULZ

Beneficial ownership: The private sector perspective

Identifying beneficial ownerships is the fundamental aspect of every anti-money laundering (AML) program. However, even though it is fundamental to every AML program, it is one of the most challenging things to do.

For decades, banks and financial institutions have identified beneficial owners as part of their AML programs. Therefore, those years of experience should make it easy to identify beneficial owners. The challenges, however, have not much changed over the years. If anything, it may be even harder today to identify beneficial ownerships than it was in the past. People who have something to hide, like money launderers, corrupt politicians, rogue employees and fraudsters, seek to channel illegitimate funds through the system. At the same time as banks and financial institutions have increased their efforts to make it harder to abuse the system, criminals are getting smarter at exploiting the system.

For criminals taking advantage of the financial system, it is like water running down a hill. If the water's path becomes blocked it will find a new path or form a new way downhill.

And so when banks and financial institutions make it harder, or even impossible, to use certain vehicles to disguise beneficial ownerships, new ways and new methods are invented to continue to disguise beneficial ownerships and the people behind companies, funds, accounts and transactions.

But has nothing changed over the last 20 years? It surely has. The efforts of the Financial Action Task Force (FATF) have set global standards for combating money laundering with a clear focus on beneficial owners, the source of funds and the source of wealth.

A strong AML regime is key to deter and undermine bribery, corruption and embezzlement, because every illegitimate fund has to enter the financial system at some stage if the rogue person wants to enjoy the benefits of the funds. What good is it when one steals funds but cannot use them? Cash funds may be used in different ways, but once funds exceed a certain sum it is difficult to handle them entirely in cash, especially when they are destined to cross borders or go overseas.

Over the past years, we have seen the benefits of the 40+9 FATF recommendations, which have set global standards. Recently, the recommendations were revised and upgraded to the new 40 FATF recommendations, which support a more homogeneous environment across jurisdictions globally. Just 10 years ago, differences between jurisdictions in different regions were highly noticeable, and they created a platform for regulatory arbitrage. These days those differences are becoming fewer, although there are still differences between key financial centres and smaller jurisdictions that have smaller, emerging financial markets. Most importantly, however, is that today the environment across all key financial centres and the markets connected to those financial centres is very similar.

Global standards have certainly helped to improve the environment overall, but there are still a number of challenges that remain unresolved. And one of those challenges is identifying beneficial owners. Identifying the beneficial ownership behind funds and transactions is particularly vital if we want to spot government officials, high-ranking officers and key decision makers who are exposed to corruption and bribery or who have the ability to embezzle government funds.

So why is it so difficult if the standards are clearly defined on paper? In reality, the task proves more difficult than it appears at first glance. To begin, we must differentiate between different types of customers. First, there is mass retail and consumer banking, which is the type of banking that focuses on mass clients, volume and low costs. This is not an environment where every customer has a dedicated relationship manager. More often than not these customers are in a pool and are served by call centres, automated teller machines and the likes to drive down costs and make banking available to everyone.

Mass retail and consumer banking and its customers pose very specific challenges to identifying beneficial owners.

Second, we have commercial banking, which is when banks deal with companies, legal persons and structures that could be locally registered or offshore companies. This particular segment has different challenges as compared to the mass retail segment and those challenges stem from the complexity of legal structures. And, finally, at the high-end there is private banking. In this segment, every customer has a dedicated relationship manager. At the high-end a financial institution is better able to know more about the customer as compared to the mass retail and consumer banking segment.

That said, high-end banking customers can require complex structures to manage their money. They may need trusts to support their estate planning, which also could involve special purpose vehicle investment companies or certain complex life insurance structures. So while high-end customers have a dedicated relationship manager who knows more information about their customers, at the same time those customers are considerably more complex than mass retail customers. Therefore, each of the customer segments brings its own unique challenges that we will look at closer.

The retail segment is the entry level of the banking structure, and it is geared towards financial inclusion. It provides the basis of the banking system in that it allows businesses to transact, and it allows everyone to have an account and to keep their money in a safe and regulated place. Therefore, providing banking services in a cost-efficient manner is critical to keeping the fees low and the services affordable. For this reason, retail banking customers cannot have dedicated relationship managers. So when it comes to identifying beneficial owners, it needs to be automated and fast. This does not mean it should be done with less prudence or rigour, but the process cannot be overly complex either. In this segment, identification and verification of the individual should take place like in all other segments by way of a passport and other identification documents. The working assumption must be that the consumer will open an account in his or her own name for personal private matters.

Of course banks are aware of exceptions to the rule, and they certainly do not neglect to check the legitimacy of a person requesting an account and their services. But these accounts usually have a low(er) turnover and low volumes of wealth relative to the market in which they operate. The source of one's wealth and the source of their funds are usually linked to the account owner's occupation and job. Questions arise when the account owner has money going through the account that is not connected to his salary. In the retail segment, it would be unusual to find a company or legal structure listed as the account owner. Therefore, the natural person should be the beneficial owner.

Screening for public officials in this segment is usually done by automated systems, which check customer lists against the so-called politically exposed persons (PEPs) lists that financial institutions usually buy from one of the commercial vendors. Should the system match an account owner with a name on one of these lists, the account owner will be flagged as a PEP. These automated checks help to flag increased risk customers who could be in a position to receive bribes or even embezzle funds. Once a PEP is identified he or she will be monitored more closely than the rest of the pool. The key to this process, however, is not the identification of the beneficial owners but rather the active and ongoing monitoring of the transactions that go through the account. Transaction monitoring is the only way to identify unusual activities and unusually high amounts of money going through a mass retail account, in which one would expect only salary payments coming in and the average living expenses going out.

Even in simple account structures, there is the potential for risk. For example, a person could open the retail account but give the power of attorney to another person. The person with power of attorney could be a PEP exposed to bribery and corruption or other illegitimate funds. Therefore, it is important to check not only account holders (or, beneficial owners) but also the people who have control of the funds and access to the account. People with power of attorney usually also get screened against PEP lists to ensure that they are not politically exposed persons in a critical position.

For banks dealing with commercial customers, the challenge is to identify the beneficial owner(s) within the complexity of corporate constructs, because the financial institution is dealing with a legal person and not a natural person. To identify the beneficial owner an institution needs to identify the natural person behind these constructs.

In some cases, that could mean going up multiple ownership levels and within layers of structure before it is clear who the natural person or persons behind the structures are. The limited information provided by corporate registers makes this a very tedious and time-consuming task. Commercial customers usually do have a dedicated relationship manager who knows more about the customer. If a company is registered and organised within one jurisdiction that also can make the identification task easier.

But, of course, when hiding illegitimate funds people become very creative. They use companies from multiple jurisdictions, none of which is the jurisdiction in which they reside. As long as there is no information regarding beneficial owners in the corporate registers of the countries where these companies are registered, uncovering beneficial owners becomes the work of the financial institution. Moreover, each financial institution is working to uncover the same information about the same company. Therefore, a company's corporate structure and beneficial ownership is being investigated multiple times. Apart from this not being cost-efficient, the bigger risk is creating inconsistencies or further potential loopholes for corrupt people to exploit.

Similarly, it becomes equally challenging to detect money laundering when private banking customers use existing legal constructs as part of their overall wealth planning. Although these customers do have dedicated relationship managers who usually know the customer well, these high net-worth individuals usually do not bank with only one institution. More often than not these individuals spread their wealth across multiple banks in multiple countries, which means that none of the banks have a complete view of an individual's assets or a holistic understanding of the customer's activities. While institutions may know the beneficial owner, they most likely do not know all the transactions made by the customer. It is therefore harder to notice if transactions are unusual, and it is more difficult to differentiate between legitimate and illegitimate funds.

Identifying the beneficial owner and other challenges do not only exist with new accounts. These challenges repeat themselves each time the customer relationship is reviewed on a periodic basis. This regular relationship review is necessary and crucial to avoid high-risk beneficial owners from slipping through the cracks.

For example, there could be a situation in which a financial institution takes on a company or any legal entity structure that has no beneficial ownership of concern. However, a person of concern could become a beneficial owner at a later stage. This person could begin to control the entity, take over the entity or make key decisions involving the manoeuvring of funds, assets and money across the world under the umbrella of the original account. As a result, these challenges apply in the beginning of a relationship, during the relationship and until the end of the relationship. The structure and frequency of periodic relationship reviews is ideally driven by the inherent risk of a customer, i.e. the more complex a relationship or customer type, the higher the risk and thus the more frequent the reviews. Each review presents the same challenges, and each review requires that the same efforts be applied to the relationship on a regular basis, which could be as often as annually. So the process of reviewing customers is not a one-time task for banks and other financial institutions. Rather, it is a challenge that requires ongoing mitigation, focus and energy.

Obviously, these challenges do not exist only for banks. They also exist for the entire financial services sector, including insurance companies, asset managers and many other regulated financial services groups.

So despite all the efforts of legislators and standard setters, the financial services community as a whole and all banks individually face the same challenges after 20+ years. So what can we do to improve the situation?

It is critical to have the ability to identify people in key public positions who have the power to influence or to be influenced – that is, people who have the power to control government funds and who have the power to control government decisions that are of great interest to individuals or companies. If every country were to create its own list of people exposed to these functions across their administrations and make those lists publicly available, financial institutions around the world would be in a better position to reliably identify PEPs and specifically monitor them for transactions that do not fit their financial profile. These lists would also help to determine if any such person is a shareholder or a beneficial owner or controller of a corporation. Lists produced by governments would further reduce institutions' dependencies on certain companies that conduct their own research to identify PEPs. These companies have their own interpretation of who may or may not have a public function that allows them to control decisions and funds. Governments know better who is exposed and who should be monitored more closely than others, and this intelligence should be made available to the private sector.

Furthermore, company registers are at the centre of many of these efforts. While they exist in nearly all countries and provide critical information about structures, directors, signing authorities and so on, they do not keep information on beneficial owners. Why not? Previously, in times of economic constraints, governments expressed concerns about the work it would require for them to maintain company registers with information on beneficial owners. It is indeed a lot of work, as everyone trying to reveal the beneficial owners behind legal persons and company structures knows.

If company registers were to assume the extra work and provide information on beneficial owners, the users of the information could share the additional costs. This scenario would still make it more efficient and effective for the industry as a whole, and more importantly it would create reliable and consistent sources of information. There would be a better defence against public officials who stole assets from their people or who accepted bribes and gained personal benefits now trying to hide the money behind complex company structures.

The private sector is committed to and is investing in identifying beneficial owners. However, as outlined above, this is not an easy task. To be successful in future asset recovery efforts, it will be of the utmost importance to reliably and consistently know the beneficial owners behind bank accounts, transactions and funds. If the public sector agrees to share with the private sector critical information that will help identify PEPs and beneficial owners, it will make illicit assets more traceable. Consequently, they will be more readily found, frozen and eventually repatriated to the countries and people to which they belong.

MELIS MAMBETZHANOV

Money laundering, corruption and the collapse of kleptocracies

Combating corruption and money laundering in the Kyrgyz Republic is one of the highest priorities of the state bodies. For nearly two decades the prevailing situation in the country was characterised by the imposition of corrupted systems of governance by the country's former Presidents Askar Akaev[1] and Kurmanbek Bakiyev,[2] their family members and associates.

The presidential system of governance has proved to be the most susceptible to corruption. Corruption in the executive branch, along with many other negative aspects of the power structures in Kyrgyz Republic, were the principal contributing factors leading up to the Tulip Revolution in March 2005 and the popular revolution in April 2010.

Growing indignation among the population fed up with their rulers' excessive greed ultimately forced both the former presidents and their entourages to flee from justice after 15- and five-yearlong reigns, respectively. Former President Akaev has lived in Russia since 2005, and former President Bakiyev found shelter in Belarus. The two fugitive former presidents clearly lacked the personal or political will to address the needs of the country, namely political and economic stability. Instead, they chose to focus on embezzling and diverting huge sums of money from the state for themselves and their closest allies.

In 2005, following Bakiyev's rise to power, his supporters were still hopeful that his government would bring progress and stability to y. Instead, Bakiyev and his family members consolidated state power

1 Askar Akaev was president of the Kyrgyz Republic from 1990-2005.
2 Kurmanbek Bakiyev was president of the Kyrgyz Republic from 2005-2010.

into their own hands and began a rule entrenched in corruption and crime. The official parliament and the rest of the government of the Kyrgyz Republic acted as servants who tended to the kleptocratic interests of the omnipotent family.

In their pursuit of profit and power, members of Bakiyev's family never ceased inventing new ways to generate criminal proceeds. They imposed upon the population increased utility, electric and mobile phone tariffs. As a result of the increased taxes, entire populations in remote areas could not afford their electricity bills, which forced them to live in medieval darkness. In April 2010, the people of the Kyrgyz Republic chose to revolt against the kleptocratic Bakiyev regime. The people paid the high price of 82 individuals shot dead by the president's guards. The conflict took place on the capitol city's main square in front of the House of Government just below the ousted president's office.

The April 2010 political upheaval in the Kyrgyz Republic that led to the deposition of a tyrannical and kleptocratic president may have been an impetus for the so called 'Arab Spring', by serving as inspiration to people in other countries also suffering at the hands of despotic regimes.

The longer the family of Bakiyev remained in power, the more it profited. As a result, dirty money badly needed to be laundered abroad – that is, it needed to be safely diverted away from the Kyrgyz Republic into other jurisdictions where the money would be protected to some degree.

Resorting to the use of local commercial banks and international criminal groups specialising in money laundering, members of the Bakiyev clan were able to transfer huge amounts of capital abroad. Findings from investigations conducted by the Kyrgyz Republic's competent authorities as well as research done by independent financial institutions provided evidence of the misuse of state loans borrowed from the international community, including a USD 300 million loan from the Russian government that was officially designed to support the country's strategic sectors of the economy (hydropower, agricultural processing, mining, etc.), in order to disguise the capital outflow from the Kyrgyz Republic from 2008–2009. The son of ousted President Bakiyev, Maxim Bakiyev,[3] hired Eugene Gourevitch,[4] an international financial fraudster, to manage the country's legitimate assets so that he could mix them with the illegal assets owned by the president and his family in order to make the illegal assets appear legitimate. In addition to being investigated by the Kyrgyz law enforcement, the criminal activities and assets of Maxim Bakiyev and Eugene Gourevitch are being investigated by competent authorities in the United States, the United Kingdom and Italy.

In the United States, the US Securities and Exchange Commission is conducting, in cooperation with the FBI, an investigation into Taiyyib Ali Munir who is accused of aiding a former high-level government official of an unidentified Central Asian country in an insider-trading scheme from 2010 to 2011. The US case against Munir draws a direct link between members of the Bakiyev family and their assets in the United States and the criminal investigations underway in the Kyrgyz Republic. It is already known that ill-gotten assets belonging to a criminal group led by Maxim Bakiyev, who is indicted in the Kyrgyz Republic on charges of state looting and other financial crimes, were used in a multinational insider-trading scheme involving securities listed on stock markets in New York, London, Madrid and Milan that netted millions of dollars.

The FBI is investigating the case, assuming Maxim Bakiyev and Eugene Gourevitch were involved in a criminal conspiracy to commit securities fraud and obstruct justice. Eugene Gourevitch has already been arrested and has agreed to cooperate with the investigation. As for Maxim Bakiyev, who is currently residing in the UK, the United States filed extradition proceedings in the United Kingdom in October 2012. On 7 December 2012, the court in London appointed the extradition hearing to begin in May 2013. Later, the United States decided to withdraw its claim until his trial in the UK is over. Unfortunately, in crimes involving politically exposed persons (PEPs) and their close relatives who claim to be victims of political persecution in their own

3 Maxim Bakiyev is ousted President Bakiyev's son, formerly the director of the Kyrgyz Central Development, Investment and Innovation Agency from April 2009–April 2010.

4 Eugene Gourevitch is a US citizen who served as financial advisor to Maxim Bakiyev and his father, former President Bakiyev.

jurisdictions – jurisdictions that are in compliance with international standards for the protection of human rights – getting justice is a complicated procedure. It requires extensive work to gather evidence and to overcome various legal barriers in countries with different legal systems. In the countries where the criminal and court prosecution of criminals takes place, the professionalism of the competent authorities plays an important role. To date even the American justice system cannot unravel the crimes committed by the Bakiyev family on the US stock exchange.

Indeed, the investigation of crimes committed by transnational financial fraudsters, who use the most advanced knowledge of banking software and IT-products and work with insider information to commit crimes involving multiple jurisdictions, requires lengthy and costly procedures on the part of law enforcement bodies in order to gather sufficient evidence and establish the proof of the crime.

Throughout the process of investigating corruption, the biggest problem authorities encounter has to do with the different legal systems in the various jurisdictions in which international criminal groups have engaged in illicit activities. In the hopes of getting away with the crime, evildoers have considered the difficulty of solving crimes involving multiple jurisdictions. The malefactors must have counted on the fact that the Kyrgyz Republic has never succeeded in a single case of repatriation of proceeds of corruption hidden in foreign jurisdictions since its independence in 1991.

In 2010, after the deposition of kleptocratic President Bakiyev, the Kyrgyz Republic adopted a new constitution that established the parliamentary system of governance. New and democratic reforms aimed at optimising the public administration have been initiated. Hopefully, the new reforms will help the people and the international community regain trust in the institutes of power that were abused by the Kyrgyz Republic's two former presidents. The biggest problems the country faces are eradicating corruption and combating criminal elements in society. Local criminal groups continue to attempt to launder money out of the country, because from 2005–2010 financial fraud groups made the practice commonplace in the country's financial sector. Some criminals are also keen to pursue, launder and export their ill-gotten funds to other jurisdictions in the hopes that the Kyrgyz justice system will not be in a position to recover the stolen assets.

In 2011, the Kyrgyz Republic's government took increased measures to combat organised crime and contributed considerably to investigations of crimes allegedly committed by a number of high profile political figures. In the M. Sadyrkulov[5] murder case the military court recently sentenced ousted President Bakiyev to 24 years in prison and his brother, Janysh Bakiyev, the ex-chief of the presidential security service, to life imprisonment. The fact that fugitive ex-President Bakiyev was, as early as August 2010, granted Belarusian citizenship, shows that he is attempting to evade justice in his home country. His actions should also be considered an indirect admission of guilt. Indeed, a former head of a state would never accept citizenship from another country unless he was unsure about his innocence.

In March 2013, a court of law in the Kyrgyz Republic found Maxim Bakiyev, the former director of the Kyrgyz Central Development, Investment and Innovation Agency, guilty of corruption and entering into contracts and public procurement deals on behalf of the state, which were harmful to the interests of the Kyrgyz Republic. He was sentenced in absentia to 24 years in prison, his property was confiscated and he was banned from public office for three years. According to the statement issued by the court, as a consequence of one particular illegal privatisation deal the state budget lost as much as KGS 123,498,700 (over USD 2.5 million). In another deal, the state lost USD 132.7 million as an intentional result of underselling a strategic company in the power sector. Based on the conviction, the Office of the Prosecutor General of the Kyrgyz Republic intends to file an extradition proceeding in the United Kingdom.

During the Kyrgyz Republic's first two presidencies, the nation moved steadily towards one of the most corrupt countries in the world. Ultimately, the Kyrgyz Republic was ranked 166 out of 180 in Transparency International's Corruption Perception Index. The existing

5 M. Sadyrkulov was the former chief of former President Bakiyev's staff. On 13 March 2009, upon return from a business trip to Almaty, he was treacherously kidnapped and brutally murdered in a criminal conspiracy. The crime was only investigated in 2011–2012.

national anti-money laundering/combating the financing of terrorism (AML/CFT) system has been heavily criticised by Financial Action Task Force (FATF), which placed the Kyrgyz Republic on the so called 'grey' list of jurisdictions that have strategic AML/CFT deficiencies and fall short of FATF standards. At the moment, the political leadership of the Kyrgyz Republic is taking measures to develop a national system for combating money laundering that includes important mechanisms that support the establishment and identification, tracing and confiscation of the proceeds of crime. Therefore, the anti-money laundering efforts are regarded as an integral part of the comprehensive anti-corruption strategy. Taking into account the above-described situation in the country, a national program aimed at eradicating corruption across all sectors of society was launched in 2012. National anti-corruption and anti-money laundering legislation are currently being reviewed and improved. Judicial and law enforcement reforms are well underway, along with efforts to weed out corrupt public officials from the bodies of the state most vulnerable to corrupt influence. Under the country's former presidents, major national corporations and taxpayers were forced to enter illegal schemes designed to profit the companies affiliated with and controlled by the ex-presidents' relatives and associates. These companies are now subjected to tight monitoring.

One particularly profitable business in the Kyrgyz Republic deals with mobile communication services. In the past, mobile communication companies in the country achieved rapid development and profit growth. Beginning in 2005, when Bakiyev's clique seized power, almost every mobile communication company was forced to give shares of their businesses to persons who represented the interests of the ruling family. In return, company owners were allowed to own the remainder of their businesses.

At some point around early 2008, the Bakiyev clan began using the services of so-called 'international consultants' who advised them on new market relationships. At this time, the largest mobile communication companies were raided by the government and taken over via fraudulent schemes. Thus, members of the Bakiyev family seized ownership and took full control of the mobile phone companies. The new, post-revolution government has decided to completely or partially nationalise the companies that were seized by the Bakiyev family. However, some of the mobile communication companies have retained the management they had under the Bakiyev regime for purposes of business development and due to a shortage of qualified specialists in the IT field.

The identification, freezing, confiscation and repatriation of criminal assets can be used to counter kleptocracy and to protect the national interests of developing states

A newly appointed set of high-level managers in the largest national mobile operator in The Kyrgyz Republic, which has a significant public ownership as a result of nationalisation, are in charge of the interim management of the company. Based on large banking transactions involving various jurisdictions, it is known that the interim managers decided also to partake in schemes of tax evasion and money laundry. A detailed analysis of contracts for the procurement of new generation IT technologies approved by the company's managers shows that instead of paying the supplier directly for the IT technologies the money ended up in banking accounts opened in advance by the suppliers in a totally different Southeast Asian country.

As a result of law enforcement officials monitoring banking transactions and investigating the illegal diversion of large amounts of cash from the mobile operator, two of the company's top managers and one of their local partners were indicted on the following charges: abuse of power by a public official, bribery, fraud and embezzlement as well as legalisation (laundering) of proceeds of crime.

The Kyrgyz Republic's financial intelligence unit (FIU), with the support of its partners at the Egmont Group, has been able to trace the cash stolen from the company and laundered abroad by the criminal schemers. Authorities have established that the cash was diverted from the company by manipulating procurement contracts. A total of USD 14 million was purported to acquire equipment at intentionally inflated prices via the use of shell companies. The scheme ultimately netted USD 6 million, which landed in the plotters' account.

In the course of the criminal investigation, authorities found out that one of the principal defendants (identified as Mr X) demanded a USD 6 million kickback during the negotiation process with the head of a supplier company. Mr X said the money must to be paid to an account belonging to a private company he controlled as a precondition to the procurement contract for the mobile operator he officially represented. The foreign supplier accepted the condition, because he realised there was potential profit for him. The USD 6 million bribe could serve as a pledge for continued cooperation between the supplier company and the major mobile phone operator. As a result of the negotiation, the illegal USD 6 million bribe was paid in full to an account belonging to a company called 'TCL' that was controlled by Mr X and registered in the British Virgin Islands. The bank account, however, was opened in a Southeast Asian country. Confident of their impunity, the malefactors proceeded to legalise their criminally obtained funds.

From July–September 2011, Mr X initiated three transfers (approximately USD 2 million each) of cash from the 'T.C.L.' bank account in an attempt to make ownership of the illicit assets appear legal. By using a banking sector in another country in the same region of Southeast Asia, he closed a USD 2 million real estate deal involving a piece of property in the capital city of The Kyrgyz Republic, which was subsequently registered under his spouse's name. Next, around USD 2 million was transferred via shell companies back to the Kyrgyz Republic and deposited in other bank accounts. The money was cashed upon fictional grounds with a view to cover the plotter's personal expenses. The remaining USD 2 million was disguised as a loan to a company called 'IC-FFC' and paid into an account in a commercial bank in Lichtenstein.

The FIU of the Kyrgyz Republic sent an inquiry concerning the abovementioned bank account to the EFFI (the state FIU of Lichtenstein). The EFFI provided relevant information regarding the account. In addition, the FIU from the Seychelles Islands assisted in confirming that the account actually belonged to a company registered in the Seychelles Islands. The company's beneficiary is no one else but Mr X, who originally withdrew the money from the national mobile operator in the Kyrgyz Republic where he worked as a top manager.

The EFFI has temporarily frozen the funds in the bank account in Lichtenstein, and it provided the Kyrgyz FIU with all relevant information. Based on the information forwarded by the EFFI, and with the invaluable support of the Basel Institute on Governance, the competent Kyrgyz prosecution body has, pursuant to the United Nations Convention against Corruption (UNCAC), sent a mutual legal assistance request to Lichtenstein with a view to freezing the illicit assets owned by Mr X.

The MLA request was satisfied by the competent court of a European state, which decided to freeze the assets in the bank account in Lichtenstein for a period of two years. In process of pursuing the freeze order, the suspects were brought to justice in a court of law. Two of the principal defendants were arrested and placed in detention, while another one is under house arrest.

Successful indictment and prosecution of the crime of money laundering is fairly difficult, especially because it means unravelling complicated and sophisticated schemes involving the movement of assets across financial sectors in multiple jurisdictions. Collecting evidence and establishing proof of the crime requires special skills and knowledge and also qualified and coordinated efforts on the part of investigators, prosecutors and judges. In the case of freezing the assets in Lichtenstein, the key roles were played by the FIUs in the Kyrgyz Republic and Lichtenstein, whose interactions with each other were based on the principle of reciprocity. The joint financial investigation that resulted in detecting USD 2 million and identifying the account's beneficiary serves as an example of the best practices of cooperation between FIUs in the Egmont Group. The Kyrgyz Republic's lack of knowledge and experience in the repatriation of illicit assets was compensated for by the technical support provided by donors.

In order to smoothly repatriate the stolen assets to the Kyrgyz Republic, the EFFI requested that a donor agency provide support to the competent authorities of the Kyrgyz Republic in the preparation of a mutual legal assistance request. Subsequently, the donor agency hired an expert from the International Centre for Asset Recovery (ICAR) with the Basel Institute on Governance along with an independent anti-money laundering expert and financially supported their missions in The Kyrgyz Republic. The Kyrgyz Republic appointed the anti-money laundering expert as a representative of the government who, in cooperation with the competent authorities in Lichtenstein, attended to the process of repatriating the stolen assets on behalf of the interests of The Kyrgyz Republic. A few months later, all relevant paperwork regarding the account in Lichtenstein was furnished to the Kyrgyz Republic and used to support the prosecution of the anti-corruption case there. As a next step, it is expected that the assets will be confiscated and returned to their lawful owner.

Silvio Antonio Marques

Political immunities: Obstacles in the fight against corruption

Political immunities are constitutional prerogatives that protect certain public officials from investigation and prosecution by precluding unlawfulness, punishment or payment of compensation when these public officials perform certain acts. Considered by many authors to be privileges, these faculties seek to promote freedom of action and self-determination for public officials, in particular parliamentarians in the exercise of their functions.

While controversial,[1] most historians believe that the origins of political immunity date back to ancient Greece, where speakers were inviolable with regards to the opinions they expressed in the tribune. In Rome, the Lex Sacrata of 494 BCE conferred immunity on the tribunes and their assistants (edis), who were not subject to punishment in connection to the opinions they expressed.[2]

The current configuration of these guarantees, however, is a result of the English Privilege of Parliament Act 1603, which prevented the arrests of Members of Parliament in particular as a result of civil debts, and the Bill of Rights of 1689, which guaranteed the freedom of speech and protected Members of Parliament against abuses and coer-

1 Luiz Pinto Ferreira, *Princípios gerais do direito constitucional moderno,* São Paulo, Saraiva, 6.a edição, 1983, p. 492.

2 The tribunes were magistrates elected by the people with the mission of defending the interests of the Roman commoner. At the time, inviolability was granted to the tribunes, and it was considered a triumph of the commoners and democracy (Charles Demangeat, *Cours Elementaire de droit romain*, Paris, Marescq Ainé, 1876, tome 1, p. 41; Michel Poizat, *Vox populi, vox Dei: voix et pouvoir,* Paris, Éditions Métailié, 2001, p. 82).

cive measures enacted by the English sovereign in response to parliamentary statements or bills.[3]

There are many cases that are remembered as inductors of political immunity in the English legal system. Certainly, one of the most emblematic cases involves Member of Parliament Richard Strode, who was sentenced in 1512 by Stannary Court of Devon to prison and a fine for having presented a project for the exploration of tin in Dartmoor. However, the Respecting Richard Strode Act declared null and void all proceedings initiated against Members of Parliament related to subject matter of assessment by the British Parliament, which was a body that simultaneously had judicial and legislative powers.[4]

In the US, the First Amendment of the Constitution (1791) forbids Congress to enact laws against freedom of speech and other civil liberties:

> Congress shall make no law respecting an establishment of religion, or prohibiting the free exercise thereof; or abridging the freedom of speech, or of the press; or the right of the people peaceably to assemble, and to petition the government for a redress of grievances.

In the past, political immunities not only protected the free expression of opinion, but they also allowed for the independence of Members of Parliament and gave them an important function in relation to the sovereign. Among parliamentarians there was a real fear of sovereigns, particularly in European monarchical regimes until the end of the Middle Ages.

Over time, however, in many countries these guarantees were expanded to include a range of public officials in addition to Members of Parliament. Currently, many immunities are no longer justified, because the legislative branch of government is guaranteed its power in democratic countries. Moreover, politicians who commit crimes or administrative irregularities before or during their term in office some-

3 The text of Article 9 of the Bill of Rights of 1689 established 'that the freedom of speech and debates or proceedings in Parliament ought not to be impeached or questioned in any court or place out of Parliament'.

4 J.P. Joseph Maingot, *Le privilège parlementaire au Canada*, McGill-Queen's Press, 1997, pp. 27 e 28.

times use immunities to avoid investigations and criminal and civil proceedings against them. In many cases related to corruption, money laundering and other serious crimes, immunities result in serious damage to investigations or criminal prosecutions, which results in impunity.

Types of political immunities in countries

Political immunities are generally granted to Members of Parliament and members of the executive or the judicial branches of government for acts performed within the exercise of their functions. There are two types of political immunities: material immunities (absolute immunities) and formal immunities (procedural or relative immunities), which have limitations foreseen under the constitutional system of each country.

Material and formal immunities

Material immunities[5] are constitutional provisions that exclude the illegality of an act and the imposition of a criminal, civil, political or disciplinary sanction. Formal immunities are immunities that exclude measures, such as arrest, investigation, the process and the obligation to testify as witnesses or those that establish privileged jurisdiction.[6]

Hence, when expressed by ordinary people who do not have immunities opinions can be characterised as crimes of defamation, slan-

5 Brazilian jurists have discussed the legal nature of material immunities concerning crimes of opinion (defamation, incitement to commit a crime, etc.). Some argue that immunities are due to the exclusion of the criminal offence (Celso Ribeiro Bastos and Ives Gandra da Silva Martins, *Comentários à Constituição do Brasil,* v. 4, p. 187; César Dario Mariano da Silva, *Manual de Direito Penal,* São Paulo, GZ Editora, 2009, 17ª ed. p. 62). Others claim that the crime remains, but the constitution excludes *the punishment that could be applied* (Damásio E. de Jesus, *Questões criminais,* São Paulo, Saraiva, 1988, p. 53).

6 Julio Fabbrini Mirabete, *Processo Penal,* São Paulo, Atlas, 2005, 17ª edição, pp. 68–70.

der and libel, among others. However, when Members of Parliament express such opinions they do not represent any wrongdoing. Because there is no crime, administrative measures or related criminal procedures, such as arrest, detention, investigation and proceedings as well as civil action for damages, are not permitted.

Although some national constitutions do not explicitly separate material immunity from formal immunity, in most cases there is a definite distinction. In the US, Section 6 of the 1787 Constitution prescribes that:

> …the Senators and Representatives shall in all cases, except treason, felony and breach of the peace, be privileged from arrest during their attendance at the session of their respective Houses, and in going to and returning from the same.

They are equally inviolable for any speech or debate in both houses of Congress and cannot be questioned in any other place.

The 1958 Constitution of France establishes in a single article but in separate paragraphs formal and material immunities. Under material immunity, Members of Parliament cannot be processed, investigated, stopped, detained or tried for opinions expressed or for votes cast in the exercise of their functions. Under formal immunity, Members of Parliament cannot be subject to, in criminal or correctional matters, detention or any other form of deprivation or restriction of liberty except when authorised by the *bureau* of the assembly to which the Member of Parliament belongs. This authorisation is waived in the case of arrest in flagrante delicto or in a final judgement convicting the Member of Parliament of the commission of a crime. Moreover, detention, deprivation, the restriction of liberty measure and the accusation against a Member of Parliament are suspended throughout the parliamentary session (Article 26).

In Spain, the Constitution of 1978 deals with material immunity by establishing that Members of Parliament and senators enjoy inviolability for the opinions expressed in the exercise of their functions (Article 71). Regarding formal immunity, the Spanish Constitution states that during their tenure Members of Parliament and senators enjoy immunity and may only be detained in the case of flagrante delicto. They cannot be charged or prosecuted without permission of the respective chamber (Article 72). Moreover, parliamentarians enjoy privileged jurisdiction, because proceedings are adjudicated by the Criminal Chamber of the Supreme Court of Spain (Article 73).

The 1983 Constitution of the People's Republic of China deals initially with formal immunity, stating in Article 74:

> ...the deputy to the National People's Congress may be arrested or placed on criminal trial without the consent of the Presidium of the current session of the National People's Congress or, when the National People's Congress is not in session, without the consent of its Standing Committee.

Regarding material immunity, the Chinese Constitution states that 'Deputies to the National People's Congress may not be legally called to account for Their speeches or votes at its meetings' (Article 75).

In Argentina, thc 1994 Constitution prescribes for material immunity in that 'No member of Congress shall be accused, judicially examined, or disturbed for opinions expressed or speeches delivered by him while holding office as a legislator' (Section 68). Regarding formal immunity, the same constitution provides in Section 69 that:

> ...no senator or deputy shall be arrested as from the day of his election until the expiration of his term, except when flagrantly surprised committing a crime deserving capital punishment or other infamous or serious punishment, in which case the summary report of the facts Shall be submitted to the Corresponding House.

It goes on to say:

> ...when a written complaint is filed before the ordinary courts against any senator or deputy, once examined if there is enough evidence in a public trial, each House may, with the concurrence of two-thirds of the votes, suspend the accused party from his office and place him under the jurisdiction of the competent court to be judged (Section 70).

Moreover:

> ...the member of Congress Shall be appointed to any civil office or commission under the Executive Power, without the previous consent of the respective House, except for employments subject to promotions (Section 72).

The 1999 Swiss Constitution in Article 176 deals only with political material immunity, which benefits not only Members of Parliament but also the Chancellor of the Confederation. 'The members of the Federal Assembly and the Federal Council as well as the Federal Chancellor may not be held Liable for statements they make in the Assembly or in its organs'. Furthermore, Article 177 provides that 'the law may Provide for further forms of immunity and extend its scope to include other persons'.

Extent of political immunities

Political material and formal immunities are neither unlimited nor uniform in all countries. As a rule, they are guarantees foreseen in the constitution of each state and may vary in relation to the person (ratione personae), matter (ratione materiae), duration (ratione temporis) and place (ratione loci) of commission of the act.

Extent of ratione personae

In most countries, political immunities are granted to Members of Parliament who are exercising their public activities. But some constitutions extend the same guarantees to others, in particular to members of the executive branch and the judiciary.

The national constitutions of common law countries, such as Australia, India, Kenya and Zambia, protect Members of Parliament and other persons who testify before a parliamentary commission. Others extend inviolability to several holders of official function, such as heads of state (as in Belgium and Switzerland), cabinet ministers (as in Belgium and Macedonia) and judges of some courts (as in Slovenia and Switzerland).[7]

Although not in line with the common law system, the 1995 Constitution of Angola provides in Article 97 immunities to Members of Parliament and others:

7 Marc van der Hust, *Le mandat parlementaire – étude comparative mondiale*, Genève, Union Interplanetaire, 2000, p. 89.

> The Speaker, the Deputy Speaker, Members of Parliament and any other person participating or assisting in or acting in connection with or reporting the proceedings of Parliament or any of its committees Shall be Entitled to such immunities and privileges the Parliament Shall prescribe by law.

Extent of ratione materiae

The constitutions of most countries grant immunity in criminal cases, excluding defamation offences, and they forbid imprisonment or detention, investigations and proceedings. However, in some countries there is also the exclusion of civil cases, especially against Members of Parliament.

The Constitution of Angola, for example, provides temporary criminal and civil immunity during the performance of the duties of the president:

> Civil or criminal proceedings may be instituted against a person after ceasing to be President, in respect of anything done or omitted to be done in his or her personal capacity before or During the term of office of that person, and any period of limitation in respect of any such proceedings Shall not be taken to run During the period while that person was President.

The Constitution of the Republic of Mozambique states that no Member of Parliament may be detained or imprisoned, except in the case of flagrante delicto, or brought to trial without the consent of the Assembly of the Republic (Article 174). In the case of criminal proceedings against a Member of Parliament, the member is heard by a Supreme Court judge and enjoys special jurisdiction, as the Supreme Tribunal can only judge a Member of Parliament in accordance with the law. Members of Parliament cannot be prosecuted, detained or tried for opinions expressed or votes cast in the exercise of their functions, except with regards to civil liability and criminal liability for defamation.

Extent of ratione temporis

Political immunities are temporary and usually conferred to public officials who are in office or in a public function. In Uruguay, the 1967 Constitution asserts 'Senators and Representatives shall never be responsible for the vote and opinions expressed during the performance of their duties' (Article 112).

Although considered personal prerogatives, some authors[8] believe that immunities cannot be waived as they arise from the public interest in the proper exercise of the term in office. However, inviolabilities do not prevail if the Member of Parliament begins exercising other functions within the state.

Extent of ratione loci

The place of commission of the criminal offence is generally not regarded as decisive in defining political immunities. Members of Parliament and other public officials who exercise their functions at the national level generally have immunity within national boundaries. Conversely, representatives of regions, provinces, member states and municipalities have prerogatives guaranteed within the limits of the territory in which they perform their duties.

Some national constitutions are more restrictive and ensure the inviolability exclusively in the Parliament building. The 1949 Constitution of Germany, for example, assigns the Members of Parliament material and formal immunities but only for votes and expressions delivered within the Bundestag or one of its committees (Article 46). Furthermore, defamatory insults are excluded from the scope of immunities, even if committed within the Bundestag.

In the Kingdom of Norway, in accordance with the 1814 Constitution:

> Members of Parliament on their way to and from the Storting, as well as during their attendance there, shall be exempt from personal arrest, unless they are apprehended in public crimes, nor may they be called to account outside the meetings of the Storting for opinions expressed there (Article 66).

8 Manoel Gonçalves Ferreira Filho, *Curso de Direito Constitucional,* São Paulo, Saraiva, 1989, p. 154.

Inconvenience of political immunities

Political immunities have had an important role since the end of the Middle Ages in preserving the independence of the legislative branch in relation to the executive branch and the judiciary. It can be argued that, although not uniform in all countries, for a long time these guarantees were a factor in the maintenance of legality and the affirmation of democracy itself.

Today, however, political immunities have been used in some countries to protect public officials accused of serious crimes, especially corruption and money laundering. It is therefore necessary to review the institute of political immunities, as it has become a privilege temporarily ascribed to some public officials and not just as a prerogative to exercise their functions.

Misuse of guarantees

Although the origin of immunities is directly related to the defence of Members of Parliament, some countries have expanded their scope to include the protection of other public officials, such as the head of the executive branch and members of the judiciary. In addition, some countries stipulate the so-called special jurisdiction, giving a court the competence to judge such authorities.

The result of this combination of factors could not be more disastrous. Even in countries where the regulatory bodies are effective, some public officials accused of serious crimes can create obstacles to investigations and criminal proceedings, thereby delaying or even preventing the enforcement of criminal and civil legislation.

Brazil is a country where the undue extension and misuse of immunities caused an increase in corruption and impunity. The 1988 Constitution, as well as texts from other countries, stipulates that congressmen and senators shall be civilly and criminally inviolable for their opinions, words and votes. Since the promulgation of the constitution, Members of Parliament have been on trial before the Supreme Court (STF). If the STF receives a complaint against a senator or a congressman for a crime which took place after having been confirmed winner the election, it will inform the respective chamber (Senate or House of Representatives), which, upon the initiative of a political party represented in it and by the vote of the majority of its members, may, until the final judgement, halt the progress of criminal proceedings.

However, in the Brazilian system, Members of Parliament are also on trial before the Supreme Court for crimes committed before the beginning of their term in office. Thus, criminal proceedings for mild and severe criminal offences are displaced from lower courts or magistrates for judgment by the STF directly. If the Member of Parliament loses his seat or his term ends before the end of the criminal proceedings, the proceedings are returned to the magistrate of first instance or a lower court.

According to surveys conducted in 2012, at least 200 Brazilian Members of Parliament (federal congressmen and senators) are under investigation or responding to criminal prosecutions before the STF. There is no forecast on when these proceedings will end, because the STF is also responsible for the prosecution of numerous actions, including on the constitutionality or unconstitutionality of statutes and other normative acts, and for interpreting the Federal Constitution. The same happens in other courts that are competent to hear cases related to other authorities.

With regard to corruption, the situation is alarming. There are criminal cases that were all but terminated several years ago, because the 11 ministers of the Supreme Court do not have time to hear all the cases. Three of these cases involve Congressman Paulo Maluf, who served between 1993 and 1996 as mayor of São Paulo, the largest city in the country. Despite having an arrest warrant issued by the Justice of New York (where he laundered part of around USD 350 million diverted from municipal coffers), the inclusion of his name in Interpol's red notice and the freezing of his assets in civil cases presented by the prosecution, the accused continues to peacefully exercise his office as congressman.[9]

9 The existing criminal cases before the STF against Congressman Paulo Maluf refer to the following facts: a) Case No. 458 – Crimes of responsibility during his tenure as mayor; b) Case No. 477 – Crimes against the national financial

Admittedly, there are risks associated with Brazilian legislators voting on constitutional amendments that jettison the prosecution from criminal investigations and assign this task exclusively to the police and other amendments that give Congress the power to decide over certain final opinions issued by the STF. In other words, Members of Parliament sometimes do not want just parliamentary immunity, but they also want to prevent independent investigations and to decide for themselves on whether to implement decisions from the STF.

Need to review the system of immunities

The fact that public servants enjoy constitutional immunity and the fact that they temporarily hold a portion of state power makes it difficult to investigate wrongdoing as well as their criminal or civil punishment. A revision of the system of immunities therefore is necessary for an effective fight against corruption and other serious crimes.

The subject matter, in fact, has occupied jurists since the 20th century. For Hans Kelsen, this 'absolutely anachronistic privilege' has always been the cause of the antipathy of the masses and the educated classes under the parliamentary system. For the same law professor, the fact that a Member of Parliament cannot be prosecuted for a common crime, and especially not be detained without the permission of the legislative branch, is a privilege that dates back to the days of monarchy when there was a violent antagonism between Parliament and the government of the king.[10] Carl Schmitt's opinion was in the same vein when he called immunity an 'amazing privilege'.[11]

In Brazil, many public authorities have spoken against the privileges associated with the constitutional rules on political immunities, especially those assigned to Members of Parliament. Chief Justice of the STF Joaquim Barbosa openly advocates for the extinction of the

system; c) Case No. 461 – Conspiracy to commit a crime, crimes against the national financial system, crime of money laundering.

10 *Apud* Enéias Xavier Gomes, *Da crítica de Hans Kelsen às imunidades parlamentares, in* Revista Jurídica De Jure, Belo Horizonte, 2012, pp. 493–494.

11 *Teória de la Constitución,* Madrid, Revista de Derecho Privado, 1927, p. 366.

'privileged jurisdiction', which leads to impunity. The chief justice further argues that the Brazilian judicial system discriminates against the poor. 'Brazil is a country that punishes a lot of poor people, African Brazilians and those without good connections', said the chief justice, referring to those who cannot afford good lawyers.[12]

Conclusion

Although this topic is vast and raises varied opinions, in conclusion the following can be mentioned:

Political immunities were designed with the function of protecting Members of Parliament from persecutions exercised through investigations or court proceedings initiated by the executive branch and related to opinions or bills presented during the exercise of their function.

In addition to protecting Members of Parliament, some countries extended such guarantees to other political agents or judges, or instituted a privileged forum. This expansion proved to be improper or inconvenient, as some public officials have been given privileges that are not just guarantees for the exercise of their functions.

Although foreseen in the constitutional text, the privileged jurisdiction for the prerogative of function, which is a manifestation of political immunities, is extremely detrimental to the investigation of corruption and other serious crimes, because the competent court to hear these cases usually has no vocation for this function, which consequently delays adjudication or generates impunity.

Political immunities should be scrapped or at least reworded to be restricted to the defence of freedom of expression for Members of Parliament in the same manner as its original configuration. In democratic regimes, such guarantees are not justified today.

12 Newspaper *Valor,* electronic edition of 03 May 2013, newsreporter Juliano Basile.

RUDOLF WYSS

Proactive cooperation within the mutual legal assistance procedure

Introduction

The main instrument for an international cooperation in criminal matters is commonly referred to as mutual legal assistance (MLA). Over the last fifty years, and especially after the codification and implementation of the European Convention on Mutual Legal Assistance in Criminal Matters, dated 20 April 1959,[1] a broad set of bilateral, regional and universal treaties has been elaborated and implemented.

It is well-known that there are significant differences in these instruments that consequently make it very difficult – even for a specialist – to have just an approximate overview of what exactly is the international cooperation law. This is even truer because many of these treaties have been supplemented through additional instruments. Their legal nature differs from non-binding Memoranda of Understanding to formal supplementary agreements that in order to be implemented must be ratified in the respective States Parties' parliaments.

Looking more closely at these treaties, one often finds that as the result of long negotiations the compromise wording generally avoids clearly binding the rights and duties of the parties. The main reason for this is that parties to the treaty try to preserve their domestic law as far as possible.

Another general rule on the cooperation in criminal matters is the old Roman principle 'locus regit actum'. This principle has led to a significant number of national legislations on MLA, which address the questions left open in the treaties, such as which domestic authorities can execute a foreign request, how to execute the request, what legal

1 ETS No. 030.

remedies are available to the accused persons as well as the requesting States against any decision taken by the requested State.

This overall situation has led to faltering in the matter and created a feeling of frustration among various stakeholders. There are numerous treaties and instruments, but for the most part they only reflect the 'acquis' (achievements) of the matter on a continental or interregional level.

A fundamental problem in MLA procedure is the passivity and legal conservatism of requested States. Every requested State demands that requesting States fulfil their own special requirements. Instead of assisting their counterparts, requested States try to teach requesting States how to act and how to draft the exact wording of their requests. This is often done with criticism rather than with supportive and encouraging words.

Major impediments to a swift cooperation

The traditional perception of the roles of the requesting and requested States often results in a passive attitude on the part of the requested State. Some requested States do not even answer requests that seem at first glance to have little chance of being accepted. In cases in which responses are provided to the requesting State, sometimes after a long period of time, the response usually includes a long enumeration of the missing elements in the request. Such attitudes and delays on the part of judicial authorities is in sharp contrast to the speed with which business transactions can be carried out by criminals. In a number of countries complicated channels of transmission for MLA requests are still in place. Consequently, not only is time lost before the request can reach the hands of the competent magistrates but sometimes the whole case-file is lost.

Other requested countries' practice is to send a standard model of a 'perfect' MLA request to the requesting magistrate who finds difficult to understand the model, because it is written from the sole viewpoint of the requested State and generally does not take into account the legal differences of the requesting countries. Requesting States are bombarded with manuals, guidebooks and links to Internet pages none of which bring any further concrete assistance. From experience, these usually well-intended tools can sometimes lead instead to a great deal of confusion amongst the investigating authorities or can even discourage them from taking further steps or actions.

The MLA procedure is formal like any other legal procedure based on written documents. However, in many cases the different parties initiate their cooperation without first informally contacting or speaking to each other. Many mistakes and misunderstandings could be avoided if the requesting and requested States communicated earlier. Initiating MLA without first communicating is like a person who is lost in a dark forest and looking for a way out without first consulting his compass. Even a high-speed run in an unknown direction will not necessarily bring one to his intended point of destination.

In summary, it can be said that a strange desire to preserve a country's own domestic legal system coupled with a passive attitude at the beginning of MLA challenges disregard the keyword 'assistance' in mutual legal assistance procedures. Are repeated promises to extend cooperation made by State Parties and included in the texts of bilateral and multilateral treaties merely empty expressions?

Remedies

The following are some thoughts on how to improve upon the existing situation with regards to MLA and how to make the MLA procedure more effective.

First, the text will analyse the existing legal instruments, and subsequently it will question whether some clauses would allow a more proactive strategy for the requested States. The analysis will primarily focus on the United Nations Convention against Corruption (UNCAC).

Whilst incorporating the pre-existing philosophy that international cooperation is primarily giving assistance upon request, UNCAC allows for different spaces for proactive cooperation. Proactive cooperation shall be understood as the cooperation that is given or offered with genuine interest in combating international crimes. In other words, the deep conviction that the international community should lead countries and their law enforcement agencies all over the world in informing their foreign colleagues about suspicious situations or activities with a possible criminal background.

Second, this text will conduct a brief analysis of four instruments that are considered to go further than a cooperation request. The implementation of these four instruments is either largely unknown or has not yet reached its full potential as outlined under UNCAC.

Cooperation without prior request: UNCAC Article 46 paragraph 4[2] and Article 56[3]

A relatively long time before the Articles 46 paragraph 4 and 56 of UNCAC allowed States the possibility of spontaneously transmitting information, in 1996 the Swiss legislator enacted the possibility in its domestic MLA-legislation.[4] A close analysis of the provision of article 67a in the Swiss Federal Act on Mutual Assistance in Criminal Matters (IMAC) of 20 March 1981 reveals how cautiously the parliament worded this particular provision.

This is not surprising, as this clause was not only the subject of controversy in the discussions of the parliamentary subcommittees but also in the discussions of the plenary.[5] When reading its wording one can clearly see the efforts made to limit an uncontrolled exchange of information. On the other hand, those involved in the practice of MLA recognise that there is, indeed, an actual need to informally exchange information with foreign investigative bodies regarding facts that may

2 '[…] a State party may, without prior request, transmit information relating to criminal matters to a competent authority in another State party[…]'

3 Under the heading of 'special cooperation'.

4 See Article 67a Swiss Federal Act on Mutual Assistance in Criminal Matters, of 20 March 1981; (IMAC).

5 Rudolf Wyss, Die Revision der Gesetzgebung über die internationale Rechtshilfe in Strafsachen in SJZ (1997) Nr. 3, espec. pages 41-43; Robert Zimmermann, La coopération judiciaire internationale en matière pénale, pages 381-387; Stämpfli Ed. SA Berne, 2009, troisième édition.

be of interest to them, because there is suspicion that these facts have to do with a crime committed abroad.

Statistical data from the Swiss Federal Office of Justice[6] shows that in recent years an average of 70 to 110 spontaneous transmissions are made from Swiss authorities to their counterparts abroad a year. It is not surprising that most of the transmissions were made to law enforcement agencies in the neighbouring countries. This information proves that Swiss authorities prefer to take proactive measures primarily with authorities with whom a certain level of confidence has been established. The author hopes that more foreign law enforcement and judicial authorities will profit from the possibility of spontaneously transmitting information in future and that the necessary confidence between the authorities can be built rapidly.

Of course the authority receiving the information would be liable to undertake every possible effort to respect the conditions of use that are normally imposed by the providing authority. Furthermore, due to the fact that Switzerland receives on average only 5(!) spontaneous transmissions of information a year from foreign countries, it is clear that this instrument is not known to many foreign investigating agencies.

Swift and complete freeze orders

Article 31 paragraph 1 of UNCAC requires the contracting parties take 'to the greatest extent possible' within their domestic legal systems the measures necessary to effectively freeze money and objects that are the proceeds of a criminal activity or destined for use in an offense. The practical value of this provision should not be underestimated, as issuing a freeze order is most often the origin of successful international cooperation. The opposite, namely complicated, lengthy and demanding freeze procedures, are often the origin of frustrating and unsuccessful cooperation.

What is the value of a complicated and lengthy freeze order if when the order is finally issued, the money has already been taken

6 Available at: www.rhf.admin.ch/rhf/de/home/straf/.html.

away? In a world where business transactions are performed very quickly, where huge amounts of money can be wired from one jurisdiction to another within a very short time, investigating authorities must be granted effective countermeasures. When UNCAC proposes that such actions should be taken – of course only temporarily – on the basis of previous oral requests (Article 46 paragraph 14) it demonstrates a clear commitment to proactive cooperation.

Naturally, the same circumstances apply to politically motivated freeze orders, such as the Swiss Federal Council decisions during the political upheaval in Tunisia and Egypt in the spring 2011. Here another proactive step could have been of immense help to Egypt and Tunisia. The freeze orders could have been combined with an indication or detailed information on the persons whose bank accounts were blocked or on properties that were seized. Initiating this second step, which could also be regarded as proactive cooperation, would have been of paramount importance to the two States. Knowing this information could have helped them focus their investigations, gain time and save costs.

The ways in which Tunisia's and Egypt's efforts to recover their presumed stolen assets were treated up to now illustrates again the existence of passive attitudes and discouraging administrative barriers rather than effective and efficient support of countries in democratic transition. It is to be feared that in these circumstances inaction or passivity in relation to international cooperation in criminal matters could have unintended consequences, which cannot be reliably predicted. The uncertainty surrounding possible consequences may, as a result, discourage these countries during their democratisation process.

Is close and proactive cooperation not exactly the sort of cooperation – in the widest possible extent – that is explicitly required from State Parties to the UNCAC?

Exchange of persons/experts

Article 48 paragraph 1 lit. (e) of UNCAC allows a requested State to support a requesting State through the exchange of specialised personnel and experts or by posting liaison officers. Also, international law provides explicitly for support to be given to another State that goes beyond merely executing foreign MLA on the basis of a written request. Of course, this kind of support cannot be provided for common cases. However, when dealing with large and complex cases in which hundreds of millions of dollars worth of assets are at stake or in which there are potential political consequences, strong efforts to provide support should be made in the early stages of the cooperation process.

Steps should be taken to ensure that the requesting State does not commit acts that will lead to an unsuccessful cooperation. In complicated investigations a fast, proactive decision on the part of the requested State to offer help in the form of specialists can be of crucial importance. Some cases' highly political nature can have implications and impacts on society that are without a doubt comparable to ecological disasters. In the case of environmental catastrophe, who would wait months or years before taking action? Who would refer the State asking for help to manuals or Internet sites with examples of good practices, etc.? Unfortunately, in the legal cooperation field this is still done as a rule. A real proactive and supportive approach is undertaken quite rarely. Requested States have specialists on hand, but if for political or legal reasons the requested State would prefer not to be directly involved in expert consulting, there are many other alternatives. For example, there are specialised lawyers and, more importantly, international organisations, such as the UN and the World Bank's Stolen Asset Recovery (StAR) Initiative, universities or specialised institutes, such as the International Centre for Asset Recovery (ICAR) of the Basel Institute on Governance.

Without going into detail, when working with a requesting State a delegation of one or more experts needs a clear legal framework – respectively, a case consultancy agreement, a detailed description of the services sought, a description of the rights and duties of both parties involved, a reporting duty for both parties, a description of the terms of confidentiality, a description of the modalities of remuneration or termination of services, etc.

Special proactive forms of cooperation in criminal investigations against political exposed persons (PEP)

To date in common criminal investigations many countries only grant MLA when the dual criminality requirement is fulfilled. This means countries are prepared to issue coercive procedural measures, such as freezing a bank account or seizing an object of special value, only when the investigated criminal offense in the requesting State could also be qualified as an offense in the requested State.

The reasoning behind this principle is that in a domestic investigation coercive measures against a citizen can be ordered only when his behaviour can be qualified as an offense. Whilst this may be a suitable solution for common investigations, it is obvious that such a requirement may sometimes be too heavy a burden at the beginning of an investigation against a PEP. Take, for example, a corrupt political leader who flees his country and takes with him as much evidence as possible or a corrupt political leader that has simply been arrested and put in jail. In order to deal with situations involving corrupt political leaders, the international community has started to issue politically motivated embargo-blocking orders. Through embargo-blocking orders all persons and legal entities are requested to freeze accounts and seize patrimonial values or financial resources belonging to the corrupt person for a specified period of time and to report their existence to the authorities.[7] In Switzerland, when a person or legal entity wilfully or by negligence does not fulfil the obligations of an embargo-blocking order by disposing of the blocked assets or making them available to the corrupt leader, this person can be fined up to ten times the value of the blocked assets. The threat of this penalty guarantees that the ordinance is respected. Switzerland is, of course, not the only country to issue blocking orders, but it was the first country to do so. Unfortunately, the Swiss government is not yet entitled to indicate to the victim State the blocked assets' specific bank account details (number, owner, amount, name of bank, etc.).

7 See Ordinance of the Swiss Federal Council of 11 February 2011 concerning measures against certain persons of the Arabic Republic of Egypt (SR 946.231.132.1) with an initial freezing time of three years.

To date strict privacy laws in financial matters do not allow communication of the customers' personal data to the victim country. The rationale behind privacy protection is that the victim country should be given sufficient time to investigate the criminal behaviour of its former PEPs and to present a MLA request according to existing treaties or laws. Is this not, however, too much to ask when in post-revolutionary countries law enforcement agencies and the court system often suffer from instability?

Can it not be understood that this situation frustrates and disappoints victim countries? The present situation is like a dog that is allowed to smell steak but never allowed to eat it. This is an unacceptable situation that must be changed. For UNCAC Member States to resist cooperating with one another in the fight against corruption is nonsensical.

Conclusions

Whilst UNCAC and a wave of national anticorruption legislation have undoubtedly made improvements in the field of MLA in criminal matters on a whole, there has not been enough notable progress in regards to proactive measures of cooperation. The first three measures described in this article could be put into practice without legislative changes; the fourth measure described – the one in which politically motivated freeze-orders should be used as a basis for an extensive exchange of information – could probably be implemented in practice only following some legislative amendments. The Member Parties of UNCAC could work to this end for the next few years. Wouldn't it be a positive initiative to further explore possibilities for proactive cooperation in the fight against corruption? Surely there are more proactive measures to be found in the UNCAC text, but a detailed investigation of the entire text would have exceeded the perimeter of this chapter.

Major stumbling blocks

Part 2: Political and practical

MARCUS DAVIES[1]

Asset recovery: An ongoing dialogue

With the adoption of the United Nations Convention against Corruption (UNCAC) by the United Nations General Assembly on 31 October 2003 and its coming into force on 14 December 2005, the international community took a significant step forward in combatting transnational corruption.[2] As UNCAC moves towards its 10-year anniversary with 167 State Parties as of July 2013, it is the most widely accepted authority in preventing and combatting global corruption. Within this framework, asset recovery has emerged as one of the most high profile tools in challenging a culture of impunity for corrupt officials, providing justice for victim States and deterring officials from engaging in future corruption. Notably, the express creation of a legal framework for asset recovery in Chapter V of UNCAC is both unique, as it is the first time that an international treaty has focused on asset recovery as a basis for combatting corruption, and innovative, because it calls for a multifaceted approach that emphasises prevention, punishment and international cooperation.

The threat that corruption poses to democratic processes, the rule of law and economic and political development has been observed in many forums.[3] Corruption undermines confidence in the State and creates unpredictability. Public officials who put personal interests ahead of those of the State fuel this unpredictability, which, in turn,

1 Marcus Davies is a legal officer in the Criminal, Security and Diplomatic Law Division at the Department of Foreign Affairs, Trade and Development Canada.

2 United Nations Convention against Corruption, 31 October 2003, A/58/422. Available at: www.unodc.org/documents/treaties/UNCAC/Publications/Convention/08-50026_E.pdf.

3 The preamble to UNCAC states: Concerned about the seriousness of problems and threats posed by corruption to the stability and security of societies, undermining the institutions and values of democracy, ethical values and justice and jeopardising sustainable development and the rule of law […].

encourages people to put their own interests ahead of the State, because they do not believe that the State will provide them with services. In this way, the perception of corruption can become self-fulfilling. Citizens deem that it is in their best interest to act corruptly out of a belief that the public sector is too co-opted by corruption to serve the needs of its citizens.

Given the potential for vast amounts of wealth to be diverted from their intended uses by corrupt officials who use the wealth for their personal gain, it is not surprising that asset recovery has come to the forefront as a key part of a meaningful response to corruption and a means to promote integrity, good governance and global security. It is estimated that USD 20–40 billion is stolen from developing States each year due to corruption. In Africa, the African Union has reported that corruption is responsible for a 25 percent loss in the continent's GDP, or USD 150 billion dollars each year.[4] Despite the gravity of the problem, practice has shown, however, that only a small percentage of assets illicitly obtained by corrupt means have been recovered and returned to the States from which they were stolen.[5]

Recent events in the Middle East and Northern Africa following the fall of former Presidents Zine el Abidine Ben Ali of Tunisia, Hosni Mubarak of Egypt and Moammar Gaddafi of Libya in 2011 have further fuelled the call for action on asset recovery as these States move to recover assets allegedly stolen by corrupt officials associated with the deposed regimes. These crises have led to unprecedented strides in asset recovery with the development of the G8 Action Plan

4 The World Bank and the United Nations Office on Drugs and Crime (UNODC), Stolen Asset Recovery: *Toward a Global Architecture for Asset Recovery*. Available at: www.siteresources.worldbank.org/EXTSARI/Resources /5570284-1257172052492/GlobalArchitectureFinalwithCover.pdf. 'Corruption risk analysis in Southern Africa', Transparency International. Available at: www.transparency.org/news room/in focus/2007/nis_africa. Cited in Mark V. Vlasic & Jenae. N. Noell, 'Fighting Corruption to Improve Global Security: An Analysis of International Asset Recovery Systems' (2010) 5:2 YJIA 106 at 108 [hereinafter Vlasic].

5 It has been reported that of the hundreds of billions of dollars stolen over the course of the last fifteen years, only USD 4.9 billion has been recovered. [see Vlasic at 108]

of Asset Recovery,[6] the passage of laws to rapidly freeze assets belonging to corrupt foreign officials and active bilateral engagement between States. Notwithstanding these successes, there is not a great deal of legal precedent nor is there a common approach to asset recovery. In many ways, the blueprint for successful asset recovery is being drafted at the same time as it is being pursued. To that end, some observations may be made about the challenges inherent in this process along with some practical suggestions to help navigate the process.

Learning as we build

As noted in Chapter V of UNCAC, State Parties shall afford each other the widest measure of cooperation in asset recovery matters. Far too often, however, such cooperation has been interpreted as a 'we ask and you give' dynamic where asset recovery is seen as an end goal objective rather than a process of technical cooperation between State Parties. As a result, requests for asset recovery are often made too early. They are made before investigations are completed and before there is sufficient evidence to substantiate a request for assistance. In turn, delays occur as the parties work to clarify misperceptions in the process, explain legal requirements and supplement a request with more evidence in order to identify, trace and seize assets for the purposes of recovery.

Whereas it is understandable that State Parties will want to move quickly to recover assets to ensure that the assets in question are not depleted further, transferred and hidden for the personal use of corrupt

6 At Camp David, on the 21 May 2012, the G8 adopted its 'Action Plan on Asset Recovery' within the overall framework of the Deauville Partnership with Arab Countries in Transition. In the plan, G8 countries committed to a comprehensive list of actions aimed to promote cooperation, capacity building efforts and technical assistance in support of the efforts of Arab countries in transition in recovering assets diverted by past regimes. G8 countries also agreed, 'to assist in the launch of an Arab Forum on Asset Recovery, which will serve in part as a coordinating mechanism on this issue, through periodic meetings and other activities, and with the support and involvement of the regional partners'. Further information on the Action Plan available at: www.state.gov/j/inl/rls/190483.htm.

officials, their associates and family members, the request for asset recovery should usually be the last step in the process and not the first. Chapter V recognises that State Parties can only cooperate in accordance with their domestic law.[7] It follows therefore that requests for assistance must take into account the domestic legal requirements of the State where assets are held if there is to be any probability of success, because the requested State will only be able to provide assistance if it can satisfy the due process of its domestic law. In this respect, asset recovery is a collective undertaking between experts from multiple States and disciplines who must work to identify what assets have been obtained through corrupt practices and to trace them through multiple jurisdictions so that they may be seized and returned to their lawful owners. The work requires close cooperation between jurisdictions, awareness of different legal systems, strong law enforcement, complete investigations and well-drafted mutual legal assistance (MLA) requests. Given its technical nature and the fact that asset recovery must often navigate diverse cultural, linguistic, legal and political environments, there are few, if any, shortcuts.

Given the aforementioned low percentages in repatriating assets derived by corruption, States seeking to recover assets will on occasion criticise delays in the asset recovery process as indicative of a lack of political will. The challenge such public statements pose is that they rarely reflect the real reasons why asset recovery is not being achieved more quickly, and furthermore they cannot be addressed directly within the public domain. States will not for the most part comment on State-to-State communication due to the confidentiality of such communication and the risk that public statement could affect the integrity of ongoing investigations. As such, there is little opportunity in the public forum to clarify misperceptions respecting the time it takes to pursue asset recovery. Such comments are also almost always counterproductive to achieving effective cooperation.

The fact that it takes time to foster cooperation between domestic authorities should come as no surprise and should in no way be seen as indicative of a lack of political will. Transnational criminal law is a relatively new area of international law for which there are no auto-

7 UNCAC, articles 52–57.

matic solutions. In this respect, the expertise required to identify, trace and seize assets tends to come from persons who are primarily expert in domestic law enforcement and not necessarily the laws of another State. As such, experts must learn how to cooperate with their foreign counterparts when the perpetrators, proceeds and harm implicate the jurisdiction of more than one State. To the extent that expertise is not always transferable from one jurisdiction to another, it is understandable that State experts require time to learn how to cooperate in order to suppress transnational criminal activity and ensure that corrupt officials cannot find safe havens for their illicitly obtained assets. Thus, the time it takes to develop appropriate modes of cooperation is both unavoidable and necessary.

Under the Action Plan for Asset Recovery, G8 States have recognised that ignorance of legal requirements and procedures can hinder asset recovery.[8] To address this common challenge, the G8 commitment to publish practical country guides on asset recovery has been very useful in promoting a greater understanding of the legal requirements and processes to recover assets from G8 States.[9] The fact that the G20 has also committed to publishing such guides suggests that the information they provide is in demand and worthwhile. Nevertheless, such initiatives can only go so far to educate experts in asset recovery about the due process requirements of foreign jurisdictions.[10] In addition to knowing about the legal and procedural requirements of a foreign jurisdiction, it is equally important to know who to talk to. Many misperceptions can be addressed and delays mitigated through informal dialogue between experts who can clarify the legal and procedural requirements for asset recovery in a foreign jurisdiction.

8 Supra note 5.

9 The country guides on asset recovery are available at: www.star.worldbank.org/star/ArabForum/country-guides-asset-recovery.

10 G20 Anti-Corruption Action Plan 2013 – 2014. Available at: www.g20.org/load/781360452.

The only bad questions are the questions you do not ask

There is no such thing as a bad question when one is trying to navigate the technical requirements of asset recovery in another jurisdiction. In particular, best practice would dictate that the experts contact their foreign counterparts to ask what is required to recover assets from the State in question before making the request. For example, the State requesting assistance in an asset recovery matter is in a better position to know what crime has been committed and what assets have been stolen. It will not always know, however, how such information can be best communicated to a foreign authority to satisfy its legal standards for asset recovery. However, if the requesting State can speak to an expert in such matters before making the request, it can find out how the request should be presented and what information should be provided. In turn, the foreign expert will almost always appreciate the informal consultation, because it will eliminate the need for them to follow-up with the State requesting assistance to obtain supplementary information in relation to a MLA request.

While we do not need to be expert in each other's systems, we do need to know who to talk to in order to navigate the legal requirements of each system. To this end, it is very useful for States to designate focal points for asset recovery matters to ensure that there are common points of contact. In addition, States should, if possible, designate a local point of contact in the embassy of the State where asset recovery is being pursued to manage linguistic barriers and time zone differences as well as to provide opportunities for frank face-to-face discussion. In this respect, good interpersonal communication is conducive to effective cooperation.

Canada's experience

In the case of Canada, the federal government has consistently said that Canada will not be a safe haven for the proceeds of corruption.[11]

11 Department of Foreign Affairs, Trade and Development, Press Release, '*Canada Enacts Freezing Assets of Corrupt Foreign Officials Act*' (23 March 2011).

Only months after the fall of the Ben Ali and Mubarak regimes in Tunisia and Egypt, Canada moved quickly to draft and adopt on 23 March 2011 the Freezing Assets of Corrupt Foreign Officials Act (FACFOA) and the Freezing Assets of Corrupt Foreign Officials (Tunisia and Egypt) Regulations.[12] These instruments were adopted to support the transition in both States to ensure that misappropriated assets held by officials of the former governments can ultimately be seized so that politically exposed foreign persons may be held accountable. To this end, FACFOA permits the government to freeze the assets or restrain property of politically exposed foreign persons at the written request of a foreign State when the Governor-in-Council has determined that the foreign State is in a state of turmoil or political uncertainty and when the making of an order or regulation is in the interest of international relations. Designated persons are listed publicly as politically exposed foreign persons in schedules annexed to the regulations, and their property shall be subject to freezing.[13] In so doing, the law and regulations give effect to written requests from States that have recently experienced political upheaval to freeze the assets of their former leaders and senior officials or their associates and family members suspected of having misappropriated State funds or obtained property inappropriately as a result of their office or family, business or personal connections. It is important to note, however, that while it is not necessary to establish that the property is a proceed of

Available at: www.international.gc.ca/media/aff/news-communiques/2011/118.aspx?lang=eng.

12 Freezing Assets of Corrupt Foreign Officials Act, S.C. 2011, c. 10. Available at: www.laws-lois.justice.gc.ca/PDF/F-31.6.pdf. Freezing Assets of Corrupt Foreign Officials (Tunisia and Egypt) Regulations, SOR/2011-78. Available at: www.laws-lois.justice.gc.ca/PDF/SOR-2011-78.pdf.

13 Section 3 of the Freezing Assets of Corrupt Foreign Officials (Tunisia and Egypt) Regulations, SOR/2011-78, provides:

3. A person in Canada must not

(a) deal, directly or indirectly, in any property, wherever situated, of any politically exposed foreign person;

(b) enter into or facilitate, directly or indirectly, any financial transaction related to a dealing referred to in paragraph (a); or

(c) provide financial services or other related services in respect of any property of any politically exposed foreign person.

crime in order for it to be frozen under FACFOA, seizure cannot occur unless the property is identified as a proceed of crime. Thus, the freeze ensures that the property remains in Canada to give the foreign State the time it needs to pursue investigations and gather evidence to support a formal request for the seizure and forfeiture. To date Canada has designated 256 persons as politically exposed foreign persons, and a total of USD 2.62 million in assets has been frozen.[14]

The requirement that property be identified as a proceed of crime is a common challenge in asset recovery matters. The challenges involved in tracing assets are beyond the scope of this chapter, but suffice it to say that merely establishing that a person has been convicted of an offense will rarely be sufficient to recover assets. Rather, there must be evidence linking the property to the crime in order for criminal forfeiture to take place for the purposes of asset recovery.[15] As

14 For greater certainty, a 'politically exposed foreign person' is defined under the Freezing Assets of Corrupt Foreign Officials Act to mean a person who holds or has held one of the following offices or positions in or on behalf of a foreign State and includes any person who, for personal or business reasons, is or was closely associated with such a person, including a family member:
- head of state or head of government
- member of the executive council of government or member of a legislature
- deputy minister or equivalent rank
- ambassador or attaché or counsellor of an ambassador
- military officer with a rank of general or above
- president of a state-owned company or a state-owned bank
- head of a government agency
- judge
- leader or president of a political party represented in a legislature
- holder of any prescribed office or position.

15 UNCAC provides for direct and indirect recovery of assets under articles 53 and 54. In contrast to criminal asset recovery (article 54), direct non-conviction based (NCB) asset forfeiture (article 53), also known as civil forfeiture, is not possible in Canada at the federal level. NCB asset forfeiture enables governments and the victims of crime to recover illegally acquired assets from an individual or an entity through a direct action against their property without the requirement of a prior criminal conviction of the defendant. However, due to Canada's constitutional division of powers, the Government of Canada cannot respond to a request for NCB asset forfeiture as such requests fall within the jurisdiction of Canada's provinces. As such, should a foreign State seek to recover assets from Canada though NCB asset forfeiture, it must hire private counsel to act on its behalf in the province where the property is located.

such, requests for asset recovery should be supported by completed investigations to demonstrate not only that a crime was committed but also that the proceeds of that crime can be traced to property located in Canada. To the extent that such evidence can be obtained by leveraging partnerships bilaterally through police-to-police communication or multilaterally through organisations such as Interpol, States are encouraged to do so to gather evidence for the purpose of seizing assets. For the latter, information sharing between jurisdictions can also help domestic law enforcement advance their own investigations as they become privy to more information in foreign jurisdictions.

Know your target

Another challenge faced in asset recovery matters is ensuring consistency in translation. Because corrupt officials often face multiple charges leading to multiple proceedings, which can in turn lead to multiple MLA requests for the same person, it is extremely important that the persons be identified in a consistent manner to avoid confusion. For example, when there are multiple requests for assistance even a minor variation in the spelling of a person's name can lead to delays due to the need to clarify whether the requests in question pertain to one person or persons with similar names. Consistency is especially important when persons have to be identified to financial institutions to prevent anyone from dealing in their property. Financial institutions can only act on the information provided to them.[16] As

16 As a matter of practice, when Canada designates a person in accordance with the Freezing Assets of Corrupt Foreign Officials Act, it notifies the Office of the Superintendent of Financial Institutions Canada, which is the primary regulator and supervisor of federally regulated deposit-taking institutions, insurance companies and federally regulated private pension plans, so that it may notify financial entities in Canada to not deal in the property of the designated person. In accordance with sections 8 and 9 of the Act, person and financial entities in Canada and every Canadian outside Canada must, without delay, disclose to the Commissioner of the Royal Canadian Mounted Police the existence of property in their possession or control that they have reason to believe is the property of any politically exposed foreign person who is the subject of an order or regula-

such, providing consistent transliteration and clear identifiers, such as a date of birth and the title of a person (i.e. former Minister of Industry, spouse of former President X, cousin of Judge X, etc.), is extremely important when requesting that assets held by politically exposed foreign persons suspected of corruption be frozen so that the assets may later be returned.

In addition to providing sufficient identification criteria in asset recovery matters, it is also good practice to indicate whether the persons believed to have illicitly obtained assets though corrupt means have also set up corporations where their assets can be hidden. While it is true that identifying natural persons is a primary consideration, a requesting State should not assume that a requested State will be able to make all the linkages to identify other persons, legal or natural, who can be used to hide funds for the benefit of corrupt officials. The more information provided, the better the chances that assets can be identified, frozen and ultimately seized for asset recovery.

Conclusion

The legal framework for asset recovery in Chapter V of UNCAC marks a significant advancement for transnational criminal law. Given the absence of strong legal precedent, however, persons working in the field of asset recovery are both witnessing and orchestrating a shift towards ever more effective enforcement and cooperation. Experts who would not have worked together previously are now engaging across jurisdictions as peers and partners. In so doing, it has become clear that asset recovery is a process of engagement premised on mutual learning, expertise and constructive dialogue to ensure that corrupt officials are not allowed to profit from their crimes. While officials working on asset recovery may not have all the answers in this common endeavour, they are learning what questions to ask, and they are seeing that the answers will come.

tion and information about a transaction or proposed transaction in respect of such property.

Olivier Longchamp and Mark Herkenrath

Money laundering, liability and sanctions for financial intermediaries – the issue of having the assets of politically exposed persons in Switzerland

In the field of the fight against illicit financial flows in general, it has become commonplace to say that there is a distinction between the law and its application. International bodies, such as the Financial Action Task Force (FATF), the Global Forum on Transparency and the Exchange of Information for Tax Purposes, in their evaluation reports examine not only the laws implemented by the jurisdictions surveyed but also their concrete practices. In the national context, such reviews are rare. Also rare are comparative studies that analyse the sanctions taken against financial intermediaries that have violated their obligations under the provisions for combating illicit financial flows and the effectiveness of those sanctions. Nevertheless, such sanctions are likely to play a decisive role in the preventive dimension of the fight against money laundering. Without conducting such an analysis, this brief article – based on the treatment of cases involving the assets of politically exposed persons (PEP) in Switzerland – aims to show how difficult it is to get an accurate picture of the effectiveness and the application of the provisions against illicit financial flows. This article will stress the need for a sanction mechanism that combines criminal prosecution with administrative proceedings against intermediaries who have failed to show due care, and it will question the usefulness of an international standard in this regard.

The effectiveness of the anti-money laundering system

Swiss financial intermediaries and their advocates are more than happy to describe the Swiss system against illicit financial flows as 'one of the most rigorous in the world'.[1] They assert that in practice black money, especially illicit money from PEPs, has disappeared from the system. In January 2011, shortly before the Arab Spring, James Nason, the spokesman for the Swiss Bankers Association (SBA), told the Financial Times that 'no Swiss bank would knowingly accept money from a corrupt head of state'.[2] Authorities readily embraced this rhetoric. In 2008, the Federal Department of Foreign Affairs (FDFA) commented that thanks to its 'arsenal of laws and procedures for combating money laundering' Switzerland could 'effectively fight against financial crime'.[3] At the same time, voices spoke out criticising the gap between the legal framework and its application. Professor of Criminal Law at Basel University and recognised international expert, Mark Pieth, points out that the Swiss system, which requires financial intermediaries to report transactions that they reasonably suspect are being carried out with illicit money to an intelligence unit financial, 'does not work. It is quite obvious that the rules exist, but they are applied with insufficient care. This also means that regulators are not doing their job'.[4] It is interesting to note that the majority of the Swiss population also considers the means of combating illicit financial

1 See for instance the Internet page of Geneva's financial centre's foundation. Available at: www.genevefinance.ch/en/financial-place/anti-money-laundering.

2 'Foreign leaders favour Switzerland', *Financial Times*, 25.1.2011. Cf. also interview with SBA director, C. A. Margelisch, 18.09.2011, *RTS*. Available at: www.rts.ch/video/info/journal-19h30/3404683-fortune-du-clan-ben-ali-un-des-hauts-dignitaires-tunisiens-a-depose-onze-millions-de-francs-dans-une-banque-ge nevoise.html.

3 FDFA, cited in *Le Courrier*, 22.4.2008. Cf. also the statements made by the Swiss minister for Foreign Affairs, Micheline Calmy-Rey, at the conference for the Stolen Asset Recovery Initiative in Paris, June 2010. Available at: www.eda.admin.ch/etc/medialib/downloads/edazen/dfa/head/spee10.Par.0019.File.tmp/StAR%20Conference%20Paris_FR_0608.pdf. Or those made by V. Zellweger, in 'Suisse : le paradis bancaire n'est plus ce qu'il était', *Jeune Afrique*, 12.02.2011.

4 'Banks Scrutinize Regimes' Assets', *Wall Street Journal*, 23.02.2011.

flows insufficient. At least, that was the opinion of 60 percent of respondents in a survey conducted on behalf of the SBA.[5]

Anyone seeking to form a balanced opinion on this rather weighty political issue will have difficulty. One could refer to the Swiss evaluation reports by FATF, the Global Forum on Transparency and Exchange of Information. In doing so, one would only obtain – at least as far as Switzerland is concerned – a partial and dated view. Switzerland is the only country in the Organisation for Economic Cooperation and Development (OECD) that is locked in phase 1 of the peer review conducted by the Global Forum, which examines the legal framework of countries.[6] That being said, the assessment conducted by the FATF in 2005 and the last Swiss biannual follow-up report made in 2011 have not yet been evaluated.[7] It may also be possible to try to form an empirical opinion on the issue by analysing the cases brought to the attention of the public through the press or the justice system. The exercise would certainly be interesting, and it would be well worth conducting a closer review, particularly of some of the PEP cases given that since 2011 their number has significantly increased.

An empirical solution based on the cases revealed by the press or the justice system of PEP assets in Switzerland

Following the Arab Spring, the Swiss authorities by means of ordinances blocked the assets of several deposed or fallen leaders and

5 Survey 'Les Questions Bancaires Actuelles 2013', conducted for the SBA, February 2013, p.33. Available at: www.swissbanking.org/fr/20130307-5740-all-schlussbericht-nko.pdf.

6 OECD, *Peer Review Report – Phase 1: Legal and Regulatory Framework – Switzerland*, 2011, §91-3. Available at: www.eoi-tax.org/jurisdictions/CH#peerreview.

7 State Secretariat for International Financial Matters, *1er Rapport de suivi bisannuel de la Suisse*, October 2011. Available at: www.sif.admin.ch/dokumen tation/00522/00835/index.html?lang=de&download=NHzLpZeg7t,lnp6I0NTU0 42l2Z6ln1acy4Zn4Z2qZpnO2Yuq2Z6gpJCDdIR7e2ym162epYbg2c_JjKbNoKS n6A.

their crownies. On 3 May 2011, Federal Councillor Micheline Calmy-Rey announced that the Swiss authorities had blocked CHF 830 million of suspicious origin (CHF 60 million of Tunisian origin, CHF 410 million of Egyptian origin, CHF 360 million of Libyan origin).[8] Since the initial reporting, the figures have grown in a way that has never been explained, but it may suggest that the intermediaries concerned had, at least initially, incorrectly identified or not reported all assets concerned. In July 2012, the Swiss Attorney General (SAG) announced that the amount then frozen as a result of Egyptian proceedings alone amounted to CHF 693 million[9] – with the investigation of nearly 140 banking relationships only halfway concluded at that point.

Certainly, nothing prevents Swiss financial intermediaries from maintaining business relationships with PEPs. However, they must clearly identify such relationships given the increased risk that they pose, and examine in a particularly precise manner the origin of the funds entrusted to them. For the moment, it cannot be confirmed that the frozen assets are indeed of illicit origin, and proving it will not be easy. Proving corruption will require that the proceedings initiated in Egypt and Tunisia reach a satisfactory conclusion and also that mutual assistance on criminal matters succeeds between these countries and Switzerland. Nevertheless, it should be noted that in recent findings the Swiss High Court confirmed that assets of the former Egyptian and Libyan regimes should be considered those of a criminal organisation.[10] This is enough to render assets illicit, which means that banks should report to the Money Laundering Reporting Office Switzerland (MROS) without waiting for a freezing order from the Federal Council. It is worth noting, as MROS documented in its report for 2011, that between 2010 and 2011 the number of communications to MROS

8 'Quelque 830 millions de francs gelés en Suisse', *RTS*, 2.5.2011. Available at: www.rts.ch/info/suisse/3116507-quelque-830-millions-de-francs-geles-en-suisse .html.

9 'Gel de nouveaux fonds de Moubarak', *20 Minutes*, 25.7.2012. Available at: www.20min.ch/ro/news/dossier/tunisie/story/21597703.

10 Decision of the Federal Tribunal 1B_175/2012, 5.9.2012, and the decision of the Federal Criminal Tribunal BB.2012.71, 20.12.2012.

concerning Egypt increased from 0 to 55, for Libya from 0 to 33, for Syria from 0 to 7 and for Tunisia from 0 to 40.[11]

On these bases, we may therefore have doubts about how financial intermediaries apply their due diligence on money laundering, particularly with regard to PEPs. Is it really so difficult for a potentate to use a Swiss financial centre to hide the fruits of his plundering? Do financial intermediaries really administer the procedures that lead to identifying the beneficial owners of the assets they host with the requisite diligence? Do they communicate effectively with the authorities when they have suspicions of money laundering or assets that should be blocked? Are their communications with authorities influenced by a risk analysis that places priority on concealing a problematic relationship rather than fulfilling a legal obligation, as the above statistics from MROS on the Arab Spring countries tend to suggest? Are these risks not weighed against the magnitude of the amounts under management that may escape the intermediary should he expose a major customer?

Since 2011, these doubts have been reinforced by the increase of stories concerning the funds of potentates. Investigations into the assets of the Obiang clan from Equatorial Guinea, whose patriarch, Teodoro, has monopolised the petrodollars since 1979, are being conducted in Switzerland where Teodoro's son, Teodorín, happily goes skiing. The press has reported that behind the famous apartment of 101 rooms on Avenue Foch in Paris, which following a raid led to several convictions of the clan in France in what has been dubbed the case of the 'Ill-gotten Gains', were five Swiss companies (with bearer shares).[12] The Swiss accounts of relatives of the Assad clan gave rise to an incredible mess, which would not be useful to recall here.[13] Suffice it to say that more than CHF 100 million was frozen in Swiss

11 MROS, *14è rapport annuel 2011*, May 2012, p.21. Available at: www.ejpd.admin.ch/content/dam/data/kriminalitaet/geldwaescherei/jahresberichte/jb-mros-2011-f.pdf.

12 'Les connexions suisses d'Obiang', *L'Hebdo*, 4.7.2012.

13 Decisions of the Federal Criminal Tribunal BB.2011.95 and 106, 11.01.2012 and decisions of the Federal Administrative Tribunal B-3488/2011 and B-5196/2011, 14.06.2012. Cf. also Jonas Mueller-Töwe, 'Die lukrative Kundschaft der HSBC'. Available at: www.freitag.de.

banks in June 2012 following embargoes enacted by the government against members of the Syrian regime. Certainly nothing proves that the funds represented illicit assets in the legal sense, but it does show that Swiss financial intermediaries do not hesitate to maintain business relationships with clans whose exercise of power is characterised by clientelism, corruption and human rights violations.

In the wake of the Arab Spring, a corruption scandal involving a leading Canadian construction company (SNC Lavalin) and a Geneva lawyer, who made use of the Geneva financial centre to pay bribes to secure public procurement contracts in Libya and Tunisia, was also reviewed.[14] In Geneva, the press revealed in late November 2012 that proceedings for corruption were under way against Victor Khrapunov, the former mayor of Alma-Aty, and his wife, who present themselves as 'political opponents' of the Kazakh president, Nazarbayev.[15] Should they ever need to defend themselves from an allegation of bias, the same Geneva authorities could point to another procedure instigated in September 2010 for money laundering, this time against Nazarbayev's son-in-law who was also based in Geneva.[16] In this case, USD 665 million was transferred in 2006 from a UBS account in Switzerland to an account at Credit Suisse in Singapore. The bank of the SBA's chairman, Patrick Odier, is for its part involved in three different PEP cases. In 2012, the SAG opened a trial for money laundering involving the entourage of the daughter of Uzbek President Islam Karimov who was residing in Geneva.[17] The Karimov family links with Switzerland and the dubious nature of their affairs have long been docu-

14 'Un avocat de Genève pris au piège du scandale de blanchiment SNC-Lavalin', *RTS*, 21.11.2012. Available at: www.rts.ch/info/economie/4458715-un-avocat-de-geneve-pris-au-piege-du-scandale-de-blanchiment-snc-lavalin.html.

15 'La famille Khrapunov visée par une enquête pour blanchiment à Genève', *RTS*, 29.11.2012. Available at: www.rts.ch/info/regions/geneve/4470714-la-famille-khrapunov-visee-par-une-enquete-pour-blanchiment-a-geneve.html.

16 'Transactions suspects du clan Nazarbaïev en Suisse', *RTS*, 17.12.2010. Available at: www.rts.ch/info/2805853-transactions-suspectes-du-clan-nazarbaiev-en-suisse.html.

17 'Plusieurs centaines de millions de francs ouzbeks sont bloqués en Suisse', *RTS*, 19.9.2010.

mented.[18] In May 2013, yet two more cases were revealed. The first concerns secret funds of Luis Bárcenas, the former treasurer of the Spanish Popular Party (PP), who has been accused of corruption in Spain; and the second involves the illicit assets of Kirchner regime.[19]

This brief overview of asset recovery cases involving PEPs is absolutely sufficient to prove that the issue of enforcing anti-money laundering standards should be raised. The review could be extended to cases of money laundering beyond PEPs, although these cases are less likely to make the headlines. However, similar questions would arise. There is the example of a certain bank that waited two years to open a safe after the holder had ceased to pay the rent. It then waited another three years before issuing a communication to MROS, on the basis of which the authorities were able to determine that the police already knew the customer of the bank because of a previous burglary conviction.[20] The conclusion that can be drawn from this empirical overview does not fundamentally change: there are legitimate doubts about how anti-money laundering standards are applied, but we cannot make any definite conclusions. First of all, only parts of cases are made public – sometimes through the financial intermediaries themselves – so it is unclear whether any cases, and if so which ones, are representative or exceptional. Also, the details of the case are rarely made public. The question of whether the financial intermediaries carried out the requisite due diligence, and are therefore the collateral victims of their clients, or whether they avoided doing so, and are therefore complicit, is generally overlooked. The proliferation of these cases can be interpreted both as evidence that the anti-money laundering system works and that it is ineffective.

One would expect that official statistics on open legal proceedings, following communications from financial intermediaries, would

18 Cf. for example: 'Usbek-Gate', *Tages Anzeiger*, 18.4.2001; 'De Tachkent à Cologny – la saga des sœurs Karimova', *L'Hebdo*, 5.1.2010.

19 'Les secrets des fonds suisse de l'ex-trésorier du Parti Populaire espagnol', *RTS*, 3.5.2013 ; 'El caso Lázaro Báez impacta en la dinámica de la justicia en Suiza', *La Nacion*, 5.5.2013.

20 MROS, *15è rapport annuel 2012*, May 2013, p.73. Available at: www.fedpol.admin.ch/content/dam/data/kriminalitaet/geldwaescherei/jahresberichte/jb-mros-2012-f.pdf.

provide more understanding of the situation. This would require, however, that judicial proceedings had been completed and a decision made regarding the financial intermediary's liability for any potential laundering. But the reality is disappointing. Not only do official statistics not exist, but also it must be acknowledged that proceedings initiated on the basis of a report to MROS – which represent only a part of the open procedures – rarely result in a court decision. Nearly 42 percent of all reported suspicions that were forwarded to law enforcement during the past decade are still being processed, and only 7.7 percent of cases have resulted in a judgment.[21] In particular, the most important cases in international crime encounter the difficulties of international assistance in criminal matters. Swiss authorities recognise the problem and emphasised in a recent report that 'establishing proof of a predicate offence mainly committed abroad represents a huge challenge'.[22] This issue could be further exacerbated in cases involving PEPs who might order the judiciary not to respond to a request for mutual assistance. Or, worse, the judiciary could discharge the accused. In any event, because of the lack of official statistics and the low number of cases resulting in a judgement, it is not possible to draw conclusions on the compliance (or lack of compliance) of financial intermediaries. The low rate of judgements mentioned above also demonstrates the difficulties associated with proving money laundering in a court of law.

The supervisory authority, its reports and the sanctions for financial intermediaries – towards an international standard?

One would hope that the supervisory authority, the Swiss Financial Market Supervisory Authority FINMA in the first instance in Switzer-

21 Ibid., p.66.

22 State Secretariat for International Financial Matters, *Rapport sur la mise en œuvre des recommandations du GAFI*, 27.2.2013, p.23. Available at: www.efd.admin.ch/dokumentation/gesetzgebung/00571/02691/index.html?lang=fr.

land's case, would provide sufficient information to enable one to get a better idea of compliance by financial intermediaries in regards to their duties of anti-money laundering due diligence. It will be recalled that apart from the criminal question – that is, whether a financial intermediary involved in a money laundering case is guilty – the administrative authorities may examine whether the financial intermediaries applied the procedures consistent with their legal obligations. Unfortunately, investigations on such issues are rarely carried out. Following the Abacha case in 2000, however, the regulatory authority did conduct a special investigation that found that financial intermediaries are sometimes unfamiliar with their duty of care. Some financial intermediaries do not apply it, and others do so in an inadequate manner.[23] A similar investigation was conducted 11 years after the Abacha case in the context of the Arab Spring. At the end of the investigation, FINMA noted that the banks had not fully complied with the prescribed due diligence process in 19 of the 29 relationships with politically exposed persons. FINMA did conclude that the banks 'are aware of their LBA (anti-money laundering) obligations' and apply them in a 'satisfactory' way but 'not always with sufficient intensity'.[24]

In conclusion, in Switzerland it is difficult to get an accurate picture of whether or not the anti-money laundering system is effective based on data available at the national level. However, an empirical examination gives grounds to doubt its effectiveness. It is even more difficult to know whether sanctions taken against offending financial intermediaries are effective in preventative terms – that is, whether they are sufficient in changing problematic common practices. It is regrettable that the regulators are reluctant to communicate openly about the sanctions they impose, to name the financial intermediaries concerned or even to simply impose sanctions. In the case of financial intermediaries singled out by FINMA for their relations with deposed groups in the Arab Spring, it is noteworthy that a year after opening

23 Commission fédérale des banques, 'Fonds 'Abacha' auprès des banques suisses' *Rapport de la Commission des banques*, 30.8.2000. Available: www.finma.ch/archiv/ebk/f/archiv/2000/pdf/neu14a-00.pdf.

24 FINMA, *Obligations de diligence des banques suisses en relation avec les valeurs patrimoniales de PEP*, 10.11.2011. Available at: www.finma.ch/f/aktuell/Documents/bericht_pep-abkl%C3%A4rung_20111110_f.pdf.

proceedings against them FINMA announced that the proceedings were closed again and that the supervisory authority had 'simply noted the deficiencies' of the banks involved.[25]

The apparent lack of sanctions, a lacuna in communication combined with the difficulty of obtaining criminal convictions in cases of financial crime involving PEPs, implies impunity or at least a lack of accountability for financial intermediaries. This perception would further be reinforced by the ratification of a draft law recently proposed in Switzerland. The draft law is a poorly conceived policy of restitution of illicit assets that proposes getting rid of illicit assets frozen in Switzerland as part of a possible compromise solution, thereby avoiding the resolution of legal proceedings initiated in the country.[26] On the basis of the Swiss example, one might wonder if international standards for combating illicit financial flows should not include requirements for the conduct of regular national surveys on the implementation of anti-money laundering standards – a form of 'stress-testing' that could act as a check to the robustness of the system – and the publication of sanctions on financial intermediaries for breach of their duty of care. To convince financial intermediaries of the need to meet their obligations, the threat of damaging their reputations by disclosing sanctions imposed in offending establishments is probably as effective as the application of hypothetical criminal penalties.

25 FINMA, *Rapport annuel 2012*, March 2013, p. 74. Available at: www.finma.ch/f/finma/publikationen/Documents/jahresbericht-2012-f.pdf.

26 A draft law on this has recently been proposed and should soon come before Parliament. Cf. art. 10 of the draft Federal Act on the Restitution of Assets Illicitly Obtained by Politically Exposed Persons, 8.5.2013. Available at: www.admin.ch/opc/fr/classified-compilation/20100418/201102010000/196.1.pdf.

Till Förster

Between restoration, adaptation and appropriation: Governance in post-conflict Côte d'Ivoire

Introduction: The legacy of an insurgency

Governance in Côte d'Ivoire, once West Africa's most promising economy, is still affected by the profound crisis that has rocked the country since the 1990s. In many parts of the country, governance arrangements are not dominated by the State and its administration. Government institutions, for instance the judiciary, are only working in certain cities and regions. The conditions for claiming justice or retrieving stolen assets depend by and large on local circumstances. During the years of crisis, Statehood and governance adopted many different forms that often varied from one city to the next. This short article outlines the underpinnings of these new figurations of governance in post-conflict Côte d'Ivoire.

For almost nine years, from 2002 through 2011, Côte d'Ivoire was divided into two halves. After the failed coup of 19 September 2002, a coalition of three rebel movements known as the *Forces Nouvelles* controlled the northern part of the country, roughly 60 percent of the national territory, while the southern part of the country remained under the control of then sitting President Laurent Gbagbo and his government.[1] Despite several peace treaties, first mediated by France as former colonial power and later by Burkina Faso as regional power, the situation remained tense until the UN-monitored presidential elections of October 2010 and the run-off between Laurent Gbagbo and his rival Alassane Ouattara a month later. When President

1 For an overview see:
McGovern, Mike, 2011: Making War in Côte d'Ivoire. London: Hurst.
Poamé, Lazare M. (ed.), 2007: Penser la crise ivoirienne. Paris: Meniabuc.

Gbagbo did not recognise his defeat in the run-off elections, the tensions rose and the country slipped into a civil war that lasted until April 2011 when the *Forces Nouvelles* conquered Abidjan, the country's largest city and important seaport, and the Gbagbo regime fell.

As a result of the insurgency from 2002–2011, Côte d'Ivoire lost its position as the region's most important entrepot. During the crisis, its main harbour in Abidjan had no or only very limited access to its hinterland. As a result, the merchants in the North and in the neighbouring countries of Mali, Burkina Faso and Niger established new trade routes towards Accra, Ghana; Lomé, Togo and Conakry, Guinea. The abrupt breakdown of State administration was a double-sided sword. In particular, the absence of custom controls opened new opportunities for long-distance trade, but it simultaneously led to harassments by vigilante groups and sometimes loosely controlled rebel groups. The insurgents, for their part, were unprepared to govern the part of the country under their control as they had hoped for a sudden takeover of the State administration. During the first and most violent period of the division, the rebels still had to work out their own modes of governance.

What emerged in the years that followed were, on the one hand, a central rebel command structured in ten 'zones of command', and on the other hand lower-level highly specialised governance arrangements adapted to local circumstances. Many villages, sometimes even entire rural areas, refused the presence of rebels in their vicinities. Partly because of lack of personnel and partly because of their image as 'children of the soil', the insurgents often respected the people's claims for more autonomy. In the towns, and in particular in the bigger cities, the rebels had to engage in governance arrangements with other actors.[2] The reasons were manifold and more often than not they were informed by the specific figuration of actors in a certain place and the social problems that needed to be addressed there. Over the years, the cities bred increasingly governance arrangements that included important urban actors, including individuals as well as groups

2 In print: Förster, Till, 2010: "Dialogue direct": Rebel Governance and Civilians in Northern Côte d'Ivoire, in: Mampilly, Zacharia et al. (Eds.): *Rebel Governance*. Cambridge: Cambridge University Press.

that successfully articulated their own interests and political claims. While the rebels executed more direct forms of domination in cities such as Man in western Côte d'Ivoire, they tolerated more segmentary forms of governance in other places such as Korhogo. The legacy of rebel governance was hence as multifaceted as the rebellion's political movement. The longer rebel domination lasted, the more stable such local figurations became. When the rebellion ended in 2011, governance had adopted localised, fairly routinized forms in many towns and cities. Furthermore, different governance arrangements co-existed according to the social problems that had emerged in the urban political spaces.

Attempts to bring some State agencies back in the rebel-held territory after the signature of the Ouagadougou Peace Treaty of March 2007 were not very successful as they met the resistance of both the rebels and the bigger merchants who were not keen to pay customs again. Finally, the re-establishment of State administration in all parts of the territory began slowly only after the military victory of the former rebel forces in April 2011. Many areas, including some cities that were controlled by the rebels until then, experienced a long period of transition. Different actors competed to secure the best position in the post-conflict political landscape. Besides the new actors that had surfaced on both sides during the years of crisis, others aimed at re-establishing the old patrimonial networks that had once dominated urban politics. Such struggles, visible as well as invisible, often emerged and still emerge around social problems that become governance issues.

Social problems that turn into governance issues

It would be pointless to list all the social problems that surfaced over the years of crisis in Côte d'Ivoire from a 'neutral', outsider's perspective. It is more appropriate to look at the structuration of these problems – that is, how the actors identified social problems and how they then engaged with them, thus making them nodal points in the politics of governance.

Many of these problems have a longer history, which needs to be outlined first. Some date back to the old regime of President Félix Houphouët-Boigny, the first president of Côte d'Ivoire who ruled from independence to his death in 1993. Widespread disregard for the youth and the lack of their participation in political decision-making was, for instance, inherited from President Houphouët-Boigny's tenure. Youth issues became one of the driving forces of the crisis that saw infuriated youth claiming more rights and, especially, better job opportunities on both sides.[3] The failed integration of migrants from the northern neighbours of Côte d'Ivoire, in particular from Burkina Faso, Mali and Niger, was another fault line. Together with the ethno-nationalist ideology of *Ivoirité* or 'Ivoirianness'[4] in the 1990s, the failed integration of migrants instigated land conflicts and violent clashes between these groups and the descendants of the first settlers in the most productive parts of Côte d'Ivoire, the coffee and cocoa belts along the northern fringes of the rain forest region. The 1990s were also a time when the police and other bodies of the administration increasingly tended 'to supplement their income' as the Ivoirian State went through a series of economic crises. Corruption attained a level previously unknown. Policemen released criminals for bribes or shared booties with them right from the beginning, as the population suspected. Meanwhile, dangerous criminals attacked travellers on the road and once even hijacked a train. The 'thieves', as they were usually called, were well armed and did not hesitate to kill if they could not get want they wanted.

3 Konaté, Yacouba, 2002: Génération Zouglou, in: *Cahiers d'Études Africaines* 42.4: 777–796.
Konaté, Yacouba, 2003: Les Enfants de la Balle. De la FESCI aux mouvements des jeunes patriotes, in: *Politique Africaine* n° 89: 49–70.

4 On Ivoirité see:
Dozon, Jean-Pierre, 2000: La Côte d'Ivoire entre démocratie, nationalisme et ethnonationalisme, in: *Politique Africaine* 78: 45–62.
Marshall-Fratani, Ruth, 2006: The war of "Who is Who": Autochtony, nationalism and citizenship in the Ivoirian Crisis, in: *African Studies Review* 49.2: 9–43.
Banégas, Richard, 2007: *Côte d'Ivoire: Les jeunes "se lèvent en hommes": Anticolonialisme et ultranationalisme chez les Jeunes patriotes d'Abidjan.* (Les Études du CERI, 137) Paris: Centre d'études et de recherches internationales.

By the turn of the century and until the outbreak of the insurgency in 2002, the attempts to prevent main opposition leader, Alassane Ouattara, who was of northern origin, from running for president led to the discrimination of almost the entire population in the northern half of the country. *Ivoirité* again legitimized this act, because Ouattara was, according to this ideology, of 'doubtful citizenship'. This time, however, it led to outright oppressive governance practices in the North where civil servants thought it best to extract as much as they could from those who, they believed, did not have the same rights as other 'true' Ivoirians. The rebels then promised to bring such 'outrageous discrimination' to an end. They were, they said, the 'real true Ivoirians', because they would not draw a line between those who came from the South, the North or any other part of the country. They would, they added, talk and listen to the people and take care of the pressing problems they learned about.

Of course, the pervasive insecurity was the first, and by far the most important, social problem that the rebels faced. At the end of the old Gbagbo regime and during the first months of the insurgency, a plethora of vigilante groups emerged all over the country – in the cities as well as in the rural villages. Most of them consisted of young men who volunteered to keep night watches, erecting barriers at village entrances or policing urban neighbourhoods. The so-called traditional hunter associations became another major group. They had already filled the void left by the weakened police and gendarmerie by the turn of the century – often against the will of the increasingly powerless State administration. As they had welcomed the insurgency, they often cooperated with the rebels and became in many places their main partners. However, the figurations differed significantly from place to place. In Korhogo, the biggest city of the North and a stronghold of the rebels, the hunters were in charge of the inner city with the main market as its centre, including the banks opposite the market's entrance. The rebels controlled access to the city centre and the large overland routes. The two groups developed a fairly stable arrangement that was also accepted and later directly supported by the Muslim traders, one of the big and powerful groups within the city. However, the rebels and hunters were not always on good terms. In the city of Man in the western part of the country, where the hunters' associations were only introduced in the late 1990s or a little later, they observed each other with some suspicion. And still in other towns, the population refused their presence altogether. The rebels often tolerated claims for more autonomy, because they carefully tried to avoid any erosion of their legitimacy as 'children of the soil' that represented the will of the majority. The lack of personnel was, however, another reason why they accepted such refusals.

Even within the city of Korhogo governance arrangements differed widely.[5] The general division of labour between rebels and hunters was a wider framework that was recognised by important actors, among them the UN peacekeeping forces, but that many ordinary people ignored. The banks, for instance, hired private security companies and simultaneously supported the hunters in their part of the city through donations, food and occasionally a meal. Some neighbourhoods had night watches that were operated by young men together with hunters but guided by a council of elders or by a local headman. In other districts, the elders participated directly in the night watches or hunters or rebels did it alone. In still other quarters, groups of young and elder men monitored the movements at night while hunters served as a kind of task force to trace and arrest criminals and all sorts of suspicious persons. Mobile phones were the main means of communication, which made it easy for quarter headmen to supervise the groups active in their neighbourhoods.

Whatever they looked like the governance arrangements at the local level where often the most stable ones. They often relied on familiarity and trust and hence created social spaces (in the sense of Lefebvre)[6] that went far beyond the mere delivery of security as a public good – though security solved, of course, the social problem that brought them together. It does not come as a surprise that the population sooner or later compared the security of their own neighbourhood with that of others, and they often very consciously com-

5 Förster, Till / Koechlin, Lucy, 2011: *The politics of governance: Power and agency in the formation of political order in Africa.* (Basel Papers on Political Transformations, 1) Basel: Institute of Social Anthropology.

6 Lefebvre, Henri, 1993: *The Production of Space.* Oxford: Blackwell.

pared the governance arrangements with the aim of improving their own situation too.

Bringing the State back in

The conquest of Abidjan by the *Forces Nouvelles* rebels in April 2011 was a relief for most inhabitants living in the rebel held parts of Côte d'Ivoire. It was their victory, they thought. The country would finally be reunited under one government with one administration. The attempts to re-establish State administration, however, made them aware that this process also meant giving up what they had acquired under rebel domination, namely the autonomy that allowed them to develop their own governance arrangements. Several attempts to establish custom controls along the northern borders to Mali and Burkina Faso failed and the re-implementation of other offices and agencies were repeatedly postponed too. For some time, the national government tolerated a sort of parallelism between the governance arrangements that had emerged under rebel domination and the older model of centralised administration that was still based on the model of the French State, the former colonial power whose understanding of Statehood had iterated deeply into post-colonial times.[7] The general policy was one of restoration. 'State building' and 'rehabilitation' were the buzzwords that many State actors repeated day in and day out. Playing with the double connotation of the words in French they could also mean the refurbishment of buildings, such as the former court that was burnt down in the first days of the insurgency. After the end of the civil war, this seemed to be a promising perspective with lots of job opportunities in the construction industry. And indeed, the first months looked like an economic boom: streets were bituminised, wa-

7 On the interaction of different forms of statehood see:
Förster, Till, 2010: Maintenant, on sait qui est qui! Re-configurations of an African society after conflict, in: *Development and Change* 41.4: 699–722.
Förster, Till 2012: *Statehood in a Stateless Society: Political Order and Societal Memory in Northern Côte d'Ivoire.* (Basel Papers on Political Transformations, 4) Basel: Institute of Social Anthropology.

ter tanks were repaired and power was supplied to neighbourhoods that had not had electricity until then.

But as time went by, some actors, in particular the hunters and their supporters, suspected the civil servants of having a hidden agenda and of conspiring to 'rob' the achievements of the past nine years. Still more outrageous, they said, was that 'these guys' often had not suffered during the war and now came with no knowledge of how things worked. The provision of water and electricity was not, as the technicians claimed, a technical exercise only. Many actors, namely the members of old patrimonial networks that had dominated urban politics for decades, had their stakes in this process. For instance, power lines did not reach certain streets and places where opponents of these old-boy networks lived. The attempts to re-appropriate the city, however, met more resistance than expected by those who turned power and construction companies into political instruments.

This became more apparent in the field of security again. The vast majority of the population saw the governance arrangements that had emerged under rebel domination as obviously superior to the former police and gendarmerie, and they did not want to give up what it had achieved. That general opinion was a known fact. So when the first policemen were re-deployed to the North, they were not reclaiming the monopoly of force. And they did not originate in the South as so many had under the former Gbagbo regime. They spoke one or the other local language, cooperated with the hunters and did not inhibit the many local groups from patrolling their neighbourhoods at night. Former rebels were partly incorporated, too – though that raised concerns about those who had committed war crimes during the rebellion that were not yet prosecuted. Although there were official forums, courts and reconciliation commissions to treat such cases, the usual way was, and still is, to search for some sort of compromise or, as it was expressed in local French, un pardon. The actors adapted to the new circumstances. Whether that was the outcome of an official government policy remained unclear. The longer it lasted, though, the more the police and gendarmerie insisted on re-establishing their former dominant position. However, many claimed that the security forces had lost their dominant position long before the insurgency began and that it would not lead anywhere if they insisted on such a monopoly. They had already become part of the governance arrangements that had iterated from the times of the rebellion into the present.

A few questions

The current situation in Côte d'Ivoire leaves many open questions. Firstly, one may ask to what degree the governance arrangements that developed under rebel domination can serve as examples for more sustainable arrangements in the future. Secondly, it is an open question to what extent such a process would affect the State as an institution and also the image of the State that the population shares. In other words: To what degree will these new governance arrangements become part of State governance, which then might lose the monopoly it claimed in the field of security? Thirdly and finally, one may ask whether these new governance arrangements are more affected by neo-patrimonialism and other forms of clientelism than the older State administration. That the new governance arrangements are highly political is as obvious as the patrimonial underpinnings of the former State that now tries to re-establish itself in the former rebel-held part of the country. But how these governance arrangements really work, to what extent they allow actors to participate and which social problems they tackle is an open question that only empirical research can answer.

With regard to governance in general and the recovery of stolen assets in particular, one may summarise the current situation as a puzzle where one would need thick local knowledge to figure out whether a particular institution would work in a specific figuration of local actors. Courts may also be viable in view of certain crimes but may not be able to handle other cases. In particular, when it comes to assets that 'disappeared' during the years of separation, it may be very difficult to bring the responsible persons to justice. Because the new president and his government owe their victory to a considerable extent to the insurgents, they may, on the one hand, be very reluctant to persecute them even if they had the means to do so. On the other, only the former leaders of the Gbagbo regime have been arrested or handed over to the International Criminal Court in the Hague – but to persecute all the former supporters of the Gbagbo regime risks fuelling underlying tensions that could generate more violence again. Under such conditions of a still fragile peace and deficient public institutions, it is almost impossible to satisfy international requests of legal assistance.

Jesse Mwangi Wachanga[1]

Hurdles in asset recovery and fighting corruption by developing countries: The Kenya experience

A brief history of Kenya's efforts to fight corruption

Kenya got her political independence in 1963. At that time, there was the Prevention of Corruption Act, which had been enacted in 1956. This statue criminalised bribery, but it did not initially provide for a specialised anti-corruption authority or anti-corruption courts.

The country registered rapid economic growth in the early years of independence, buoyed by public investment and encouragement of small-scale agriculture production as well as incentives for private (often foreign) industrial investment. The gross domestic product (GDP) grew at an annual average of 6.6 percent from 1963 to 1973.[2]

In 1971, the government allowed public officers to simultaneously run private businesses.[3] This action seems to have encouraged corruption, because public servants took advantage of weak systems in order to do business with the government often in conflict of interest.

In the years between 1974 and 1990, Kenya's economic performance declined due to several factors. In the decade of 1990s, Kenya had its worst economic performance since independence.[4] The country registered negative 0.3 economic growth in 2000.[5]

1 The views expressed are solely those of the author and do not represent the view of the UNODC.

2 See *Economy of Kenya*. Available at: http://en.wikipedia.org/wiki/Economy_of_Kenya.

3 See the *Report of the Commission of Inquiry (Public Service Structure and Remuneration)* published by the Kenya Government Printer in 1971.

4 See *Economy of Kenya*. Available at: http://en.wikipedia.org/wiki/Economy_of_Kenya.

5 See page 17 of *The Economic Survey, 2001, Kenya.*

In 1978, the country went through the first political transition after the death of the first president. When the second president took office there was great optimism that things might improve. But an attempted military coup in 1982 seems to have sent the government into a panic, which thereby resorted to political repression policies and patronage. Illegal and irregular allocation of public land was accelerated in the 1980s, and a series of monumental financial scandals occurred between the late 1980s and early 2000s. In 1997, the Kenya Anti-Corruption Authority (KACA) was created to try to address the scourge of corruption, but it was disbanded in 2000.

The general public was largely dissatisfied with the state of corruption in the country. They got the chance to correct the situation during the general elections of 2002. The then regime was overwhelmingly removed in an election that was largely contested on the anti-corruption platform. The new regime set out in 2003 to reinvigorate the fight against corruption in the country. In his inauguration speech the new president declared that

> Corruption will now cease to be a way of life in Kenya and I call upon all those members of my government and public officers accustomed to corrupt practice to know and clearly understand that there will be no sacred cows under my government.[6]

A series of anti-corruption laws[7] were enacted between 2003 and 2005. The Kenya Anti-Corruption Commission (KACC) and anti-corruption courts were created in 2003. All public officers were required to submit an annual declaration of wealth from the year 2003. A public investigation was opened into the conduct of all judges in 2003. In the same year two Commissions of Inquiry were established – one inquired into the illegal and irregular allocations of public land and the other probed the Goldenberg scandal. The new regime also contracted a UK firm (Kroll and Associates) to investigate and report on stolen assets, which were stashed abroad by the former regime. It

6 Full speech available at: www.statehousekenya.go.ke/speeches/kibaki/2002301201.htm.

7 Most notably the *Anti-Corruption and Economic Crimes Act 2003; the Public Officer Ethics Act 2003; The Public Audit Act 2003; the Government Financial Management Act 2004; and the Public Procurement and Disposal Act 2005.*

was estimated that the amount of funds stashed abroad were in excess of USD 2 billion. In 2009, the country enacted the Proceeds of Crime and Anti-Money Laundering Act, albeit after some delay.[8]

The United Nations Convention against Corruption (UNCAC) was introduced at a time when Kenya had strong momentum to fight corruption. The new political regime, which had entered office on an anti-corruption platform, had been in office for barely a year when UNCAC was unveiled for signature in Merida, Mexico on 9 December 2003. Kenya became the first country to sign and ratify the Convention. The then Kenyan Minister for Justice Mr Kiraitu Murungi told the delegates as follows:

> For us in Kenya, the fight against corruption is a matter of life and death. It cannot wait for tomorrow. We believe we are doing the right thing by ratifying this Convention today. It is not by accident that Kenya has become the first nation to sign and ratify the Convention. The country has been one of the most corrupt nations on Earth.[9]

Unfortunately, in 2004 it was alleged that a fresh scandal of mega-corruption had taken place within the new political establishment.[10]

The outbreak of the alleged scandal in the new regime in 2004 seems to have affected the impetus of the fight against corruption in Kenya. The report written by Kroll and Associates was submitted to the government in 2004, but it was neither made public nor implemented. The reports of the two Commissions of Inquiry were also submitted to the government in 2004 and 2006, respectively, but there has been little effort to implement their findings. The country has not yet established an Asset Recovery Agency, although it is provided for in the Proceeds of Crimes and Anti-Money Laundering Act that was enacted in 2009. The wealth declarations submitted by public officers have simply been stored and have not been subjected to verification.

In 2010, the country promulgated a new constitution,[11] which contains several measures for good governance and integrity. For exam-

8 The Act was initially presented to Parliament in 2007 but it faced opposition.

9 See Press Release available at: www.un.org/webcast/merida/statements/pressrelease2-eng.htm. Also see the full official presentation at pages 20-23 of *Global Action against Corruption: The Merida Papers*, which is available at: www.unodc.org/documents/corruption/publications_merida_e.pdf.

10 The scandal was given the name 'Anglo Leasing'.

ple, the new constitution bars all state officers from maintaining bank accounts abroad unless authorised by parliament. It also bars state officers from running private business that lead to conflicts of interest. The new constitution has also separated the Office of the Attorney General from the Office of Public Prosecutions. This is largely intended to ensure that public prosecutions are done professionally and are not affected by political considerations.

Some financial and procurement scandals and efforts to recover the stolen assets

We will now highlight two major financial and procurement scandals suffered by the country, the Goldenberg and the Anglo Leasing scandals, that illustrate some challenges associated with asset recovery discussed later in this paper.

The Goldenberg scandal occurred in the early 1990s and involved a company that had been established to export gold and diamonds. Two persons owned the company and one of them was the former head of the National Intelligence Service. It was alleged that he was a nominee of the then president who was the real shareholder. The company received public monies from the Central Bank of Kenya (CBK) through various schemes, such as payment of illegal export compensation, cheque kiting, sale of fictitious US dollars, pre-shipment financing, illegal transfers from the Paymaster-General account, among others. It is alleged that the bulk of this money was stashed abroad by powerful individuals and some of it was used to finance elections and political activity. The scandal came to light in April 1993 when a clerk at the Central Bank of Kenya blew the whistle. The whistle-blower was promptly arrested and charged in court for communicating confidential documents to unauthorised persons and he was remanded in prison custody. In September 1993, he was dismissed from employment by the CBK. Efforts to get him back into employment were thwarted, because 'there was no legislation in Kenya protecting the

11 The Constitution can be accessed at: www.kenyalaw.org/klr/index.php.

employment of whistle-blowers therefore his dismissal was technically legal'. He died after a life of poverty and unemployment in August 2006.[12]

In 2003, the government established a Judicial Commission of Inquiry into the Goldenberg Affair. The Commission gave its report to the government in February 2006.[13] The report found that about USD 1.97 billion of Goldenberg money was transacted with 487 companies and individuals, with Goldenberg Company receiving about USD 440 million. The report concluded that the country lost at least USD 387 million in the scam. It recommended further investigations of four persons including the former president. It also listed the names of fourteen persons to be prosecuted, including the former vice president and ministers and high ranking public officers. Prosecutions were commenced against only five persons. The cases proceeded at a snail's pace, and by 2012 three of the accused persons and some witnesses had died. In March 2013, a judge of the High Court of Kenya issued an order declaring that the prosecutions should terminate forthwith and never be instituted again, ostensibly because the cases had taken too long and the accused had received negative publicity.[14] The Director of Public Prosecutions has appealed against this decision. Other than the prosecution, there has not been any major effort to recover the stolen funds.

The other scandal, the Anglo Leasing scandal, is not a single transaction but rather a series of transactions that commenced in the late 1980s. It involved entering into government contracts for supply of goods or services at heavily inflated prices. The government would pay for the goods or services against some promissory notes, whereas the suppliers would either not supply anything at all or they would supply insufficient quantities. Whereas the human actors behind the scam were the same people, the contracts were entered in the names of

12 See the book *The True Story of David Munyakei* (ISBN 9966-7008-9-7).

13 The Report of the Judicial Commission of Inquiry into the Goldenberg Affair is available at: www.marsgroupkenya.org/Reports/WebsiteJudicialDecisions/Goldenberg_Commisson_of_Inquiry_Report_November_2005.pdf.

14 See *Republic* v *Attorney General & 3 Others*, ex parte Kamlesh Pattni, Judicial Review Application No. 305 of 2012, available under case law at: www.kenyalaw.org.

different companies most of which were not registered (although they were alleged to be foreign companies). All the contracts were for the supply of goods or services to the security agencies (the police, military, intelligence and immigration), which made them very difficult to detect because of the level of secrecy involved. But after a new regime of government took office in 2003, the then Presidential Advisor on Governance Mr John Githongo got wind of a new scam in 2004. He commenced enquiries about it and soon discovered that the scam was one in a series that had been going on for decades. When he realised that his colleagues in the new regime were alleged to be involved in perpetuating the scam, he resigned from government and escaped into self-imposed exile in the UK in February 2005.[15] The matter was then forwarded to the anti-corruption agency for investigation. The total project cost of the eighteen cases under investigation in this scam amounted to approximately USD 857 million.

Since the supplier companies were said to be foreign and payments were made to foreign banks, it was necessary to seek mutual legal assistance (MLA) with several countries in Europe and the United States. Several requests for MLA were sent to the foreign countries, but in 2007 the High Court issued an order prohibiting the local and foreign authorities from executing the MLA requests. The anti-corruption agency appealed against the decision. In 2010, the court of appeal reversed the decision of the High Court and allowed the foreign investigations to continue.[16] Then in 2011, the legislature repealed the section of the anti-corruption law that had allowed the anti-corruption agency to request MLA.[17] In the result, it is not expressly clear whether the anti-corruption agency can independently conduct MLA requests.

In 2008, the anti-corruption agency was hit with another court order in another Anglo Leasing case. The High Court declared that the contract should be forwarded to arbitration and not be subject to crim-

15 See *It's Our Time to Eat: the story of a Kenyan Whistleblower* by Michela Wrong.

16 See *Kenya Anti-Corruption Commission* v *First Mercantile Securities Corporation* (Civil Appeal No. 194 of 2008). Available at the Kenyalawreports website.

17 Section 12(3) of the Anti-Corruption and Economic Crimes Act 2003, repealed by section 37 of the Ethics and Anti-Corruption Commission Act 2011.

inal investigations. The court argued that the contract had an arbitration clause, which precluded the application of public law to the contracts.[18]

The Anglo Leasing cases therefore have remained unresolved mainly due to difficulties in conducting the foreign investigations. It is worth mentioning that the authorities of the UK, France, Switzerland and the United States have expressed their willingness to give their fullest assistance in the investigations, but Kenyan authorities have been unable to progress the investigations.

Corruption and asset recovery

Asset recovery is gaining increased prominence.[19] The main justification for asset recovery in this context is twofold: first, to combat crime through its financial lifeline and second, to return the property to the rightful owners.

Asset recovery could arise in various circumstances and thus there are a variety of terms in use, such as recovery of stolen property, recovery of proceeds of crime, confiscation and forfeiture of instruments of crime, combating illicit financial flows, amongst others.

In the context of this paper, we shall use the term mainly in reference to recovery of proceeds of crime and recovery of embezzled public assets.

Corruption has been defined as the abuse of public office for private gain.[20] The crime of corruption therefore results in some form of gain for the criminal. Asset recovery seeks to remove the profit from the criminal. Corruption also facilitates the commission of other serious offences, such as drug trafficking, trafficking in persons, terror-

18 See *Nedermer Technology Bv Limited* v *Kenya Anti-Corruption Commission* and Another (No. 390 of 2006). Available at: www.kenyalaw.org.

19 Article 51 of the United Nations Convention against Corruption declares that the return of assets is a fundamental principle of the Convention, and that the State Parties shall afford on another the widest measure of cooperation and assistance in that regard.

20 This is the definition adopted by the World Bank.

ism, among others. Combating corruption is therefore useful in deterring these other crimes as well. Corruption has also been said to be a violation of human rights.[21] In grand corruption cases, the offences involve massive plunder of public property. Developing countries have particularly suffered economically and socially from the misappropriation of public resources and funds.[22] The recovery of proceeds of crime and stolen assets is therefore important not only for combating crime but also for the economic and social development of developing countries.

Challenges to asset recovery

As a matter of fact, there are very few asset recovery success stories in developing countries. The recovery of assets stolen from African countries has been hampered by a multitude of challenges. In this chapter, we shall only highlight a few of them.

(i) The persons who engage in grand corruption involving embezzlement of huge amounts of public funds in developing countries are often persons in powerful positions of leadership (or persons connected to such persons). They find it easy to plunder the public assets, because they have the opportunity and access to do so. The powerful positions they occupy enable them to prevent or frustrate the recovery of the assets in a number of ways. For example, they may have control over the legislative machinery which enables them to obstruct the passing of any laws that would criminalise their conduct, and if such laws are nevertheless passed, they can ensure that the laws are weak or incapable of implementation; they also have control over the law enforcement agencies, and this enables them to nip any de-

21 See *Corruption and Human Rights: Making the Connection*, a report of the International Council on Human Rights Policy, which is available at: www.ichrp.org/files/reports/40/131_web.pdf.

22 The annual Global Corruption Reports by Transparency International and also the national and regional Bribery Index (eg the East African Bribery Index) show that developing countries are most affected by corruption.

tection or investigation in the bud; they have control over the national security apparatus, and they may use and misuse the national security agencies to intimidate and harass or otherwise harm any opposition or any person who may be tempted to report or investigate their corruption; they have the means and opportunity to ensure there are no records of their wrong-doing, or ensure that the records are falsified or destroyed, or are not accessed by persons who may report them, and they can also coerce or influence the junior public officers into facilitating the embezzlement and keeping quiet about it.

(ii) The political economy of corruption shows some patterns of prevalence of patron-client networks, politicisation of the bureaucracy, dominance over the legislature, capture of electoral processes and oversight institutions and blurred lines between business and politics. These patterns are shaped by the dominant elites.[23] A law enforcement regime may find obstacles in reigning cartels for drug trafficking and looters of public resources, because they are protected at high levels of the ruling political regime. Owing to the huge profits they get from illicit activity, the corrupt people can influence the actions of those in public service and legislature. They can also hire the services of top lawyers from private practice and accountants to help them launder the money and hide it abroad. They can hire these expensive services either at the expense of the government or from the proceeds of the crime.

(iii) The looted funds are often stashed abroad. Any initiative towards recovery of such looted funds would inevitably require the tool of mutual legal assistance and cross-border repatriation of assets. Africa faces a lot of capacity challenges in adopting the tool of MLA, especially because of lack of proper training, lack of requisite technology and lack of funding. Also, the MLA process is difficult in terms of procedural formalities, formal requirements (eg dual criminality, etc.), delays, bureau-

23 See the report *Can UNCAC Address Grand Corruption? A Political Economy Analysis of the United Nations Convention against Corruption.* Available at: www.u4.no/publications/can-uncac-address-grand-corruption.

cracy, language barriers, differences in legal systems, cost and provisions, which allow a requested State to refuse to give co-operation in certain circumstances. To make matters worse, requested States are usually empowered to share the stolen assets at best or retain the whole proceeds at worst. In Australia, the Attorney General (or the Minister for Justice and Customs) has the discretion to direct how the proceeds of a registered foreign order will be dealt with. S/he can direct that the money belongs to Australia or that it be paid in part or in whole to the requesting State.[24] In the UK, the authorities seek to enter into an asset sharing agreement wherever possible.[25] Developing countries would easily consider this to be an injustice to their citizens whose public funds have been stolen.

(iv) There is another serious problem facing repatriation of assets to Africa, and it is that the government invariably controls the process of seeking the return of stolen assets and yet the persons against whom the recoveries are sought are often the leaders of that government. The leaders who are the subject of the request are often in a position to prevent the competent authorities from initiating the request. And if the request is nevertheless initiated (perhaps after pressure from the public or donors), they might be able to use the judicial arm or prosecution services to terminate or frustrate the execution of the MLA request. As a matter of fact, the inability of Africa to recover stolen funds from abroad is often caused by local problems rather than non-cooperation from requested States.

(v) Recovery of stolen assets may become a vicious cycle if the country does not have a strong regime of prevention measures.

24 See pages 86 and 102 of *Mutual Legal Assistance, Extradition and Recovery of Proceeds of Corruption in Asia and Pacific* ISBN 978-92-64-04370-1. See also Article 57(4) of UNCAC; Article 14 of the UN Convention against Transnational Organised Crime; and Article 5 of the UN Convention against Narcotic Drugs and Psychotropic Substances; which allow a requested State to deduct certain costs and expenses.

25 See *Obtaining Assistance from the UK in Asset Recovery; A guide for international partners*. Available at: http://star.worldbank.org/star/sites/star/files/UK-Guide-to-Asset-Recovery.pdf.

If corruption is a rampant feature within the government of a country, then there is no assurance that the recovered funds will not be stolen again or that there will not be any further thefts. Requesting States must remember that the requested States expend time and money to execute the request, and therefore must exercise diligence both in the handling of the recovered funds as well as in ensuring such thefts are minimised. It would be useful therefore to include a mechanism in the asset recovery policy, which guarantees that the recovered funds will be properly utilised for the benefit of the victims (usually the general public). It would be commendable also to appoint an autonomous third party, as happened in the case of the assets recovered from Sani Abacha, whereby the third party is given authority to receive and disburse the recovered stolen assets. In this case, the World Bank, for instance, would be an ideal choice to oversee the disbursement of recovered funds.

(vi) Where a new regime seeks to recover funds allegedly stolen by the outgoing regime, there could be accusations of a witch-hunt. In other situations, the new regime may strike a deal with the members of the outgoing regime so that they protect each other. After all, all politicians are birds of a feather.

(vii) The justice systems of many developing countries are ineffective in adjudicating cases against the ruling elite and wealthy interests. All the major cases of asset recovery by developing countries were rendered successful mainly because of the effectiveness of courts in the requested States rather than their own courts. Also, it is a fact that some alleged stolen properties have been frozen in Europe mainly because of the actions of civil society and courts in Europe not because of requests from developing countries.

(viii) Asset recovery becomes difficult and sometimes impossible due to lack of information. In absence of laws allowing access to information and in absence of financial intelligence units, many African countries find it difficult to detect or investigate the trail of stolen assets. The corrupt public officers can invoke secrecy laws to prevent the disclosure of information to third parties. The investigation agencies themselves often lack the facilities for proactive detection and investigation of corruption. In many countries in Africa the laws on freedom of the media and access to information are quite weak, which enables the leaders to keep the public ignorant of crucial facts.

(ix) Many African countries still have the paramount chief syndrome, which makes it virtually impossible to question, remove or act against corrupt leaders. When the corrupt leaders find there is a threat of legal proceedings for corruption, they may use the government machinery and patronage to entrench and consolidate their position to make sure they cannot be removed from office.

(x) In the case of non-criminalisation, if the legal system has not declared the embezzlement or misappropriation of public resources a wrongdoing, then it becomes difficult to lay a claim for restitution.

(xi) Many African countries have weak prevention mechanisms. Even when a new regime deposes a corrupt regime, the members of the new regime soon find themselves embroiled in corruption because of the many loopholes.

Concluding remarks

From the foregoing, it should be clear that whereas developing countries are entitled to expect requested States to return stolen assets, they themselves have important roles to play for the success of this initiative.

Asset recovery ought to be given top priority by any regime, first, as a tool to prevent crime, and second, for the justice of the citizens. It is therefore sad to note that asset recovery has not achieved much over the years. But we must not give up. Despite the challenges and the few success stories, we must persist in our endeavours to recover stolen public assets and restore them to the rightful owners, the citizens.

Emerging trends, good practice

Part 1: Overarching themes

Dimitri Vlassis, Dorothee Gottwald and Ji Won Park[1]

Chapter V of UNCAC: Five years on experiences, obstacles and reforms on asset recovery

Background

The United Nations Convention against Corruption (UNCAC), and particularly its Chapter V, has seen unprecedented progress in the past years. In 2005, the dynamics of the negotiations of Chapter V of the Convention brought about a landmark agreement. For the first time, the return of assets to the countries of origin was stated as a fundamental principle (article 51 of the Convention), and the unconditional return of proceeds of embezzlement to the States of origin was made an obligation for all State Parties (article 57 paragraph 3 of the Convention). When the Basel Institute on Governance published one of the first books on the market on recovering stolen assets in 2008,[2] there were only a few (yet famous) asset recovery cases. Countries had only emerging experience in the area and the new legal framework was so recent that it had hardly been used. This paper takes stock of the progress achieved since.

On one hand, this paper shows how the policy discourse on asset recovery has advanced. Intense discussions in intergovernmental fora have brought about a number of resolutions and recommendations, especially in the Conference of the States Parties to the Convention ('the Conference of the States Parties') and its Open-ended Intergovernmental Working Group on Asset Recovery ('the Asset Recovery Working Group'). In 2008, the Stolen Asset Recovery (StAR) Initiative (launched in 2007) began its work. Apart from providing capacity

1 The views expressed in this article are those of the authors and do not necessarily reflect the views or position of the United Nations or the World Bank.
2 Mark Pieth, ed.: Recovering Stolen Assets (Bern: Peter Lang, 2008).

building and technical assistance, the StAR Initiative has enriched the policy discussion with a number of policy papers that put experiences of the most advanced practitioners and scholars on asset recovery at the disposal of practitioners around the world. In this paper reference is also made to the work of the Group of 20 and the Group of Eight, whose members include many financial centres and typically requested States as well as the European Union and other regional organisations. Following the policy debates, this paper will show that a number of countries have amended their laws on identification, freezing, seizure, confiscation and return of assets.

On the other hand, as a prominent practitioner noted, 'In the end, the UNCAC is and must be about actual recoveries.'[3] The final purpose of all policy reforms is to make asset recovery easier and make more recoveries possible. Whether the international community has achieved this goal to a satisfying extent is more difficult to measure and describe, since there is no mechanism to collect comprehensive information on all international asset recovery cases. However, the StAR Initiative has a powerful tool to monitor asset recovery both quantitatively and qualitatively. The StAR Asset Recovery Watch database[4] is an outcome of a recommendation by the Asset Recovery Working Group, which suggested a database of asset recovery cases be created as a mechanism by which the international community could share knowledge about successful asset recovery practices and measure to what extent the goals expressed at the highest policy levels are carried out by concrete actions at the operational levels. Launched in fall of 2011, StAR Asset Recovery Watch is the most comprehensive database of its type. Still, it does not purport to be exhaustive due to persisting knowledge gaps and the inevitable time lag until cases are known and documentation is available, which allows the cases to be added to the database. Asset Recovery Watch currently contains 96 completed and active cases; some of the cases are internationally known while others are less known outside of their countries of origin.

3 Daniel Claman, "The promise and limitations of asset recovery under the UNCAC", in Mark Pieth (ed), Recovering Stolen Assets, p. 350.

4 StAR Asset Recovery Watch, available at: http://star.worldbank.org/corruption-cases/arwcases.

The cases are organised into separate entries by the jurisdiction(s) of recovery effort and/or asset location. The cases span a wide range of time, from the early 1980s to the present.

Policies and reforms

When the United Nations Convention against Corruption was negotiated, the chapter on asset recovery proved to be particularly difficult. The spirit of cooperation and mutual understanding, which characterised the entire negotiation process, prevailed also in this case and resulted in the solution of article 57 that established the unconditional return for proceeds of embezzlement of public funds.

The Conference of the States Parties has since its first session in 2006 placed particular emphasis on the further development of its work on Chapter V, and therefore established the Open-ended Intergovernmental Working Group on Asset Recovery. The Group focused its work on three lines, which the Conference endorsed in its following sessions: developing cumulative knowledge, building confidence and encouraging cooperation between requesting and requested States and capacity-building and technical assistance.

The development of cumulative knowledge is an area in which progress is easily visible. Different from five years ago, when asset recovery was generally considered a scarcely known and relatively new field of international law, practitioners and policy makers nowadays have a number of tools at hand. The laws of 178 countries on asset recovery can be found and searched for by different criteria in the Legal Library, which is part of the United Nations Office on Drugs and Crime (UNODC) online information database known as TRACK (Tools and Resources for Anti-Corruption Knowledge).[5] Since 2008 the StAR Initiative has developed a number of new knowledge products. Some of the products aim primarily at informing the policy debate and create inspiration for legislators, such as the studies on asset declaration systems (Public Office, Private Interests: Accountability

5 Available at: www.track.unodc.org.

through Income and Asset Disclosure, 2012), on follow-up on the Accra Agenda for Action (Tracking Anti-Corruption and Asset Recovery Commitments: A Progress Report and Recommendations for Action, 2011, in collaboration with OECD) or on illicit enrichment (On the take, Illicit Enrichment, 2012). Other knowledge products are designed for practitioners, such as the Asset Recovery Handbook which provides a step-by-step guide to asset recovery cases and offers guidance on how to deal with typical problems in different legal systems (Asset Recovery Handbook, 2012) and the good practice guide on non-conviction based forfeiture (Stolen Asset Recovery).[6] A digest of asset recovery cases will soon be launched. UNODC also expanded the Mutual Legal Assistance Request Writer Tool to cover more typical situations in mutual legal assistance requests related to asset recovery.

Capacity building and technical assistance directly follow the logic of enhanced knowledge, which has to be distributed to asset recovery practitioners to be applied in their everyday cases. Work in this field has started, but it needs to be continuously strengthened. The language barrier that StAR knowledge products meet is increasingly overcome by translations into all official United Nations languages. A new generation of training materials has been developed on the basis of enhanced knowledge, and a high number of practitioners have been trained by StAR in regional and national training courses, many of them in cooperation with the International Centre for Asset Recovery (ICAR). Strategies of South-South cooperation should be explored increasingly, since some of the regional financial centres have been found to be central in asset recovery. StAR has further developed and applied strategies for case-specific preparatory assistance and is currently working with 28 countries. A visible success of this engagement was the recent return to Tunisia of USD 28.8 million from Lebanon.[7]

6 All StAR publications are available at: http://star.worldbank.org/star/publications?keys=&sort_by=score&sort_order=DESC&items_per_page=10.

7 Available at: http://blogs.worldbank.org/psd/tunisias-cash-back-the-start-of-more-to-come.

The building of confidence and trust between requesting and requested States is a question that touches on the political will of countries, but it also has important implications at the technical level. Creating contact points and building networks have been found to be helpful in developing working relationships between practitioners that result in more effective cooperation. Work has been initiated, but a number of key issues are to be addressed. Following a request by the Working Group, 53 States have designated their focal points on asset recovery. They complement the 101 central authorities for mutual legal assistance designated under article 46 paragraph 13 of the Convention.[8] The StAR-Interpol Asset Recovery Focal Point Initiative is linking contact points of 102 countries, mainly at the law enforcement level. Building on the experience of the Camden Asset Recovery Inter-Agency Network (CARIN), the Asset Recovery Inter-Agency Network of Southern Africa (ARINSA) and the Network for Asset Recovery of the GAFISUD countries (*Red de Recuperación de Activos de GAFISUD* or RRAG)[9] have been established. The establishment of similar networks is under discussion in various other regions. However, a clear picture of the most functional global asset recovery network has yet to be envisioned. Given the existing networks and their specific advantages, a network of central authorities could be one possibility. Discussions are on going and the Conference of the States Parties is in the process of developing a clear vision of the most functional network for time-sensitive and complex asset recovery cases.

The political discourse on asset recovery has significantly changed since the adoption of the Convention. In recent years, in-depth political discussions have taken place in the Group of Eight and the Group of 20. These groups of countries include many of the financial centres and States that are typically requested for asset recovery. In 2009, the Group of 20 recommended the review and proposal of mechanisms to strengthen international cooperation on asset recovery, the enforcement of standards related to the identification of beneficial ownership and the monitoring of politically exposed persons. Its Anti-

8 See for a full list of central authorities document CAC/COSP/2011/CRP.10.

9 GAFISUD stands for Financial Action Task Force on Money Laundering in South America.

Corruption Working Group has addressed the work on asset recovery further. Responding to the specific situation of the Arab Spring, the Group of Eight in 2011 launched the Deauville Partnership and its action plan. The first Arab Forum was held in Doha in September 2012. Both the Group of 20 and the Group of Eight have published country guides to mutual legal assistance and asset recovery, which aim to make requests to their jurisdictions more efficient.[10] Further, the Financial Action Task Force (FATF) and the Wolfsberg Group have recently referred directly to asset recovery and the StAR Initiative.

Operations and obstacles

As noted previously, by including both completed and active cases Asset Recovery Watch seeks to measure how expressions of political will and policy reforms translate into concrete actions. More specifically, Asset Recovery Watch provides an indication of how active cases are faring in the three distinct and necessary stages of asset recovery: (i) location and freezing, (ii) confiscation or forfeiture and (iii) return of assets. In summary, the Asset Recovery Watch records a good deal of progress made by countries to foster asset recovery, but it also points to further work needed if the international community truly aspires to fulfil the promise of UNCAC.

Location and freezing

There is an ever-greater awareness of the importance of rapidly locating and freezing assets lest they dissipate. The mentioned country profiles for asset tracing elaborated by the Group of 20 Anti-Corruption Working Group[11] show that there is still much work to be done in this area. For example, while a small number of countries

10 Group of Eight: Country Guides for Asset Recovery; Group of 20: Asset Tracing Country Profiles (2012), Requesting Mutual Legal Assistance in Criminal Matters from G20 Countries (2012). Available at: track.unodc.org.

11 Assets Tracing: Country Profiles (2012), see reference above.

have central registers of bank accounts that authorities may access without a court order in order to prevent money laundering, in other countries, to identify and locate unknown bank accounts a request must be sent to all financial institutions upon a court order or decision, thereby delaying the asset location and freezing process. For identifying real estate holdings, registration is not always mandatory or it may be done at the state/provincial level, which makes the identification process cumbersome. Past research by StAR, FATF and The Organisation for Economic Co-operation and Development (OECD) has shown that in large-scale corruption cases public officials often hide their beneficial ownership of bank accounts and real estate properties by placing these assets in the name of legal structures, such as shell companies. Yet, company registries do not always exist at the national level nor do they hold beneficial ownership information. Banking secrecy and insufficient mechanisms for rapid freezing upon request by another State have been identified as two of the major barriers to asset recovery in StAR's research.[12]

Despite these obstacles, the cases in Asset Recovery Watch show that there is progress, and countries are cooperating and exchanging information, which has led to the location and freezing of assets. Additionally, countries such as Canada and Switzerland have departed from the past practice of waiting for a request from the jurisdiction of origin of the public official before freezing assets located within their own countries. Canada's 2011 Freezing Assets of Corrupt Foreign Officials Act targets assets of foreign politically exposed persons when 'the foreign nation is in a situation of "internal turmoil" and the freezing of assets is in the best interests of the "international community"'. In February 2011, the day after the Mubarak government fell from power in Egypt, Switzerland announced that assets associated with the Mubarak family and close associates had been located and frozen. In 2012, the Financial Action Task Force Recommendations were revised to give greater guidance to countries in the implementation of concrete measures to promote transparency, availability and

12 Kevin M. Stephenson et al., Barriers to Asset Recovery, An Analysis of the Key Barriers and Recommendations for Action, barriers No. 10 and 12. Available at: www.worldbank.org/star.

accessibility of information on beneficial ownership of legal entities and legal arrangements, which, as noted above, has been misused in large-scale corruption cases to conceal the origin and/or destination of corruption proceeds.

Asset Recovery Watch reports USD 2 billion as currently frozen. In comparison to the tens of billions allegedly stolen, this figure points to the clear need for more work. Further, while this is a significant figure, it should be noted that more than USD 1.3 billion of the total amount is the result of three cases. At the same time, in the aftermath of the fall of the Gaddafi regime in Libya, several countries announced the freezing of tens of billions of dollars in Libyan assets. Those figures have not been included in the total USD 2 billion frozen, as it was unclear how much of those assets were specifically connected to the Gaddafi family and associates.

Confiscation

Even when alleged corruption proceeds have been located and frozen, it is far from certain that they will be subject to forfeiture and confiscation. Asset Recovery Watch contains examples of successful confiscations, including successful non-conviction based confiscations by the US Department of Justice's Kleptocracy Asset Recovery Initiative and a private civil action undertaken by Libya in London against a mansion legally owned by an offshore company that was held by the UK court to be beneficially owned by the son of the late Colonel Gaddafi. At the same time, experts point to confiscation as the most challenging phase of the asset recovery process, because it requires that authorities prove the nexus between the assets and specified corrupt acts. The US cases, for example, involved foreign public officials who had been criminally convicted in their own countries, which cooperated with the US in the civil proceedings. However, a court ruling in an active US case involving the current vice president of Equatorial Guinea dismissed the US government's complaint for failure to state specific links between the assets in question and unlawful acts (as opposed to general allegations of corruption) and on going efforts in post-Arab Spring asset recovery efforts demonstrate the evidentiary challenges that must be met in order for assets to be confiscated. Further obstacles to confiscating assets are shown by StAR research to be insufficient legal frameworks, especially for value-based confiscation and for the enforcement of foreign confiscation orders, and barriers to efficient mutual legal assistance, such as onerous mutual legal assistance requirements and lack of accessible knowledge of procedures.[13]

At the same time, more countries have established and/or reorganised units within their law enforcement agencies to focus specifically on 'kleptocracy' cases and asset recovery, which utilise specialised investigators and prosecutors in order to better meet these challenges.

Return of assets

Asset Recovery Watch reports that USD 4 billion has been returned. Returned assets can be put into three categories: (i) embezzled or misappropriated funds and laundered public funds, in accordance with Articles 17 and 23 of UNCAC, (ii) other proceeds of crime mainly resulting from foreign bribery and related cases and (iii) others, such as voluntary reparation payments.

For the first set of assets – embezzled or misappropriated funds – Article 57 (3)(a) provides for the mandatory return of the confiscated property to the requesting State Party. The bulk of the returns recorded in Asset Recovery Watch fall under this category, but it should be noted that a good deal of the amounts relate to two large pre-2008 cases, the Marcos and Abacha cases.

Article 57(3)(b) of UNCAC provides that, 'In the case of proceeds of any other offence covered by this Convention' the requested State Party shall 'return the confiscated property to the requesting State Party, when the requesting State Party reasonably establishes its prior ownership of such confiscated property […] or when the requested State Party recognises damage to the requesting State Party as a basis for returning the confiscated property'. Asset Recovery Watch contains a small number of foreign bribery (UNCAC Article 16) cases

13 Barriers (see reference above) No. 14 and 19, 21-26.

in which asset return took place, including the UN Oil-for-Food related criminal enforcement actions undertaken by the US Attorney General's Office for the Southern District of New York against a number of US companies and individuals. In those cases, criminal proceeds were forfeited to the US and then transferred to the Development Fund for Iraq as restitution for the benefit of the people of Iraq.

Article 57(3)(c) of UNCAC states that State Parties also shall consider 'compensating the victims of the crime'. Asset Recovery Watch contains a small number of cases in which jurisdictions considered who the victims were in a given case and sought various means to provide reparations. The most notable cases have taken place in the UK, and they include the BAE Systems case in which the company agreed to make an ex gratia payment for the benefit of the people of Tanzania, the Messent case in which restitution was ordered to the Costa Rican state-owned entity that the customer harmed and the Oxford University Press case in which the company agreed to make a voluntary payment for education-related purposes for the benefit of peoples in the affected region. Switzerland also ordered Alstom SA to make a reparation payment to an international charity for its programs in the three countries where the company had secured public contracts through foreign bribery. Lastly, the USD 100 million Siemens Integrity Fund set-up as part of the company's 2009 settlement with the World Bank in which the funds were to be used to support anti-corruption efforts, including initiatives aimed at helping countries recover assets stolen by their leaders, is a welcome development even if it does not fit neatly into the UNCAC asset recovery framework.

Asset Recovery Watch also records about USD 1.3 billion in total pending returns. This figure, again, needs to be considered in context. It includes over USD 400 million in restitution ordered in one case, and it is unknown if the defendants have the ability to pay. It also includes the USD 356 million judgment awarded by a US court to the Marcos-era victims of human rights violations, which is still under appeal by the Marcos family.

Outlook

More asset recovery efforts are currently underway than ever before, and this should serve as cause for optimism. Asset recovery, as embodied in Chapter V of the Convention, is no longer a novel idea but rather an idea that has come to be accepted and expected. Countries around the world, albeit to varying degrees, have put or are putting into place the policy, legislation and institutional frameworks needed to facilitate the recovery and return of stolen assets. At the same time, the practitioners both in the public and private sectors working in the field as investigators, prosecutors or civil lawyers now include more knowledgeable professionals who have worked on past asset recovery cases and who are experienced in navigating the complex terrain of multijurisdictional recoveries. With new cases, new professionals are coming on board and the field of asset recovery experts is growing.

However, much remains to be done. The Convention is built on the fundamental principle of shared responsibility, and the area where most work remains is in the capacity building of developing countries to undertake asset recovery efforts both within and beyond their borders. Asset identification and tracing, freezing and confiscation are yet to become a standard feature of investigations in economic crime. As mutual legal assistance to this effect comes closer to a standard procedure, one can expect that trust and confidence between practitioners will grow and that consensus on the operational mechanisms, including efficient networks, will also grow.

A clearer picture about the legal and operational needs will emerge from the Mechanism for the Review of Implementation of the Convention in its second cycle (2015-2019), in which the State Parties to the Convention (166 in May 2013) will be reviewed on the implementation of Chapter V. The basic tool for collecting information on domestic legislation and other measures designed to implement the Convention is the self-assessment checklist. The Conference encouraged State Parties to use the self-assessment checklist as a way to assess their efforts in implementing the provisions of the Convention relating to asset recovery with regard to legislation and regulations, statistics and case law. Furthermore, information regarding the challenges in implementation and technical assistance needs is to be collected. Some State Parties have already used the self-assessment checklist on Chapter V of the Convention for their national analysis of implementation gaps. From 2015 onwards each State Party will undergo a peer review by two other State Parties. The result of this peer review will be contained in detailed country reports. The Executive Summaries of these reports will be public as part of the official documentation of the Implementation Review Group and the Conference of the States Parties. The reports and Executive Summaries are sure to contain a wealth of information on the implementation of Chapter V, implementation gaps and technical assistance needs. General trends will be described in thematic reports and regional addenda. The review of Chapter V will create an unprecedented momentum for asset recovery, which will complement and continue the positive developments of the last years.

RITA ADAM AND VALENTIN ZELLWEGER[1]

The proposed Swiss comprehensive act on asset recovery

The year 2013 marks the tenth anniversary of the United Nations Convention against Corruption (UNCAC). Chapter V of UNCAC, which specifically addresses asset recovery, for the first time laid the framework for tracing, freezing, forfeiting and rcturning funds obtained through corrupt activities in an international legal document and was therefore a significant innovation. By adopting the text, the community of lawmakers and practitioners involved in asset recovery created the first major tool in international law to address the challenge of stolen assets.

Switzerland played a key role in the elaboration of the UNCAC chapter on asset recovery and led negotiations on Article 57 concerning the return and disposal of illicit assets. Involvement with UNCAC enabled Switzerland to put its already considerable experience in the area of asset recovery to good use. The first Swiss case of asset recovery dates back to 1986 with the fall of the Filipino dictator Ferdinand Marcos. Within hours of the political upheaval in Manila the Swiss Federal Council (the Swiss government) froze all of the assets deposited in Switzerland that belonged to Marcos and his entourage. The case of Duvalier in Haiti occurred in the same year and was followed by a series of other cases of restitution, including those of Abacha in Nigeria, Montesinos in Peru and Salinas in Mexico. Efforts to return the assets of the former President of Zaire (Democratic Republic of the Congo) Mobutu had to be abandoned in 2009 due to weakened institutions in that country. Before abandoning their efforts, the Swiss

1 The views expressed in this article are those of the authors and do not necessarily reflect the views of the Swiss authorities.

authorities worked for 12 years exploring every available avenue of restoring the funds to the Democratic Republic of the Congo (DRC).[2]

At the time of the UNCAC negotiations in 2003, Switzerland already had vast experience in dealing with asset recovery questions. In handling the different cases outlined above, Switzerland acquired a considerable amount of substantial, well-differentiated know-how, but it also suffered setbacks. Both the Duvalier and Mobutu cases were characterised by requesting States with severely weakened institutions. The States were unable to provide for mutual legal assistance proceedings that would have eventually allowed for lawful restitution. The impending failure of restitution efforts to Haiti in 2010 prompted the preparation of a new legal basis that would enable Switzerland to confiscate stolen assets originating from fragile States with a view to sending them back to the countries of origin. The new act, called the Federal Act on the Restitution of Assets of Politically Exposed Persons obtained by Unlawful Means (RIAA), came into law on 1 February 2011.

The beginning of the political unrest in North Africa in early 2011 was in many ways a turning point. This historical phenomenon opened a new chapter in worldwide asset recovery initiatives. Suddenly a whole series of countries with important financial centres found themselves simultaneously confronted with requests for legal assistance and immersed in restitution procedures of an exceptional nature. Among these countries was Switzerland. Thanks to its past experience, the Swiss Confederation was the first country to block all funds of deposed President Ben Ali just days after the upheavals in Tunisia. Following the unrest in Egypt, the assets of former President Mubarak were frozen half an hour after his ousting. High on the list of Swiss priorities in such cases is the earliest possible restitution of all illicit assets in the framework of cooperation with the countries in which the assets originated.

2 For further information on the various cases see the Dispatch on the Federal Act on the Restitution of Assets of Politically Exposed Persons obtained by Unlawful Means (RIAA). Available at: www.eda.admin.ch/etc/medialib/downloads/edazen/topics/finec/intcr.Par.0018.File.tmp/Message%20LRAI%20in%20English.pdf.

Against the backdrop of the political turmoil in Northern Africa and its repercussions on Switzerland, the Swiss government decided to take action at the legislative level. In May 2013, the Swiss Federal Council presented the draft of a new act on asset recovery. While constitutional considerations were at the origin of this legislative project, the government decided to seize the opportunity to create a comprehensive act on asset recovery. When enacted this law should ensure that the Swiss procedures in relation to the restitution of illicit assets are properly codified. The draft law covers the following stages that occur in most cases involving so-called 'potentate funds':

- Administrative procedures to block funds as a precautionary measure
- Support for criminal investigations in the country of origin, including mutual legal assistance (capacity building, secondment of experts, etc.)
- The possibility in certain circumstances, once legal assistance has proved of no avail, to introduce administrative procedures for confiscation of the funds in question
- Provisions for the restitution of confiscated funds to the country of origin

The law is not intended to provide new solutions in the case of on going procedures. And despite views expressed in certain media, it is not a 'Lex Mubarak' tailor-made for the situation in Egypt. On the other hand, should certain provisions in the new law prove useful in the future for the North African cases, then so much the better.

A comprehensive act devoted entirely to asset recovery, such as the one currently under consideration in Switzerland, will be a world premiere. After the adoption of key standards on asset recovery at the international level, in the framework of UNCAC, legislation at the national level will be taken one step further. The comprehensive nature of the Swiss act has substantial advantages. The law applicable in asset recovery cases will be clear and immediately understandable. Codification of the procedures employed to date adds to the legal certainty and transparency. At the same time Switzerland will be sending a strong signal regarding its determination to combat efforts to make wrongful use of its financial centre. Its long-standing policy to return illicitly acquired assets to the countries of origin will be continued.

A parliamentary debate on the draft law is due to begin in 2014. The main provisions of the law are outlined in the text.[3]

Key aspects of the law

Blocking of assets as a precautionary measure after the downfall of a corrupt regime

Practitioners and experts unanimously agree that freezing assets of dubious origin as soon as possible is key to the success of asset recovery. This kind of precautionary measure prevents the siphoning off of stolen funds from financial centres, and it allows law enforcement authorities sufficient time to devise a strategy for proceeding and, in particular, time to choose the most promising model case. In the more complex cases that involve several jurisdictions such a measure can be essential for continuing with the case.

The Swiss Federal Constitution allows the government to take steps to freeze assets as a preventive measure. In the past, the Federal Council has done this on several occasions, including during the Marcos case in 1986 and during the upheavals in North Africa at the beginning of 2011. The aim of freezing assets at the very beginning of these cases was to facilitate the establishment of mutual legal assistance proceedings with the countries of origin. The new draft law provides a firm legal basis for the continuation of this practice by setting

3 The draft law with explanatory remarks of the Swiss Federal Council is available in German at: www.admin.ch/ch/d/gg/pc/documents/2259/SRVG_Entwurf_de.pdf and www.admin.ch/ch/d/gg/pc/documents/2259/SRVG_Erl.-Bericht_de.pdf. Available in French at: www.admin.ch/ch/f/gg/pc/documents/2259/LBRV_Projet_fr.pdf and www.admin.ch/ch/f/gg/pc/documents/2259/LBRV_Rapport-expl_fr.pdf.

out the prerequisites for a freezing order. The prerequisites include the loss of power of the government or some government members in the country of origin and also a notoriously high level of corruption under the former regime. The decision to freeze assets must be made with a view to establish mutual legal assistance proceedings in the near future, and it must be necessary to preserve the interests of Switzerland.

The suspicious assets of politically exposed persons (PEPs) are usually not limited to just one financial centre. Rather they are typically spread across several jurisdictions through a complex network of investments. Coordinating preventive freezes among the countries involved can thus increase the freezes' effectiveness. It is for this reason that the draft law calls for consultation with the authorities of the most important partner countries before proceeding to freeze assets. Whenever possible the nature of the proceedings and the timing of the freeze should be decided in consultation with the partner countries, as is already the Swiss practice. In the years ahead, Switzerland will campaign for the creation of international standards aimed at improving the coordination of such measures among all countries involved.

Support for requesting States

It is usually impossible for a requesting or requested State to manage a case of asset recovery alone. Therefore, a close partnership between the two States, based on trust and dialogue, will determine the success or failure of the case. In this context tailor-made measures in support of the country of origin often play a key role in successfully recovering stolen assets. The range of possible measures is wide. For example, regular meetings between experts make it possible to establish mutual trust, clarify open questions related to the other State's legal system, clear up misunderstandings and determine the future course of action. These meetings can be undertaken at a bilateral level or, as in the case of the Lausanne Conferences that Switzerland has organised since 2001, at a multilateral level. Additionally, experts can be deployed to the requesting State to explain the peculiarities of the legal system of the requested State. Experience has shown that deploying

Swiss experts can help considerably to accelerate the process of mutual legal assistance. Also, training modules for the authorities of post-revolutionary States in the process of reorganising their justice systems may prove worthwhile in the medium- to long-term. All of these measures designed to support the country of origin are used consistently by Switzerland, and they are included in the new draft law. The above list is far from an exhaustive review of the possible forms of cooperation. Whenever necessary additional support measures should be devised to meet new requirements.

Although the vast majority of the new draft law is the codification of Switzerland's on going practices, parts of the draft law also allow for targeted innovation. In the experience of Switzerland, the judicial authorities in the countries of origin sometimes struggle to provide sufficient justification for requests for legal assistance. This is particularly true when political upheaval has made criminal investigation possible for the first time. In such cases, the authorities in the countries of origin of illicit assets often lack the experience and special know-how needed to investigate complex cases involving 'white collar' crime with international ramifications. This usually becomes evident in their efforts to formulate a request for legal assistance. Indeed the authorities of the requested State will not be able to act on a request in the absence of sufficient grounds. In such cases when a mutual legal assistance request is not sufficiently substantiated it may lead to detrimental delays and ultimately to a failure to provide legal assistance.

Deploying experts to the country of origin is a possible way to alleviate the deadlock. In addition to deploying experts, the Swiss Federal Council proposes action in accordance with Article 13 of the draft law. A new feature for the Swiss legal system, Article 13 would allow the forwarding of information to the country of origin even before cooperation within the framework of mutual legal assistance has been established. The information passed to the requesting State would normally concern assets that have been frozen in Switzerland on the basis of an administrative preventive measure by the Swiss Federal Council. For the transfer of information to be possible under Article 13 of the draft law the requesting State must first meet certain obligations, including a written declaration confirming that the information will be used exclusively for the preparation or completion of a request for Swiss legal assistance.

Administrative confiscation in the case of weakened institutions

The normal recourse for the restitution of potentate funds is through international mutual legal assistance in criminal matters. This recourse can however lead to failure despite intensive efforts on the parts of both the requesting and requested State. Ultimately, failure may be due to weak state structures in the requesting State. Taking this possibility into consideration, Switzerland created the federal act known as RIAA. RIAA came into force on 1 February 2011, and it allows the confiscation of potentate funds on behalf of a failed State on the basis of Swiss administrative court procedures. In such cases, the law allows a reversal of the burden of proof in so far as the legal or illegal origin of the assets is concerned.[4] In doing so, despite its European continental legal tradition, Switzerland introduced a kind of administrative 'non-conviction-based forfeiture' in certain asset recovery cases. Thereby, Switzerland consciously went beyond its legal obligations under UNCAC.

The power to confiscate stolen funds in certain cases is slightly extended under the new draft law. Recent experiences with asset recovery cases were the decisive factor in proposing an expansion of confiscation powers. The provision of mutual legal assistance presupposes that certain minimum requirements can be met by the requesting State, in so far as the rule of law and human rights are concerned.[5] Meeting these minimum requirements generally implies a certain institutional stability in the requesting State. In post-revolutionary situa-

4 Further information available at: www.eda.admin.ch/etc/medialib/downloads/edazen/topics/finec/intcr.Par.0018.File.tmp/Message%20LRAI%20in%20English.pdf.

5 See in this context the provisions in Art. 2 of the Federal Act on International Mutual Assistance in Criminal Matters. Available at: www.admin.ch/ch/e/rs/3/351.1.en.pdf.

tions, a requesting State may not find it easy to satisfy these minimum requirements. In practice, it could mean that years pass before there is a guarantee of minimum standards enabling legal assistance, or the standards may never be met. In such cases, the assets in question must be released, despite clear indications of their criminal origin. Such a result would be entirely unsatisfactory for all parties involved.

To avoid such an issue, the draft law proposes extending in such cases the administrative confiscation procedures created by RIAA. The Swiss Federal Council would henceforth also be able to launch a confiscation procedure when mutual legal assistance is not possible due a country of origin's failure to comply with human rights standards. The launch of such a confiscation procedure is subject to the condition of a prior preventive freezing order by the Federal Council. The inability to provide legal assistance in specific cases would be determined on the basis of the relevant provisions of the Federal Act on International Mutual Assistance in Criminal Matters.[6]

Extending the powers of confiscation would enable Switzerland to return assets to the country of origin on the basis of rule of law principles even if the institutions in the country of origin are weakened and unable to guarantee the required minimal procedural safeguards.

The restitution phase

The draft law stipulates that restitution should be implemented through the financing of programmes of public interest. The objective of returning illegally acquired money is to improve the living conditions of the population and to strengthen the rule of law. These general requirements are flexible enough and leave sufficient room for manoeuvre in individual cases to find appropriate, tailor-made solutions together with the country of origin. Solutions should take into consideration special conditions in specific cases as much as possible (no 'one-size-fits-all'). Switzerland's experience of several decades allows for a wide spectrum of possibilities, ranging from the transfer of funds

6 See footnote 4.

to an escrow account in the country of origin to restitution through a World Bank programme. Another option of proven worth is restitution through projects of the Swiss Agency for Development and Cooperation (SDC).[7]

Conclusion

Asset recovery is a relatively new policy area, and one that has grown significantly in importance at the international level as a result of the political unrest in North Africa. The 'Arab Spring' has thus acted as a catalyst. Since many countries today are faced with asset recovery requests from Tunisia, Egypt and Libya, the restitution of assets of illicit origin receives increasing attention on the international level. Given the financial dimensions and the complexity of such cases, there is heightened need for an exchange of experiences and for coordination between financial centres. Relevant questions have been raised in a number of international forums, such as the European Union and the G8.

These developments are likely to have an impact on international standards and practices for the restitution of stolen funds. Switzerland intends to play an active and constructive role in the elaboration of new solutions and would like to share its considerable experience in this area with other actors. The comprehensive draft law on asset recovery could contribute to the international debate and play a useful role in this context. Moreover, the draft law could be relevant for reflexions on how to make UNCAC more effective. In fact, the Convention has been criticised for being incomplete and for providing inadequate solutions to concrete asset recovery problems. Switzerland is convinced that important progress in this field can be achieved without reopening the Convention. A more consequent and dynamic use of UNCAC's provisions by its Member States could make the existing UNCAC more effective. The new comprehensive Swiss act might stimulate discussions on how to achieve this important goal.

7 For a general idea, see footnote 1.

CHARLES MONTEITH

Case and investigation strategy

Establishing the investigative strategy and tactics

Investigators conducting complex investigations involving economic crime or corruption have to sift through an alarming and ever increasing volume of material and data. In the midst of such detail it is easy to lose the way. Added to this challenge are the aggressive strategies and tactics used by proactive defence lawyers (challenging each and every move made), a disinterested public (because there does not appear to be an obvious victim) and the lapse of time before the corrupt activity is uncovered – all of which can put enforcement agencies on the back foot. It therefore becomes critical for such agencies to have their own strategy and tactics. A well-made, proactive investigation strategy is designed to provide and maintain some degree of essential control to enforcers. Establishing a clear methodology, strategy and investigative plan is crucial in assisting agencies to build upon initial allegations and conduct successful investigations.

Case strategy: divided we lose

There are often many different enforcement agencies involved in corruption cases. In one example, there were seven different agencies in one country involved to some degree in investigating the same suspect: the Financial Intelligence Unit (FIU), the Anti-Corruption Commission (ACC), the Asset Recovery Office, the International Division, the Prosecutor's Office, the Illegal Enrichment Office and the Fiscal Office. In the first meeting with all seven agencies, they were asked to reveal to each other what information they held on the suspect. As it turned out, each agency held different information. It is essential that cooperation between all relevant agencies be established from the beginning. And so, at the onset of an investigation the first task is to establish which are the relevant agencies. The group of relevant agencies should then identify one agency to lead, which should provide proactive strategic leadership with roles and responsibilities clearly defined. Information sharing should be the first priority. This is how cases should be 'CLASPed':

CLASP

- Cooperation: It is important that all relevant agencies cooperate effectively with regular strategic meetings (at least quarterly).
- Leadership: One agency should provide the strategic leadership.
- Allocation: Roles and responsibilities should be allocated.
- Sharing: Relevant information must be shared as part of a communication strategy.
- Proact: Those involved in the strategy must be creatively proactive and not wait for events to unfold. The investigation strategy, tactics and plan should be disseminated.

Case tactics

A multidisciplinary team of intelligence officers, financial investigators, analysts and lawyers must be established as quickly as possible. A lot of investigations and cases falter because of a lack of the right expertise in the right place at the right time. Thereafter, the following points should be covered:

- Establish a budget
- Make sure that roles and responsibilities known and understood
- Establish an intelligence plan
- Set up a mechanism to audit trail all relevant material
- Ensure all team members have tasks and milestones to meet
- Document all areas of responsibility and accountability

- Form regular meetings and share with operational leads in other agencies
- Coordinate covert resources, including electronic and human surveillance
- Update the intelligence plan
- Establish the key feature of the corrupt activity (see below)
- Identify the proposed evidence gathering strategy
- Assign the administrative tasks and assignments for the investigation
- Access expertise for mutual legal assistance (MLA) requests.

Pre investigation

The degree of information available to an agency during the early stages of the investigation is a critical factor in determining how an investigation will be conducted, and it helps to inform the strategy. Information analysed in the intelligence phase of the investigation will form the heart of the subsequent plan.

The aim of all investigations should be how to turn relevant intelligence gathered into admissible evidence. Where there is a duty of disclosure, the appropriate safeguards must also be put in place at the earliest possible stage to prevent its revelation, particularly when sensitive tactics have been employed.

Investigation strategy and plan

The investigative plan is intended to serve as a guide to the strategy. The investigative plan should assist in identifying the nature of the corrupt activity, developing the evidence necessary to prove the corruption and evaluating the most effective use of investigative powers throughout the course of the investigation. It is a living document that should be revised throughout the life of the investigation. As an investigation proceeds, it is critical to revise and update the features of the investigative plan to ensure that it accurately reflects the evidence gathered at various stages, the developments in the case and the understanding of the case.

There are five essential features in investigation planning:

- The features of the corrupt activity
- The proposed evidence-gathering strategy
- Use of investigation powers and tools
- A media communication strategy
- Evaluation

Features of the corrupt activity

The features are best captured via the 5W 1H approach:

- Who (subjects of the investigation): identify the businesses and individuals related to the corrupt activity and their relationship to each other. Financial profiling of assets (family and business) is important.
- What (types of corrupt agreement or arrangement): identify the events or actions.
- Where (geographic area affected): identify locations where participants have held meetings and the geographic area affected to assess jurisdictional reach.
- When (duration): identify all time factors related to the corrupt activity, assess statutory limitations.
- Why (motive of the participants): identify causes for events or actions related to the corruption.
- How (the way the corruption operates): identify the sequence of events and generation of the proceeds of crime. Assess whether intermediaries were used to move assets.

Determination of evidence required

Determining the evidence required to establish an offence is an essential part of strategic planning, which begins with intelligence:

- Analysis of intelligence and information obtained via the preliminary inquiry/intelligence sources to determine potential offences
- Planning how to turn this into admissible evidence
- Determination of the most effective strategy to obtain other evidence
- Consideration of the use of special powers to collect required evidence
- Determination of businesses, persons and locations to be investigated
- Factual issues relevant to determining and proving guilt
- Identification of any gaps in the evidence
- Identification of any evidence needed to address critical issues, including any relevant documentary evidence
- Identification of potential witnesses and whether they should be interviewed
- Identification of evidence held abroad.

The evidence itself will depend on the type of corruption under investigation and frequently includes:

- Meetings or telephone conversations between participants
- Testimonies from participants
- Documents, emails and/or faxes, etc.
- Bank statements and supporting documents, savings accounts, shares, trusts, property, land, businesses, etc.

Financial institutions have a lot of information relating to customers in their due diligence and risk assessments and potential suspicious activity reports, all of which should be routinely requested. In bribery cases, the bribe is often disguised in the form of payments for children's school fees or property or given to children, parents or siblings, which may need evidencing. It is of particular importance to identify the proceeds generated by the corrupt activity and to evidentially link assets back to the corrupt activity.

Analysis of the evidence required to prove the offence allows the investigation team to identify any gaps in the evidence gathered to date and thus focus on acquiring any further relevant evidence from appropriate sources. Some agencies draft an outline of the evidence gathered ('evidence matrix'), which sets out an evidence trail. An evidence matrix is a useful reference throughout the course of the investigation to determine whether the evidence obtained would be admissible and likely to withstand judicial scrutiny.

Use of investigation powers and tools

The success of an investigation often largely depends on the choice of investigative tools and powers. Inappropriate choices and improper uses may lead to the investigation being ineffective and/or challenged. The choice of investigative tools should be re-evaluated as facts and evidence come to light during the course of the investigation.

Several factors may influence the choice of investigative tools at particular stages of an investigation. The element of surprise is often a key factor when conducting searches to ensure that all relevant evidence is secured. But searches often prompt cooperation, which may provide a valuable source of evidence.

Intelligence

Information on its own can be of little value, particularly when there is so much of it. A systematic method of collecting, assessing and prioritising information into effective intelligence (which, ideally, can be then turned into admissible evidence) is therefore paramount. Intelligence-based techniques are particularly useful in tracing the proceeds of serious economic crime and corruption. The intelligence plan should cover:

Open source intelligence

Open source intelligence involves finding and selecting information from publically available sources and analysing it. There has been a huge growth of publically available personal and corporate information across the Internet, such as social networking sites, databases of registries, government reports, etc. The best way to sift through it all is to use an effective search method that will extract and aggregate only relevant data. The International Centre for Asset Recovery (ICAR) has developed the Asset Recovery Intelligence System (ARIS) as one such tool.

Human intelligence

Nothing is more pleasing to an investigator than someone voluntarily doing difficult, complex work for you. Many countries offer immunities and/or plea bargain arrangements in order to turn participating suspects into cooperating witnesses. Witnesses are particularly valuable, because they can assist in identifying the target of the investigation and in prioritising the businesses, individuals and locations for investigation. They also can provide the best direct evidence of the corrupt offence. Even when they are not willing to become formal witnesses and testify against the main offenders, they are often able to offer valuable information throughout all stages of the investigation and are under a duty to cooperate fully throughout. With so much data to sift through, witnesses are of particular use in identifying where in the world crucial evidence lies, and thus they play a vital role in focusing the investigation.

Whistle-blowers also provide essential information and evidence. As with cooperating suspects, considerable caution is required when evaluating motives, because misleading or wrong information will compromise and taint the whole investigation. Care must be taken in the verification and debriefing process to ensure the integrity of what is offered (with leniency best not offered to the main offender). Also the risk of personal harm to whistle-blowers must be carefully assessed along with the duty to provide protection and care. Finally, acquiring evidence or reporting on the activities of the suspects has its own risks, not least of which is to compromise the human source in the actual offending, thereby providing the suspects with the opportunity of a defence, abuse or entrapment argument.

Financial intelligence

When assets are transferred from one account to another it usually leaves an audit trail record, which can be tracked and detected by financial investigators. But because the stolen assets are often distributed among different accounts and under different corporate names, investigators usually also need to refer to external information, such as financial documents and suspicious transfer reports filed in banks and with law enforcement agencies. Financial Intelligence Units are now established in most countries in the world. They receive, analyse and disclose information from financial institutions relating to suspicious or unusual financial transactions. They also compile profiles of individuals and money laundering techniques. Critically, they exchange information with foreign counterparts.

Investigator analysts should build-up a financial profile of the suspects (as outlined in determining the evidence above) while also tracing their assets. It cannot be stressed enough that it is of critical importance to connect assets back to the corrupt activity that generated them. Otherwise, it will not be possible to recover the assets as proceeds of crime. This step is often overlooked and becomes a frequent issue when making MLA or information requests in relation assets held abroad.

Use MLA laws proactively to obtain information

Requesting countries often face difficulties in extracting financial information from foreign countries that cannot provide information without a solid legal basis. This has proved to be a particular problem in connection with sanctioned individuals where there may have been no suspicious activities to report.

This problem can be overcome by persuading the requested country to open its own investigation under its own money laundering laws. (This may have to be achieved through an initial letter of request). Thus the requested country makes its own request for further information (or sends a letter of request) back to the requesting country and in doing so supplies the originally requested information or evidence. Moreover, based upon its own investigation, the requested country would then generate suspicious activity reports relating to the suspect's assets, which would then be passed to the requesting country's FIU.

Freezing assets

The need to act quickly to secure assets generated by crime before they can be dissipated is of paramount importance. Using the MLA laws is a practical and convenient way to do this, particularly with assets held abroad. Engaging the foreign agency in freezing under its own powers is often the quickest and most effective way. Usually the foreign agency can agree (on behalf of the Treasury in its country) that sums recovered or confiscated will be returned to the home country, minus its reasonable costs. Best practice is to include this in the Memorandum of Understanding between the respective agencies. Again the link from the assets back to the corrupt activity must be established.

Cooperation with foreign enforcement agencies

Cooperation with foreign enforcement agencies can involve coordinating simultaneous searches, raids or inspections, exchanging information or gathering information and interviewing witnesses on behalf of another agency. The coordination of surprise inspections across relevant jurisdictions, particularly in the early stages of a full-scale investigation, is a particularly effective way to minimise the potential destruction of evidence.

Cooperation also plays an important role even in cases in which parallel investigations are not being conducted in other jurisdictions. Other counterpart agencies may provide assistance by sharing information that may be located outside the investigating agency's territorial borders. In such cases, it can be useful to secure cooperation from an agency in the jurisdiction where potentially relevant evidence may be located.

An increasing number of agencies have established international agreements, or Memoranda of Understanding, which may include state-to-state cooperation agreements, inter-agency cooperation agreements, mutual legal assistance agreements as well as bilateral agreements.

The investigative plan should consider any timeframe issues for joint operations envisaged with other agencies and other factors relevant to coordination.

Time constraints

Effective planning is important to ensure that all aspects of the investigation are completed within the prescribed statutory period. The investigative plan should include a basic schedule that identifies tasks, assigns responsibilities and sets deadlines and timeframes for completion. Such a schedule ensures that time constraints (such as statutes of limitations) are taken into account appropriately.

Prioritising and tasking

Some agencies create case agenda, task lists and timetables. These tools will become more important as staffing resources grow. In some cases, more than one method may be useful. In all cases, the investigation schedule should cover tasks to be accomplished, prioritising the most critical items. Agencies may also use software packages that assist with the creation of case agendas.

Covert actions

Agencies will often conduct their investigations in a covert manner before taking public investigative action, such as dawn raids or searches. Conducting an investigation covertly ensures that the suspects are not alerted to the investigation before the public searches begin, which reduces the opportunity for evidence to be hidden or destroyed. Accordingly, in the covert investigatory phase – with the exception of cooperating suspects – agencies usually do not communicate with individuals or corporations that may be implicated in the alleged violation.

Electronic surveillance is a practical investigative tool if the agency has sufficient information about the details of the suspects' operations. Electronic surveillance can provide valuable and powerful evidence of corrupt activity and may be a viable option when an agency has secured insider cooperation to assist with the use of hidden recording devices. Infiltration as an investigative tool may involve an agency sending an undercover agent inside a business for a period of time to obtain evidence.

Searches and seizures

Searches can be a very effective method of gathering evidence. They minimise the opportunity for document destruction and concealment, and they can avoid deliberate or inadvertent failure to produce documents following an agency request. But the problem usually lies in the amount of material gathered which is why an informer or (when there is little risk of destruction) a compulsory disclosure order helps to focus on the relevant material.

Compulsory requests for information

Compulsory information requests can result in the production of valuable information. Agencies should first identify the parties to which it is appropriate to issue a request for information and should then draft the request accordingly. Compulsory information requests should not be sent when there is a risk of destruction or interference. Unnecessarily broad requests for information may cause investigational delays because of the time required to respond. Agencies should take special care to keep compulsory requests for information as specific and targeted as possible. Often a succinctly drafted document-production order with minimal instructions and definitions and a very limited number of requests can encourage a prompt response.

Compulsory interviews

In some circumstances, and when an agency has such powers, it may be necessary or desirable to compel individuals to appear in a compulsory interview, usually when:

Interviews must be conducted quickly because of time constraints.

The individual concerned is willing to speak with the agency but wants to be compelled to do so in order that he or she is not seen as voluntarily providing information.

- An individual has a contractual or other legally binding confidentiality obligation, and compulsion is required to override that obligation.

- The individual refuses to consent to a voluntary interview or tries to stipulate conditions that are not acceptable (eg privilege against self-incrimination).
- The investigator suspects the interviewee may not be truthful in a voluntary interview.
- The investigator wishes to confront the interviewee with a more formal environment to reinforce the need to give truthful accounts.

One drawback of a compulsory interview is that anything said might not be directly admissible against that person, which is why compulsory interviews should not be used against the main suspects. It is also of vital importance to independently verify anything said in these interviews. Consideration of the potential impact on covert activity would also need to be assessed. However, incriminating documents supplied by the person in a compulsory interview may be admissible in some jurisdictions and often allow collection of evidence that may be used against a company in subsequent legal proceedings. Further, compulsory interviews often unearth valuable information, which provides leads to admissible evidence from other sources.

Outcomes

Never lose sight of the desired outcome, both in terms of imprisonment and the proceeds of crime recovered. There are also civil remedies and civil actions to be considered alongside or as alternatives to the criminal penalties. If a settlement or civil action is preferred then the rule is: the stronger the investigation, the greater the chances of recovering most of the assets.

Arrest and interview

Deciding when to arrest and interview suspects is one of the key decisions facing an agency. The timing will often depend upon the information gathered up to that point. Some prefer to wait until their gun is fully loaded before pulling the trigger; others like to act fast and quickly, even with an empty gun. Often, because corruption offences have taken place some time before they are discovered, there is a tendency to arrest and interview at a later date. In general, there is much to be gained from an early interview, preferably one as near as possible to the offence committed. However, much depends upon the state of readiness of the agency concerned, which is often determined by the quality of the pre-investigative and planning work conducted by the agency. The more prepared the agency, the more proactive the interview view can be. And likewise, the more prepared an interview, the more effective it will be. The interviewing team should prepare for an interview by outlining the issues, the responses expected from the interviewee, the prepared questions and the follow-up questions based on anticipated responses.

Media communications

One of the key issues in asset recovery is that the public does not understand the legal processes that have to be undertaken before any assets can be recovered. Hence agencies often have to deal with unrealistic expectations from the public. It is best to address expectations right at the beginning of an investigation (when it can safely be made public) and stress that the recovery of illegally obtained assets has to follow the due process of law (and court decisions) both in the country where the corruption occurred and in the country where the assets lie – all of which takes time, unless the suspects agree to return the assets or a settlement is reached. This is also true of the assets of sanctioned individuals or entities.

Thus an important part of creating and maintaining public confidence is to communicate appropriately with the media. Whilst it may not be possible to confirm or deny that an investigation has started, once elements of the investigation become public – that is, after searches, seizures, arrests, etc. – it is important to engage with the wider public as much as possible.

Evaluation

Throughout the course of the investigation it is good practice to revise and adapt the investigation plan and strategy to reflect the evidence as it is obtained, to evaluate the relevant issues, to consider emerging issues, to assess evidence-gathering strategies and to redistribute administrative tasks. Periodic team meetings are an effective way to ensure that the investigative plan is kept up to date and incorporates all relevant issues. In particular, the investigation team should discuss the investigative plan at key stages of the investigation, such as prior to conducting dawn raids or inspections, interviewing parties or following evidence evaluations. In addition to team meetings, agencies often hold more formal internal meetings periodically to update senior staff and decision makers on the progress of the investigation at critical stages when decisions need to be made. Agency staff may prepare papers setting out updates, proof issues and case agenda for presentation and distribution at such mcctings.

Conclusion

Investigations of corruption cases no longer appear to routinely fail because of capacity issues, as was the case in the near past. Much time and effort has gone into building the skills and experiences of enforcers around the world. More, though, needs to be done on the strategic level, as successful cross-border cases by definition must have good cooperation, coordination and sharing – none of which is achievable without planning and mutual trust. Trust can only be established through personal contacts, respect for each other's systems and ways of working and, ultimately, through partaking in a wider strategy to get justice for victims and to recover stolen assets.

PHIL MASON

Being Janus: A donor agency's approach to asset recovery

From the beginning of its anti-corruption efforts in 2000, the UK Department for International Development (DFID) adopted an expansive view of how to meet the challenges presented by modern international corruption.

Money laundering has often been graphically described as the 'getaway car' of corruption. Donor agencies, traditionally looking outward and with eyes only in the direction of their partner countries, have all too often ignored the getaway car carrying illicit funds that is rushing past in the other lane, in the opposite direction. Managing the traffic on this two-way street is an essential requirement for tackling modern international corruption as it relates to developing countries.

DFID recognised that the traditional development assistance approach of focusing on action in the partner developing country, on the partner country's systems and problems and working only with the partner country authorities, misses the crucial point when it comes to the dynamics of modern day, cross-border financial crime, particularly money laundering and asset recovery. To tackle the realities of modern corruption, where illicitly acquired funds are able to rapidly leave the 'victim' country for a safe haven in another jurisdiction, a development agency needs to look inward as well as uphold its traditional outward perspective to partner developing countries. DFID recognised the need to look in both directions early on. Its approach indeed exemplifies the importance of conceiving of corruption as a 'two-way street'.

This chapter illustrates the DFID experience. It describes the development of a DFID-funded donor agency 'footprint' within the UK domestic law enforcement architecture that enables dedicated attention to be given to intelligence gathering, investigation, criminal law enforcement and asset recovery relating to 'grand' corruption money laundering cases that emanate from developing countries.

The policy rationale for donor agency involvement

An immediate question to be addressed is why a donor agency should need to become involved at all in what would appear to be entirely domestic investigative or law enforcement activity. Should not the role of the development assistance donor be confined to helping the victim country, for example to be competent at gathering evidence locally, to provide technical assistance for investigation or to prepare mutual legal assistance requests?

In an ideal world, that would, of course, be the case. However, DFID's experience showed that a different reality obtains in the practical world. DFID's ambition to see domestic agencies taking on foreign bribery and money laundering cases that originate in developing countries encountered a number of severe obstacles. These obstacles were very practical. They derived not from a lack of underlying will amongst law enforcement but from constrained resources and the tyranny of prioritisation.

It became clear to DFID from consultations with UK domestic law enforcement authorities that it was unrealistic to expect that most cases emerging from developing countries would receive due attention when competing with cases emanating from other jurisdictions given the over-demand on stretched resources.

The logic of the argument DFID heard from their law enforcement authorities was incontestable: the kinds of investigatory and law enforcement capacity required for complex, international cases is highly specialised and usually in short supply. Inevitably, across the board, there has to be prioritisation. A set of considerations has to be applied by domestic law enforcement authorities in reaching judgments about where to devote scarce resources. For a number of practical reasons, these militated against cases coming from developing countries.

Given the hard choices they must make, and other factors being equal, law enforcement are likely to opt to deploy their scarce resources:

- On the biggest cases
- To countries where they have established and trusted working relationships, especially at the operational level
- Where there are good chances of practical and reliable co-operation on legal matters
- Where the prospect of gathering and exchanging evidence is strong.

These considerations aside, there is also an inherent tension facing domestic law enforcement authorities that are democratically controlled and subject to the priorities of a domestic citizen constituency. They are expected by their domestic taxpayers to concentrate on domestic law enforcement priorities.

All of these factors weigh heavily against the interests of developing countries:

- Often the cases are too small, comparatively, to rank sufficiently high in prioritisation decisions. However, while a case involving, for example, £20 million may be magnitudes smaller than what law enforcement will be taking on from other sources (such as another developed country), this amount may be a very significant sum proportionately in the finances of a developing country. But nonetheless these cases get squeezed out.
- It is a well-acknowledged, practical reality that law enforcement officers are more successful doing business with opposites with whom they have worked previously and with whom they have developed a degree of professional confidence and trust. Not surprisingly, DFID found that law enforcement in a developed jurisdiction like the UK is likely to be happier and more ready to deal with international cases from other European countries, or from North America or from other developed jurisdictions. Co-operation with developed jurisdictions will look to be a far more

predictable and familiar prospect than it will with a developing country with which previous ties do not exist.

- And even if it is judged important to engage with a developing country, the quality and predictability of doing what is required on evidential case-building will usually be seen to be riskier and more difficult with an unfamiliar developing country than with a traditional partner.

DFID recognised that if due attention was going to be devoted realistically to asset recovery cases coming into the UK from developing countries, additional input was going to be essential to counter the inherent disadvantages these countries face in the domestic competition for scarce law enforcement resource.

The rationale for using aid

Having developed a compelling policy rationale for intervention at home, DFID had to consider the administrative and legal contexts too. Expending aid resources at home, at first sight, looks counter-intuitive. DFID reports (and the Organisation for Economic Co-Operation and Development [OECD] has accepted) such expenditure as Official Development Assistance (ODA) eligible, as the activities supported are, in DFID's view, no different from those that donor agencies regularly support in partner countries, for example through supporting anti-corruption agencies. The ultimate purpose of the activity – recovering stolen assets for their return for productive developmental use – satisfies DFID's own legal confines that require all aid to be used for the primary purpose of poverty reduction.

In short, DFID considers such provision of aid funds for these purposes to be fully compliant with the required norms.

DFID's support for domestic action

DFID supports aid-funded components within the UK law enforcement architecture across the full intervention chain – from initial intelligence gathering, to investigation and case development, to prosecution and asset recovery. Figure 1 sets out the DFID 'footprint' and its relationships with other parts of the UK system.

Supporting the UK supply-side: DFID intervention chain

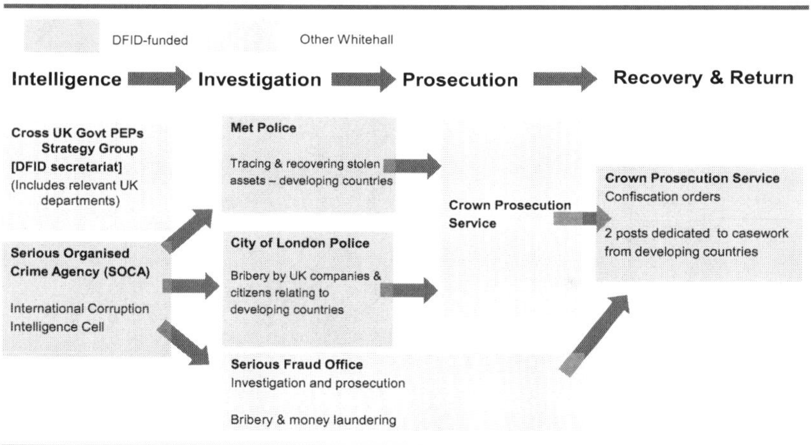

This account deals primarily with the unit based in the UK Metropolitan Police, the Proceeds of Corruption Unit (POCU), which is dedicated to tracing, freezing, seizing and returning illicitly acquired funds from developing countries. For completeness, the figure shows DFID's complementary aid-funded anti-bribery unit based in the City of London Police, the Overseas Anti-Corruption Unit (OACU). This also has a dedicated developing country mandate.

Both investigative units are supported by dedicated intelligence feeds focused on developing countries from the International Corruption Intelligence Cell (ICIC) based in the UK Serious Organised

Crime Agency (SOCA) – due to become part of the new National Crime Agency in late 2013.

At the end of the chain (DFID does not directly fund the prosecution stage on account of the independence of the prosecutorial process), DFID supports dedicated posts for developing country cases within the Crown Prosecution Service (CPS), which is responsible for executing confiscation orders handed down by the courts and realising the assets ready for return.

DFID also provides the secretariat function for a cross-Government Politically-Exposed Persons (PEPs) strategic group that brings together all the main agencies with an interest in international PEPs issues – such as the national Treasury (the lead government department for anti-money laundering policy), the Serious Fraud Office (the lead UK agency for investigating complex fraud and international corruption cases from all sources), the Financial Services Authority (the chief UK financial regulator) as well as CPS, SOCA and the Ministries for Business, Justice and Foreign affairs.

Experience to date

The U4 Anti-Corruption resource centre published a review of the working of the Metropolitan Police POCU since its formation in 2006 ('Making development assistance work at home', 2011).[1] The report provides fuller details of working practices, cases handled, operational issues confronted as well as an assessment of the impact of the initiative and some lessons learned.

Since the review, POCU has delivered its highest profile achievement to date – the successful conviction in a UK court of former Nigerian state governor James Ibori and several of his associates including members of his family and his UK-based solicitor who was found to have played a key facilitating role. In 2012, Ibori received a

1 Available at: www.u4.no/publications/PublicationSphinxSearchForm?PublicationSearch=making+development+work+at+home&Category=&ThemeID=&Year =&Country=&SearchLocale=en_US&locale=en_US.

prison sentence of 13 years in a UK jail for his offences of money laundering using stolen Nigerian public resources.

Over the six years of operation so far, POCU has cost DFID approximately £5 million in running costs. The 'return' on that investment has been over £100 million in frozen illicit assets. These frozen assets are currently subject to judicial procedures with a view to confiscation and eventual return to the countries of origin.

Few developmental initiatives in a donor agency's traditional portfolio of interventions are likely to match this magnitude of return on effort.

The end game

In the Ibori case, which has depended on strong and professional co-operation between the Metropolitan Police in the UK and the Economic and Financial Crimes Commission in Nigeria, discussions are under way with the Nigerian authorities in regard to the modalities for returning the seized assets, pending final conclusion of confiscation procedures in the UK courts.

Both the UK and Nigerian authorities recognise the importance of ensuring an open and transparent approach to demonstrating the end use of the returned funds. Putting returned funds to clear developmental purposes – with clarity on their disbursement – offers for both receiving and returning countries a mutually beneficial assurance on the value of pursuing these long and complex undertakings. Transparency on end use has the prospect of reinforcing confidence on both sides in the merits of persevering with such cases and to continue with new co-operation into the future.

The future

Over time, it is expected that the POCU can and will become financially self-sufficient. The United Nations Convention against Corruption (UNCAC) permits the deduction of reasonable costs prior to returning recovered assets. Once a reasonably predictable pipeline of recoveries has been established, the need for external financing for the POCU should disappear.

As such, upfront investment by a donor agency in a unit such as POCU represents a contribution to developing country interests that repays its costs by magnitudes in return. Additionally, the investment develops specialist capacity in an arena where such specialist skills are scarce, and it bypasses the domestic prioritisation dilemmas that are often fatal to developing country interests.

Concluding remarks

The DFID approach and experience described in this chapter is, it is believed, unique for a donor agency. While the conceptualisation of the modern corruption problem as a two-way street is often shared by many donors, the responsiveness of national systems in many developed countries to practically address the challenge has, in the main, been inadequate.

DFID's development of an inward-looking agenda with its domestic agencies has stemmed from an appreciation of the constraints that operate at home. It also has stemmed from a very practical appreciation of how to advance DFID's development assistance mission in its partner countries. DFID's ability to work credibly with developing country partners on issues such as their governance, their institutional soundness and their anti-corruption efforts is seriously undermined if our partners can point back to inaction in our home arena as a sign that the 'supply' side is not being addressed.

A donor agency cannot do its business abroad effectively if part of the problem is not being addressed back home. Being Janus – looking forward and backward – is essential to the cause.

Emerging trends, good practice

Part 2: Tracing and freezing

Daniel Thelesklaf and Amar Salihodzic

The role of financial intelligence units in fighting corruption and asset recovery[1]

The international community has identified corruption as one of the main causes for lack of economic development and the unsuccessful establishment of a framework of effective governance and rule of law in many countries around the world. According to studies, the least developed countries are least likely to fully benefit from development aid, as up to 30 percent of development disbursement 'disappears' as payoff to corrupt individuals and organisations.[2]

A large amount of those assets do not remain in the country where the corrupt act occurred, but rather they are laundered abroad. This flight of capital may lead to a severe shortage in the allocation of resources to the important areas of infrastructure, health care, education, homeland security as well as the establishment of effective democratic structures. Corruption has a strong negative influence on the distribution of wealth as well as the social harmony within a society. Furthermore, corruption fuels insurmountable political tensions, periods of economic and political stagnation, ethnical tensions and in some cases even civil wars and acts of war crimes.

The relevant international Anti-Corruption (AC) Conventions[3] have established several offences for a range of corrupt behaviour.

1 This article is based on an Egmont Group White Paper published in 2012. Available at: www.egmontgroup.com. It represents solely the personal opinion of the authors and is not necessarily in line with the Egmont Group's views.

2 Development Assistance, Asset Recovery and Money Laundering: Making the Connection, Basel Institute on Governance, Basel. 2010, page 24.

3 Organisation for Economic Co-operation and Development Convention on Combating Bribery of Foreign Public Officials in International Business Transactions; The Council of Europe Criminal Law Convention on Corruption; The Inter-American Convention against Corruption and the UN Convention against Corruption.

The most recent Convention with the widest outreach – currently 158 State Parties[4] – is the United Nations Convention against Corruption (UNCAC). It encompasses the following mandatory offences:

- Bribery of national public officials
- Bribery of foreign public officials
- Bribery of officials of public international organisations
- Embezzlement and misappropriation of property by a public official
- Obstruction of justice
- Laundering the proceeds of corruption

The Financial Action Task Force (FATF) and UNCAC standards require the criminalisation of these offences and that they be considered predicate offences to money laundering.[5] To enable international co-operation, it is important that the notion of 'corruption and bribery', as referred to in FATF, includes as a minimum all mandatory offences listed above. Progress would be likely if the full coverage of all mandatory offenses was assessed under FATF country reviews and possible shortcomings were made public.

Corruption as a predicate offence and the role of financial intelligence units in asset recovery

All around the world, and especially in developing countries, local financial intelligence units (FIUs) and competent law enforcement authorities report an increasing number of corruption related predicate offences in their annual statistics on analysis of suspicious transactions and money laundering investigations. Not surprisingly, more and more international financial centres also report equally increasing numbers regarding corruption related offences. Often in these jurisdic-

4 As of April 2013, available at: www.unodc.org/unodc/en/treaties/CAC/signatories.html.

5 Art. 23 para. 2 (b) UNCAC; Definition of 'designated category of offences' in the FATF glossary.

tions, the corruption related offences were not committed by domestic public officials but by foreign politically exposed persons (PEPs), their relatives or close business associates who tried to channel incriminated assets into the financial system through jurisdictions other than their own.

Interestingly, there seems to be a general discrepancy in dealing with the supply side of corruption (i.e. bribe giver) versus the passive side of corruption (i.e. bribe receiver). Very few cases have been identified in which the proceeds of the supply side of corruption (eg the revenues from a contract that was concluded with the involvement of a corrupt act) have been detected. In a number of jurisdictions, the giving, offering or promising of a bribe is not considered a predicate offence to money laundering, because such payments are not considered proceeds of crime until they have been received by the bribe taker. This is worrisome because the international standard requires that bribe taking as well as bribe giving shall be covered equally.

The 2012 Egmont Group[6] White Paper on Corruption illustrates many cases in which the FIU analysis identified corruption related crimes as predicate offences.[7] In addition, according to the same paper a survey showed that 37 FIUs worldwide (about 30 percent of all Egmont member FIUs) do have a specific domestic AC mandate by their respective government.

To date the work on corruption has focused too narrowly on what the recipient of a bribe, typically the public official that has abused his powers, has done with the money once it has been received illegally. Two more aspects need to be addressed[8] in order to fully comprehend the extent of the problem:

The first aspect is to follow the bribe transaction upstream. Bribes paid are supposed to be hidden. Hence, the individuals and organisations paying the bribes have a strong interest in making sure they re-

6 The goal of the Egmont Group is to provide a forum for FIUs around the world to improve cooperation in the fight against money laundering and financing of terrorism and to foster the implementation of domestic programs in this field.

7 The Role of Financial Intelligence Units in Fighting Corruption and Asset Recovery, An Egmont Group White Paper, 2013. Available at: www.egmontgroup.org/library/egmont-documents.

8 More information on the OECD website. Available at: www.oecd.org/corruption.

main undetected. Therefore, bride payers often make use of intermediaries in order to hide corruption related transactions[9] and the transfer of funds through financial centres that could result in suspicious activity reports (SAR) filed to an FIU. Because bribes are frequently paid to employees of state-owned or state-controlled enterprises (SOEs), tracking these transactions can be difficult due to the fact that these individuals sometimes are not recognised as politically exposed persons (PEPs) by local reporting entities.

The second aspect relates to the supply side of the bribe. The origin of these bribes lies characteristically in companies or individuals most often from large exporting countries with the greatest amounts of outward foreign direct investment. In particular, so-called 'slush funds' – funds that are specifically established by companies in order to fund bribes – are to be monitored closely by reporting entities. The sole establishment of such funds may already constitute a suspicious transaction, because offering or promising bribes is, or should be, a predicate offence to money laundering.

Analysing suspicious activity reports (SAR) and detecting possible links to corruption

In an ideal scenario, FIUs could have the following impact on a major (international) corruption case as follows:[10]

- A senior public official from country A receives a series of payments from a company located in country B.
- The financial institution that holds the account for this company detects that the payments are made to a senior foreign public official and reports these transactions to its FIU.

9 See OECD Typologies on the Role of Intermediaries in Business Transactions. Available at: www.oecd.org/dataoecd/40/17/43879503.pdf.

10 See Egmont Group White Paper on Corruption: The Role of FIUs in Fighting Corruption and Asset Recovery, p. 13–14. Available at: www.egmontgroup.org/library/egmont-documents.

- The FIU in country B requests information from its counterpart FIU in country A.
- The FIU in country A requests additional information from the domestic competent law enforcement agency (or AC Agency)
- The FIU in country A informs its counterpart in country B of these facts. Thereafter, a SAR is disseminated to competent law enforcement agencies in country B who are also made aware of the on going investigation in country A.
- The law enforcement agency in country A informs its counterpart in country B ('spontaneous' mutual legal assistance, see Article 56 of UNCAC) of the assets held in the bank account. This information will allow competent law enforcement agencies to pursue their investigations and confiscate the proceeds of crime.
-

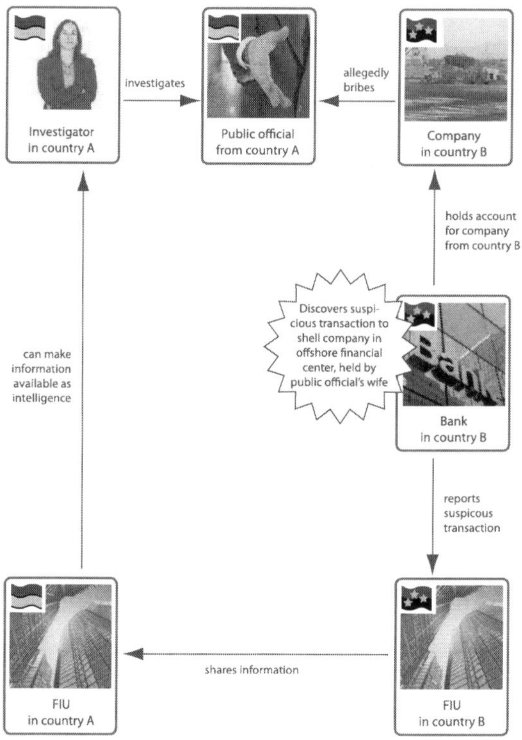

The core function of the FIU, the process of receiving, requesting and analysing financial information, is also the most important part of an FIU's contribution to anti-corruption and asset recovery. In this operational analysis,[11] the key challenge is linking financial information to possible underlying forms of crime.

The following case scenario reiterates the necessity for operational analysis conducted by FIUs:

> A banking sector SAR led to an investigation which identified a solicitor as an active facilitator for three organised crime groups engaged in various criminal offences, i.e. political corruption. Later in court, the subject was found guilty and sentenced to five years imprisonment. A confiscation hearing assessed that the subject benefited from a USD seven-figure amount and the confiscation of these assets was ordered. The detective inspector for the investigating police force said, 'This case was one of the most significant we have investigated concerning a corrupt professional and all born from a SAR.'

FIUs use a wide range of analysis network and related software programs in order to trace perpetrators of transactions linked to illegal activities. Analysts are well trained in their fields and are able to find links within a short time span. The work of operational analysts facilitates the work of law enforcement agents and public prosecutors to a large degree as they are provided with well-structured and thoroughly analysed data, which allows them to prosecute suspects in an efficient and timely manner.

Secondly, as many FIUs have been operational for a number of years, they have in most cases collected substantial amounts of operational intelligence. This information can be used for strategic analysis[12] in order to acquire knowledge in areas that could not be easily acquired unless strategic analysis was conducted. In the case of cor-

11 Operational analysis uses available and obtainable information to identify specific targets, to follow the trail of particular activities or transactions and to determine links between those targets and possible proceeds of crime, money laundering, predicate offences and terrorist financing (FATF Interpretative Note to recommendation 29, section 3).

12 Strategic analysis uses available and obtainable information, including data that may be provided by other competent authorities, to identify money laundering and terrorist financing related trends and patterns (FATF Interpretative Note to recommendation 29, section 3).

ruption, the FIU can first collect relevant information related to potential instances of corruption stemming from:

- Reports provided by the reporting entities (SAR/STR and/or cash transaction reports [CTRs])
- The FIU's own operational intelligence
- Public sources
- Commercial databases
- Anti-corruption law enforcement agencies
- Other AC bodies
- Specialised and trusted NGOs.

When combining all these elements properly, strategic analysis conducted by FIUs can produce the following output:

- A typology analysis (i.e. schemes to launder the proceeds of corruption that appear to be constructed in similar fashions)
- A geographic/region analysis (i.e. in which jurisdictions the possible offenders [bribe giver/taker] are located)
- A behaviour analysis (operations used by a group of persons, eg how companies establish and use slush funds)
- An activity analysis (i.e. which sectors are most likely to be used for illegal activities).

This part of an FIU's work will become even more important in the years to come. The current FATF standard introduced in early 2012 recommends that jurisdictions conduct a so called National Risk Assessment, in which countries should identify, assess and understand the money laundering and terrorist financing risks for the country. Authorities should then take action and apply resources in order to ensure the risks are mitigated effectively. As the content of this particular recommendation[13] will have cascading effects on a number of other recommendations, countries will have to be sure to invest their resources in conducting proper National Risk Assessment analyses. It will be interesting to see how the risks related to laundering the proceeds of corruption will be addressed in these assessments.

13 FATF Recommendation 1.

Exchanging information domestically and internationally

Close and timely national and international cooperation is required when dealing with cross-border corruption. By using existing and well-established information exchange mechanisms developed by the Egmont Group (The Egmont Secure Web [ESW]), FIUs again add value to the process of recovering illegally acquired assets. The Egmont Group's mechanisms have a crucial advantage over the traditional formal legal assistance mechanisms in criminal matters, because they are faster and more efficient. They encourage the informal exchange of information, which often paves the way for a submission of a formal request for legal assistance and therefore accelerates the entire process drastically. Both methods of information exchange are complimentary. However, the informal exchange of information should precede the formal exchange.

Typically in large-scale corruption cases, simply checking national databases will not be sufficient, as often the location of the predicate offence (bribery or another corruption related offence) is different from the location where the proceeds of corruption are laundered. In addition, the structures and legal arrangements of companies are not always made transparent for the public.[14] Therefore, FIUs play a vital role in informing their counterparts about specific information, as they have the power to access information on beneficial ownership as well as asset and income declarations (i.e. all relevant information from tax authorities, customs, police, etc.).

> The domestic FIU in country A received a request through the ESW from another FIU in the region (country B) seeking information on a domestic national detained on several criminal charges, including bribery. The requesting FIU revealed that funds were transferred to several destinations among which were the suspect's personal bank accounts held at a bank in country A. The FIU in country A revealed the presence of the mentioned accounts and decided to lift bank secrecy off said accounts, freeze their balances and forward their findings both to the requesting FIU and the General Prosecutor.

Hence, the FIU is uniquely positioned and uniquely trained to assist domestic and foreign corruption investigators regarding financial in-

14 'The Puppet Masters: How the Corrupt Use of Legal Structures to Hide Stolen Assets and What to Do About it', World Bank (StAR), 2011.

vestigations. Most importantly, however, this sensitive and confidential information must not be improperly disclosed or disseminated at any times. The Egmont Group has developed a set of binding rules for the information exchange between FIUs. These 'Egmont Principles of Information Exchange'[15] must be applied in order for the process to work properly and remain trustworthy. Some FIUs reported that they shared classified information related to foreign corruption cases with other FIUs and that the information was then disclosed, by the recipient FIU, to third parties in an unauthorised manner. This undermines the long-term aims and effects of international cooperation on an FIU level and does not positively contribute to its cause.

Other ways in which FIUs can add value

Only major banks will be able to systematically screen all relevant news channels and other media for potential allegations against clients from developing or transition countries. Thus, FIUs can play a pivotal role in proactively informing reporting entities on new information, which in turn might trigger STRs. However, this practice is not being applied in all jurisdictions, because sometimes the fear of leaking sensitive information is simply too great and cannot be risked (i.e. if at the same time a broad international investigation is on going).

Furthermore, many countries have already or are now establishing anti-corruption working groups and steering committees in order to form a coherent and broadly supported approach to fighting corruption. FIUs are playing an important role in these working groups. In some countries they are even chairing the competent committees.

15 Available at: www.egmontgroup.org/library/egmont-documents.

Conclusions

As a result, FIUs can add value to anti-corruption investigations and the recovery of stolen assets in the following ways:

- Uniquely trained and experienced operational analysts can thoroughly analyse financial information and link it to criminal origin.
- FIUs can elaborate typology, geographic and sector specific reports by deducting information from their own analysis and databases or by using external information compiled by strategic analysts.
- FIUs can use the Egmont Secure Web as a well-established channel to exchange information informally, which is faster and more efficient than formal legal assistance request procedures.
- FIUs can provide reporting entities from the private sector with relevant sensitive information (i.e. on PEPs) when the reporting entities are unaware of such information, which in turn can possibly trigger STRs and protect the financial sector from possible detriment.
- FIUs can be involved in national, regional or even international anti-money laundering and anti-corruption fora and working groups and influence current and future relevant policies.

Two case scenarios illustrate all the advantages FIUs can provide in fighting corruption and recovering stolen assets:

Case 1

The competent law enforcement agency for anti-corruption in country A in collaboration with the FIU from the country conducted an investigation into Mr X. During this investigation the authorities found that Mr X – an employee in a managerial position at company XYZ – had withdrawn around USD 14 million from the public company XYZ's account. Falsified contracts and verifications were used as disguises to facilitate real estate purchases and cash withdrawals under fictitious circumstances for the personal use of Mr X.

The FIU in country A detected a suspicious payment transaction from Mr X's account to a bank in country C. When enquiring about more information from the competent authorities in country C, it was revealed that Mr X was the beneficial owner of that specific account. The FIU of country A also learned that USD 2 million was immediately transferred to another bank account in country B and then to another bank account in country D. Together with another transfer back to country A, a total of USD 6 million in transfers was detected and analysed.

The FIU from country A then requested information on the bank account from the FIU from country B. The competent FIU from country B obtained all relevant information on the account. The FIU was able to confirm that the beneficial owner of the account held by a company from country E was indeed Mr X, who had stolen the assets in question as an employee in a managerial position at company XYZ. Based on the FIU's powers, the assets in the account in country B were frozen for five working days and all relevant information was shared with the FIU from country A. After the freeze of five working days had expired, the FIU in country B requested to prolong the freeze of the account. The competent court granted this request. The FIU from country B then forwarded all relevant information to the FIU from country A.

Close collaboration with the FIU from country B revealed that Mr X's wife used the account held in a bank in country B for the transmission of assets to purchase real estate. USD 2 million from that account was used to fund a real estate deal in the capital of country A. The property was registered under the name of Mr X's wife. The real estate was then seized and confiscated in country A.

In order to enable a smooth asset recovery process, the FIU from country B asked a donor agency to support the competent authorities from country A by drafting a request for mutual legal assistance addressed to the competent authorities in country B. Subsequently, the donor agency hired anti-money laundering experts and funded their mission to country A. In the course of the asset recovery process, country A appointed the aforementioned experts as representative of the government, who were authorised to follow-up with the competent authorities in country B with a view to seize and repatriate the assets to country A. Only a short time after, all bank account documents on the bank account in country B were transferred to country A to support their domestic anti-corruption investigation. In a next step, it is planned that the assets will be confiscated and returned to their rightful owners.

Case 2

In January 2011, the FIU of country A received a request for assistance from another FIU requesting the freezing of the accounts in the name of the ex-president's wife in the banks of country A. In addition, it was requested to freeze all other assets, money and shares of the 48 names listed in the request.

Following a sector wide search, the FIU in country A decided to immediately freeze the quickly identified account of 'Mrs Ex-president', which held a total of USD 28.75 million. The FIU in country A continued to search for and inquire about the listed names at all banks. The search also was extended to the Real Estate Registry and Commercial Registry, in order to identify other properties and entities owned by any of the listed names.

The FIU in country A advised the FIU in country B of the frozen account and other actions taken. Most importantly, the FIU in country A informed the FIU in country B that it awaits the appropriate legal action that must be pursued by the authorities in country B. Once the legal action is pursued, the judicial authorities in country A can then enforce it.

In December 2012, following the conclusion of the legal actions taken in country B and its communication to the judicial authorities in country A, country A's tribunal allowed country B to enforce its final verdict.

In April 2013, the concerned bank issued a check in the amount of USD 28,800,818 to the order of the central bank in country B in accordance with the FIU's decision.

PHYLLIS ATKINSON

Asset tracing

In the May 2011 Declaration of the G8 on the Arab Spring, it was stated:

> The changes under way in the Middle East and North Africa (MENA) are historic and have the potential to open the door to the kind of transformation that occurred in Central and Eastern Europe after the fall of the Berlin Wall.[1]

Whilst social and political upheaval have radically altered the face of the MENA region, the ousting of politically exposed persons (PEPs) has led the citizens of those nations and indeed the world to ask one question: Where is the money?

As countries in the MENA region, such as Egypt and Tunisia, move forward from the gripping drama of 2011 that brought down governmental regimes with far-reaching consequences, there are multiple issues on the agenda. One of the most important is the recovery of stolen wealth from the assets of former presidents and their families, colleagues and cronies. The task of recouping the stolen wealth has proven difficult, as it requires political will, technical competence and international co-operation amongst many countries.

Asset tracing and recovery cases often span multiple jurisdictions and pose a range of challenges to asset recovery practitioners across the globe, most notably law enforcement agencies (LEAs). In light of these challenges we must ask: How does one trace assets globally? How does one obtain freezing orders in multiple jurisdictions? How

1 G8 Summit of Deauville – 26–27 May 2011, Government of Canada g8.gc.ca, 'Declaration of the G8 on the Arab Spring', 9 December 2011, viewed on 11 April 2013, available at: www.canadainternational.gc.ca/g8/summit-sommet/2011/g8declaration-arab-arabes-2011-05-27.aspx.

does one achieve international co-operation in asset tracing investigations?

A large portion of the assets acquired through acts of corruption can never be recovered by victim countries for the simple reason that it is not possible to locate them. Corrupt officials and bribe payers, often multi-national companies, frequently use the opportunities presented by financial services providers and so-called 'gatekeepers' to conceal and enjoy the proceeds of their unlawful activities. The profits generated by crime are often transferred to financial centres in an attempt to thwart or complicate LEAs' efforts to identify and trace assets acquired in the process. Today's financial centres include not only long established places such as New York, London, Geneva and Tokyo but also a growing number of newer financial hubs in the Middle East, Asia and beyond. The success of public corruption, money laundering and most financial crime investigations therefore depends largely upon the ability of the criminal investigator to track the ownership trail of money and other assets that leads away from the crime or the criminal.

With the chances of recovering stolen assets significantly improved through the use of mechanisms within the international infrastructure, the first step in the asset recovery process is to trace the assets or identify where the assets are held. Integrated financial investigation is an essential element of any strategy for targeting proceeds from crime. The investigative process is the core activity and forms the basis of any asset recovery effort, which of necessity (particularly at an international level) involves an overlapping of anti-corruption, anti-money laundering and broader law enforcement agendas. A jurisdiction where funds have been secreted will not confiscate or repatriate the assets to the country of origin unless evidence is presented linking them to an illegal activity. This evidence must furthermore be admissible in court proceedings. As a preliminary activity to the recovery of stolen assets, LEAs thus must be able to identify and trace the proceeds of crime and secure the property for final confiscation as an essential part of this process.

Asset tracing investigation

Purpose of asset tracing

Asset tracing in a corruption or money laundering investigation inevitably requires a financial investigation (to be dealt with later),, and will actually have multiple goals:

- The investigation will aim to connect the asset to the corrupt or illegal activity. This will form the basis for confiscation and can be accomplished through the collection and presentation of either direct or circumstantial evidence.
- The investigation will aim to establish sufficient evidence to prosecute the corrupt official on criminal charges of both corruption and money laundering.
- The investigation will aim to gather evidence that will enable the country to trace and identify assets that have been stolen or misappropriated. Therefore, the asset tracing, the money laundering investigation, the establishment of the corruption charges and the seizure of assets are all, in essence, the same investigation. This will form the cornerstone for the eventual repatriation of the stolen funds.

In addition to linking the perpetrator to the crime, it is essential to be able to link the asset to the underlying criminality. Even with the assistance of robust international and national legal frameworks, which in many instances are not gainfully employed, assets can only be identified, traced and recovered through proper investigation. With a few exceptions,[2] which also in any event require a financial investigation,

2 In terms of the European Union (EU) Council Framework Decision 2005/212/JHA of 24 February 2005 on Confiscation of Crime-Related Proceeds, Instrumentalities and Property, a criminal conviction may be followed by the (extended) confiscation not only of the assets associated with the specific crime but of additional assets which the court determines are the proceeds of other similar crimes (under certain conditions). The aim of this Framework decision is to ensure that all EU Member States have effective rules governing the

such investigation must draw a link between the stolen assets and the proceeds-generating criminal conduct.

Proceeds of crime represent criminal income and manifest themselves as assets – some of which are the object of the crime itself, such as stolen funds. However, in more complex financial crimes, the asset to be linked to the offence is more likely to be the product of an intervening transaction. As a result of the intervening transaction, the asset is in a fungible form, which makes it easy to exchange for a different asset. Tracing the proceeds of crime is premised on the assumption that through transformation the origin of assets as criminal income can

confiscation of proceeds from crime, *inter alia*, in relation to the onus of proof regarding the source of assets held by a person convicted of an offence related to organised crime. Article 3 of the Framework Decision covers extended confiscation which, in essence, involves the confiscation of assets which go beyond the direct proceeds of a crime so that there is no need to establish a connection between suspected criminal assets and specific criminal conduct.

The obligation to provide for extended confiscation is limited to a restrictive list of commonly defined offences including euro counterfeiting and money laundering for which Member States are required to lay down penalties of a maximum of at least between five and ten years of imprisonment and at least four years of imprisonment in the case of money laundering. Furthermore, the obligation to provide for extended powers of confiscation applies only to offences committed within the framework of a criminal organisation and insofar as the offence is such as to generate financial gain.

Members States are required to adopt extended confiscation measures corresponding to at least one of the three situations referred to respectively in subparagraphs (a), (b) and (c) of Article 3(2) of the Framework Decision. In each of these cases property derived from criminal activities not directly linked to the offence for which the person has been convicted may be confiscated, i.e. there is no link between the offence for which the person has been convicted and the property which is confiscated either in regards to the nature of the property or its value, which is the principle of extended confiscation of the property of a convicted offender (Report from the Commission pursuant to Article 6 of the Council Framework Decision of 24.02.2005 on confiscation of crime-related proceeds, instrumentalities and property (2005/212/JHA) at p. 5):

- Property derived from criminal activities during a period prior to conviction (sub-para. (a))
- Property derived from 'similar activities' (sub-para. (b))
- Property, the value of which is disproportionate to the lawful income of the convicted person (sub-para. (c))

be concealed, and they can be easily and speedily moved between locations or across borders. The assets can be mingled with others and converted into other forms.

To benefit from profit-generating crime, criminals are usually forced to launder the proceeds to hide the origins thereof, hence the inevitable link between corruption and money laundering. If the investigator knows how and where to look, he will find there is always a connection between criminals' assets and their crimes. In addition to often providing evidence of criminal intent and identifying otherwise unknown accomplices, tracking the ownership trail may also lead to the seizure of property constituting illegal proceeds.

To trace money and property successfully and link it to the underlying criminal conduct, the investigator must be equipped to uncover and identify ownership interests often camouflaged by changes in the form and nature of the ownership. The investigator must know how to unravel accurately the cleverly disguised control over – and interest in – property. He must also know who to approach for information, where such information can be found, what can be used to create a financial profile and how to manage the collated information in the most efficient and effective manner. Most importantly, evidence that links the asset to a criminal offence must be secured both domestically and abroad. In the absence of a link showing that the asset was derived from criminal activity, the country where the assets are stashed may freeze such assets but refuse to return them to the victim country.

Process of asset tracing

The process of tracing assets and ultimately recovering assets basically comprises the following steps:

- Investigation into allegations or suspicions
- Gathering evidence to prove or disprove such allegations or suspicions
- Tracing the proceeds of unlawful activities
- Recovery and forfeiture of such proceeds or assets

In practice, asset recovery actions can commence either at the onset of a criminal investigation or at some other point during the investigation when information is received that warrants an asset recovery action. Alternatively, the knowledge of a suspect transaction or property can lead to the action. These actions may commence without the institution of criminal proceedings, but there is normally a reasonable suspicion that there may be corruption.

It is particularly important to note that one often has two or more separate investigations. In some criminal confiscation cases, depending on the jurisdiction, legal system or practice, the asset recovery work does not start until after final judgment in the criminal corruption matter. This, however, often serves to delay or complicate the tracing of assets given that they may have been dissipated or transferred to foreign jurisdictions in the *interim*.

Othcr countries allow investigations to happen in parallel but the rules differ significantly on the extent to which these different actions can be linked. However, the bottom line is that the asset recovery process cannot be divorced from the underlying criminal investigation, which commences with the tracing of the stolen assets and ultimately culminates in their confiscation and return. In the case of criminal confiscation, the success of the case is dependent on the success of the criminal investigation.

Importance of a financial investigation

During the 2012 revision of the FATF (Financial Action Task Force) Recommendations, greater attention was given to the operational Anti-Money Laundering and Counter Terrorist Financing (AML/CFT) framework. One goal was to strengthen the law enforcement standards (Recommendations 30 and 31) to enhance the functions, responsibilities, powers and tools of law enforcement to effectively conduct money laundering, terrorism financing and asset tracing investigations. The revised standards now recognise financial investigations as one of the core elements of the FATF's operational and law enforcement Recommendations.[3]

Of particular importance to LEAs is the new and mandatory global standard, i.e. Recommendation 30,[4] which emphasises the need for designated LEAs to bear responsibility for ensuring that money laundering, predicate offences and terrorist financing are properly investigated through the conduct of a financial investigation. Countries should also designate one or more competent authorities to identify, trace and initiate freezing and seizing of property that is or may become subject to confiscation.

A 'financial investigation' is defined[5] as an enquiry into the financial affairs related to a criminal activity with a view to, *inter alia*, identifying and tracing the proceeds of crime, terrorist funds or any other assets that are or may become subject to confiscation. It also includes an enquiry with a view to developing evidence that can be used in criminal proceedings – this emphasises the need for LEAs to be equipped to conduct thorough and effective financial investigations that achieve multiple goals. As stated in the FATF Operational Issues Financial Investigations Guidance referred to above:

> The major goal of a financial investigation is to identify and document the movement of money during the course of criminal activity. The link between the

3 Financial Action Task Force, *"FATF Report – Operational Issues Financial Investigations Guidance"*, June 2012, p. 3, para. 1, viewed on 26 April 2013, available at: www.fatf-gafi.org/topics/methodsandtrends/documents/operationalissues-financialinvestigationsguidance.html.

4 Countries should ensure that designated law enforcement authorities have responsibility for money laundering and terrorist financing investigations within the framework of national anti-money laundering/counter financing of terrorism (AML/CFT) policies. At least in all cases related to major proceeds-generating offences, these designated law enforcement authorities should develop a proactive parallel financial investigation when pursuing money laundering, associated predicate offences and terrorist financing. [...] Countries should ensure that competent authorities have responsibility for expeditiously identifying, tracing and initiating actions to freeze and seize property that is or may become subject to confiscation or is suspected of being proceeds of crime. [...].

5 See Interpretive Note to Recommendation 30 (Responsibilities of Law Enforcement and Investigative Authorities), para. 2.

> origins of the money, beneficiaries, when the money is received and where it is stored or deposited can provide information about and proof of criminal activity.[6]

A 'parallel financial investigation' refers to conducting a financial investigation alongside, or in the context of, a (traditional) criminal investigation into money laundering, terrorist financing and/or predicate offences.[7]

Asset tracing is a demanding task that should be conducted in parallel to the investigation of the criminal offence generating material benefit. It requires intense co-operation between law enforcement agencies or those tasked with tracing assets, Financial Intelligence Units (FIUs) and, in most instances, the prosecutor. When an investigation focuses, for example, on a public official's receipt of bribes or otherwise unlawful financial enrichment it will require the involvement of investigators experienced in gathering and analysing financial evidence. In many instances, it will also require the involvement of a forensic accounting expert to assist in unravelling complex financial transactions. The investigation furthermore requires an understanding of the role played by gatekeepers in assisting (sometimes unwittingly) criminals dispose of their criminal profits.

6 FATF Report, p. 3, para. 2.

7 FATF report, p. 9, para. 22:

Conducting a parallel financial investigation of the predicate offence is being proactive, as it identifies the proceeds of the crimes currently under investigation for seizure/restraint. It therefore ensures that the assets will not dissipate/disappear and prevents the infiltration of illegal profits into the legal economy, thereby removing the instrument for committing future crimes. The practice thus contributes to upholding the principle in both law and society that no person should benefit from crime.

Follow the money

Proving financial aspects of the case

In tracing the assets in most large-scale corruption and money laundering offences and, indeed, in proving the financial benefit obtained by the official, the question is: How can one best obtain the evidence regarding these financial aspects of the investigation? Corrupt officials often use the services of skilled accountants and lawyers to assist them in forming complex financial structures consisting of numerous shell companies and trusts in offshore jurisdictions. Many hidden assets will not be identified through commercial database searches or other open source information.

The answer to the question is: Follow the money. This must be done by tracing all financial flows. If corporate and trust entities have been formed to hide the true ownership of the funds, the financial tracing will often penetrate the web of confusion by identifying the beneficial owner of the money. The person enjoying the fruits of the crime – that is, the person driving expensive cars and living in luxury vacation properties – is the beneficial owner. The financial portion of the investigation involves tracing the purchase of each asset and the source of each identified income.

Three basic methods can be used to prove the financial aspects of the case, thus facilitating the identification and tracing of assets. The type of evidence available will dictate which method is most appropriate for a particular case. These methods are as follows:

- Specific item (using direct evidence)
- Direct proof of a bribe (using video and audio recordings)
- Indirect method of proving illegal income (circumstantial evidence)

The specific item method is used when there is evidence that can directly trace the flow of money from the corrupt activity to the official. For example, if Company A paid a bribe to a public official by sending a wire transfer from the company's bank account directly to the bank account of the official, this is direct evidence of a specific payment by the company to the official. Clearly, additional evidence would be needed to establish that the official performed a particular action as a result of having received the money in order to prove his guilt. Proof of a bribe is also sometimes obtained by using video and audio equipment to document the illegal action. This would be another method of using direct evidence to prove the crime and trace the assets in question.

The third technique that may be used to prove the amount of illegal income is an indirect method of proof. The two most common methods for proving illegal income using an indirect method are net worth projects (NW)[8] and the Source and Application of Funds.

The NW method is considered to be somewhat confusing and difficult to explain at trial. The concept of the Source and Application of Funds method is relativcly simple and remains the preferred indirect method of proving income in most cases. The basic theory for this method is that the person under investigation spent far more money during a set period of time than he had legally available to him.

8 A NW project, simply stated, is an organised process by a LEA in which intelligence is gathered to determine if public officials are living significantly above their legitimate means. The project is not an initiation of criminal proceedings; it is merely the collection of public and government database material and other non-public law enforcement information relating to a group of public officials, such as all persons at or above Deputy Minster level or all procurement officers. This data is used to make a comparison of total assets owned by a person relative to their tax returns and asset declaration statements. If the computation discloses a significant increase in the net value (excluding appreciation) of assets that is many times more the known and legal income of the official, then the possibility of corruption may have been detected. Additional information will be needed to further support this suspicion.

Source and application of funds analysis to prove amount of illegal income

Proving corrupt income often will require the use of circumstantial evidence and an indirect method to establish the amount of income.[9] It will not always be possible to trace the specific corruption income from the illegal activity directly to the receiver of the bribe or the one who benefited from the misappropriation of the government funds. The Source and Application of Funds method of proving the amount of illegal income is used when direct evidence is not available and the investigation discloses that the subject spent far more money during a set period of time than he had legally available to him. This set period of time can be any amount of time that demonstrates an increase in spending or wealth far above the legal means of the subject. This concept expressed in a formula would appear as follows:

For the set period 1 January 2012 to 31 December 2012 the defendant had:

Total expenditures and other applications of money	USD 50,000,000
Total of known and legal sources of income	USD 2,000,000
Equals illegal or unexplained income	USD 48,000,000

It is important to understand that this method standing alone does not prove illegal income. It simply demonstrates that the person was spending money far above his legal means and can assist in tracing assets. The investigation must also develop evidence that indicates that the subject committed some criminal offence such as bribery or abuse of office. This evidence combined with the financial analysis will prove the amount of the illegal income.

9 In keeping with the provisions of Article 28 of the United Nations Convention against Corruption (UNCAC), Member States are required to put in place measures which allow the knowledge, intent or purpose element of offences to be established through inference from objective factual circumstances. Similarly, the use of circumstantial evidence in proving the financial aspects of corruption or money laundering offences is to be encouraged, particularly as it will, in turn, also assist in drawing inferences regarding an offender's state of mind.

Analysing bank records

As stated in the Legislative guide for the implementation of the UNCAC:[10]

> Bank secrecy rules have often been found to be a major hurdle in the investigation and prosecution of serious crimes with financial aspects. As a result, several initiatives have sought to establish the principle that bank secrecy cannot be used as grounds for refusing to implement certain provisions of international and bilateral agreements or refusing to provide mutual legal assistance to requesting States. The same applies to the Convention against Corruption, as we have seen above with respect to seizure and confiscation of proceeds of crime (art. 31, para. 7; see also para. 8 of art 46 (Mutual legal assistance)).

In cases of domestic criminal investigations of offences established in accordance with the UNCAC, State Parties are required to ensure that their legal system has appropriate mechanisms to overcome obstacles arising out of bank secrecy laws (Article 40).[11] In accordance with Article 31,[12] State Parties must – to the greatest extent possible under their domestic system – have the necessary legal framework to enable, *inter alia*, the empowerment of courts or other appropriate authorities to order that bank, financial or commercial records (such as real estate transactions, shipping lines, freight forwarders and insurers) be made available or seized.[13] Bank secrecy should not be a legitimate reason for failure to comply.

The analysis of bank records is a task that many investigators fear. However, the process can be performed quite easily even by non-financial experts. The first step is to organise the records in an elec-

10 United Nations Office on Drugs and Crime (UNODC), United Nations Publications, 2006, p. 153, para. 487.

11 UNODC Legislative guide, p. 153, para. 488.

12 The legislation required by Article 31, paragraphs 2 and 7, involves:
(a) Such measures as may be necessary to enable the identification, tracing, freezing or seizure of proceeds or other property (Article 31, para. 2);
(b) Powers for courts or other competent authorities to order that bank, financial or commercial records be made available or be seized (Article 31, para. 7).

13 United Nations Convention against Transnational Organised Crime, 2000 (Palermo Convention), Article 12(6).

tronic database (i.e. an Excel spreadsheet). Once all data from the bank account has been entered into the spreadsheet, either manually or by a computer process, the analysis will be divided into three relatively easy tasks, namely the analysis of the deposits, the analysis of the disbursements and the identification of balances on certain dates.

The deposit analysis will include reviewing each item deposited into the account and determining its source: legal, illegal or unknown. For some deposits, such as salary payments, their type (legal, illegal or unknown) may be easily determined by simply reviewing the bank documents. However, if the source is unknown, the investigator will have to make third party contacts to inquire about the purpose of the payment that was made to the subject. By developing a list that summarises and totals each type of deposit, the investigator can focus on what leads are most important to follow.

The analysis of the disbursements can be accomplished in the same manner. The investigator can now quickly identify which items require additional follow-up or detective work. This disbursement analysis assists in identifying assets purchased, business associates, transfers to other bank accounts, international money movements and spending that exceeds the subject's legal income.

In some cases, it may be important to identify the balance that is in the bank account on a particular date or on a series of dates. This also can be quickly accomplished by adding a column in the Excel spreadsheet that automatically calculates the balance following every transaction.

These are the three basic types of analysis that should be completed for each bank account. In addition, there are other records maintained by banks that should be reviewed, such as account opening documents, bank due diligence reports, loan files, electronic funds transfers and correspondence files.

Conclusion

Asset tracing, in anticipation of the successful recovery of assets, is a lengthy and complex process where one cannot and should not expect quick results. Indeed, the process involves a series of stakeholders whose activities need to be well coordinated and appropriately timed on both a domestic and international level.

Cross-border criminal activities demand effective international co-operation during the investigation and proceedings aimed ultimately at the confiscation of the proceeds of crime. International co-operation should facilitate the provision of investigative assistance in identifying and tracing property, obtaining documents and enforcing provisional measures aimed at freezing or seizing the proceeds of crime. Knowing how to approach an investigation with a transnational component is a vital tool in the toolkit of any investigator tasked with tracing assets.

It is internationally recognised that a critical aspect of criminal investigations into corruption and related offences is the financial investigation. The main goal of the investigation is to follow the flow of the money in order to prove the link between the origins of the money, the beneficiaries and the underlying criminal activity. The financial tracing will often penetrate the web of confusion by identifying the beneficial owner if corporate and trust entities have been formed to hide the true ownership of the funds.

Through the strengthening of law enforcement standards, significant emphasis has been placed on the proper investigation of crime, such as money laundering and corruption and the identification, tracing and subsequent recovery of assets. Therefore, it is increasingly important that law enforcement agencies enhance their knowledge and skills to conduct thorough and effective financial investigations that achieve multiple goals. It is equally important that they embrace techniques that facilitate an investigation within the context of internationally recognised standards.

In addition to specialised technical skills needed to trace assets, a financial investigation will often require the expertise of a forensic accounting expert to assist in unravelling complex financial transactions and an understanding of the role played by gatekeepers. However, basic methods such as the use of the Source and Application of Funds method and Excel can go a long way towards enabling investigators to follow the trail of the money. The effective analysis of bank records facilitates the identification and tracing of assets. The same applies to proving the financial aspect of a case through the use of circumstantial evidence and an indirect method to establish corrupt income. Although this method standing alone does not prove illegal income, it can show that the person was spending money far above his legal means, prove beneficial ownership and assist in tracing assets.

Richard E. Messick[*]

How financial disclosure laws help in the recovery of stolen assets

As part of their strategy to curb corruption, more and more nations require public servants to disclose information about their personal finances. The World Bank/United Nations Office on Drugs and Crime Stolen Asset Recovery Initiative's most recent survey found that of 176 jurisdictions reviewed, over three-quarters require at least some public employees to reveal details of their personal financial data – either publicly or to an anticorruption authority or other government agency.[1] This chapter explains how these disclosures can aid the recovery of stolen assets. It begins with a description of financial disclosure laws, follows with an analysis of how they support asset recovery actions and ends with some recommendations for making them more useful.

Financial disclosure laws

Disclosure laws help combat corruption in two ways – by revealing potential conflicts between personal financial interests and the public interest and by alerting law enforcement authorities to sudden changes in an official's wealth that could be the result of corruption. The level of detail officials must disclose depends upon the law's purpose.

* Mr Messick consults for development agencies and non-government organizations on rule of law and anti-corruption measures.

1 Ivana M. Rossi, 'Public Officials Disclosure: An Effective Mechanism to Prevent and Detect Conflicts of Interest -- Global and Regional Perspectives', presentation to UNODC Workshop on Conflict of Interest Legislation, Cairo, 23 March 2013.

Where the purpose is to flag potential conflicts of interest, the laws may require filers to report only the source of any outside income and ownership interests in private firms. This is the rule in Canada, for example, where members of the upper house of parliament are expressly instructed not to report the value of their assets or the amount of outside income earned.[2]

Most financial disclosure laws now aim not only to curb conflicts of interest but also to monitor changes in employees' wealth, and wealth-monitoring laws demand far more detail from those required to file.[3] Typically, not only will the sources of outside income have to be reported but the amount as well. Likewise, assets will generally have to be individually listed and the current value, and sometimes the acquisition price, reported. Argentina goes so far as to require that bank account and credit card numbers be provided.[4]

Additional items that laws often require to be reported are outstanding debts, gifts received, reimbursements for travel and positions held in profit or non-profit organisations. A few countries make special provision for the disclosure of bank accounts in foreign jurisdictions. Some also require officials to report the assets and income of their spouse and minor children.[5]

Other important differences in financial disclosure laws are the number and identify of individuals required to report, the frequency of reporting and the penalties for the failure to file or knowingly filing a false declaration. Most statutes require senior officials in the executive, legislative and judicial branches whether elected or appointed to

2 Government of Canada, Office of the Senate Ethics Officer, Conflict of Interest Code for Senators, Confidential Disclosure Statement. Available at: http://sen.parl.gc.ca/seo-cse/eng/Home-e.html.

3 Richard E. Messick, Income and Assets Declarations: Issues to Consider in Developing a Disclosure Regime, Begen: U4 Anti-Corruption Resource Centre, 2009. Available at: www.cmi.no/publications/file/3396-income-and-assets-declarations.pdf.

4 Government of Argentina, Ética En El Ejercicio De La Función Publica, Ley 25.188, article 6(e), promulgated 26 October 1999. Available at: www.infoleg.gov.ar/infolegInternet/anexos/60000-64999/60847/texact.htm.

5 Stolen Asset Recovery Initiative, Public Office, Private Interests: Accountability Through Income and Asset Disclosure, Washington, D.C.: World Bank, 2012, pp. 36 – 37.

file, and some laws reach far down into the ranks of career employees. In Tanzania, all officers in the armed forces must submit an annual statement showing their income and assets.[6] Reporting periods vary too. Some statutes require annual reporting; in others a report must be submitted upon assuming office and a second upon leaving it. A few, such as Mongolia,[7] require updates whenever there has been a significant change in a covered individual's wealth, and others, like Thailand, demand a report after an official has been out of office a certain period.[8]

Penalties for failing to file or lying on the submission range from stiff prison sentences to fines to administrative sanctions, such as the withholding of salary, but in many countries non-reporting or falsely reporting is not considered a serious offense. A September 2012 survey of the laws in 82 countries by the World Bank's Public Accountability Mechanisms Initiative found only 26 countries treated a failure to file or a false statement as a serious criminal offense and in 14 no sanction at all could be imposed for any violation no matter how severe.[9]

Use in asset recovery actions

The value of a financial disclosure law for asset recovery begins with the support it can provide in establishing a predicate offense for an asset recovery action. The most direct way is where there is an incon-

6 Alan Doig, David Watt and Robert Williams, Measuring 'Success' In Five African Anti-Corruption Commissions, Bergen: U4 Anti-Corruption Resource Centre, 2005. Available at: http://www.acauthorities.org/publications/measuring-%E2%80%98success%E2%80%99-five-african-anti-corruption-commissions.

7 Stolen Asset Recovery Initiative, Income and Asset Disclosure: Case Study Illustrations, Washington, D.C.: World Bank, forthcoming.

8 Government of Thailand, Organic Act On Counter Corruption, section 33, B.E. 2542, 1999. Available at http://www.nacc.go.th/ewt_news.php?nid=943.

9 World Bank, Public Sector and Governance Group, Public Accountability Mechanisms Initiative, Financial Disclosure Systems: Declarations of Interests, Income, and Assets, September 2012. Available at: https://agidata.org/Pam/Documents/FD%20Primer_24Sep2012.pdf.

sistency between what an individual reports on the financial disclosure form and what other records show. A motor vehicle registry might reveal a car registered in an official's name that is not reported on the disclosure submission. Tax returns and land and corporate registries are other sources that can expose assets that a public servant owns but has failed to report.[10]

While through accident or carelessness some employees do reveal property that they have not declared on their financial disclosure submission, more commonly they take care to disguise their ownership, registering the property in the name of another or holding it through a corporation or trust that cannot be linked to them. Financial disclosure laws are still useful in these situations. Civil society or law enforcement can compare the value of an employee's residence, amounts spent on vacations and children's education and other indicators of lifestyle against what has been disclosed. Where there is a significant discrepancy between what the employee claims to earn or to own and the way the employee lives, further investigation may show unreported earnings or undisclosed assets that are the result of corrupt activities. In the Philippines, a journalist found employees of the tax authority were understating the value of their residences and driving cars registered in the name of a friend or relative,[11] and a subsequent investigation revealed widespread bribery and corruption among agency employees.

The consequences of a failure to disclose assets or income information for asset recovery will depend upon the particulars of the financial disclosure statute, the asset recovery act and national criminal law. Where the financial disclosure law makes a knowing false statement a serious crime, non-reporting alone may be sufficient to support an asset recovery action. This was the case in Trinidad and Tobago where a trial court held that assets not disclosed must be forfeited.[12] In other instances, non-disclosure may provide a link in the chain of evi-

10 Stolen Asset Recovery Initiative, Public Office, Private Interests, pp. 60 – 69.

11 Clarissa S. Batino, '4BIR, BOC Officials Fail Lifestyle Check', Philippine Daily Inquirer, 21 July 2003, p.1.

12 'Basdeo Panday Guilty As Charged', Trinidad & Tobago News Bulletin Board, 25 April 2006. Available at: www.trinidadandtobagonews.com/forum/webbbs_config.pl/noframes/read/3573.

dence needed to obtain a conviction that can support asset recovery. The most common example may be their use in prosecutions for illicit enrichment, a crime resulting from a 'significant increase in the assets of a public official that he or she cannot reasonably explain in relation to his or her lawful income'.[13] Evidence that an official is hiding assets or income can support an inference that the assets were obtained illicitly or the money earned unlawfully.[14]

Financial disclosure laws can be useful in civil actions to recover assets located in foreign jurisdictions as well. The most notable examples are two successful civil recovery cases the Federal Republic of Nigerian brought in the United Kingdom in the mid-2000s. Evidence obtained through a variety of means had shown that former Governor of Plateau State Joshua C. Dariye had accumulated significant assets through corrupt activities, including GBP 2.85 million deposited in a British bank, and that former Governor of Bayelsa State D. Solomon Peter Alamieyeseigha had purchased London properties worth over GBP 4 million with monies obtained through bribery and embezzlement. Nigeria filed suit against each seeking return of the assets and noting in the pleadings that each defendant had submitted a series of financial disclosure statements in accordance with Nigerian law. Dariye's disclosures did not reveal the bank account and Alamieyeseigha's did not reveal the properties. Accordingly, in both actions Nigeria argued that non-disclosure should be considered evidence that the assets were obtained unlawfully.

In the *Alamieyeseigha* action Nigeria argued in addition that the large disparity between what the former governor had reported on his financial declaration and his British assets was additional evidence that the assets were stolen: '[it should] be inferred that the bank balances, cash, and other investments accumulated by Mr. Alamieyeseigha outside Nigeria since May 1999 [. . .] represent bribes or secret profits obtained by Mr. Alamieyeseigha through the abuse of

13 United Nations Convention against Corruption, article 20. Available at: www.unodc.org/unodc/en/treaties/CAC/index.htmla

14 Lindy Muzila, Michelle Morales, Marianne Mathias and Tammar Berger, On the Take: Criminalizing Illicit Enrichment to Fight Corruption, Washington, D.C.: The World Bank, 2012.

his position as a public officer in Nigeria'.[15] The court agreed. In ordering forfeiture of the assets, the High Court relied both on the non-disclosure and the disparity between what was disclosed and what was concealed.[16]

In a subsequent presentation on civil asset recovery actions, Nigeria's counsel underlined the evidentiary value of income and asset declarations. Indeed, given the lower standard of proof in common law countries in civil proceedings, they noted that a civil action for recovery could perhaps be maintained solely 'on the basis of unexplained and undeclared wealth substantially in excess of what declared assets could justify'.[17]

Making financial disclosure more useful for asset recovery

Financial disclosure laws can be an important aid to asset recovery, but as this chapter suggests, some laws will be more useful than others. To ensure national law maximizes the chances that stolen assets will be recovered, lawmakers should be sure that their financial disclosure statute:

- Treats the knowing submission of a false declaration or non-filing as a crime at least as serious as bribery or embezzlement
- Follows Trinidadian law and makes forfeiture of the asset automatic where the filer knowingly omitted it from the disclosure statement.

15 *Federal Republic of Nigeria* v *Santolina Investment Corp., et al.*, Particulars of Claim Against the First to Fifth and Eleventh Defendants, In the High Court of Justice, Chancery Division, Claim No. HC05 C03602, 17 January 2006, §45. Available at: www.assetrecovery.org/kc/resources/org.apache.wicket.Application/repo?nid=bedccbf6-ca92-11dd-b3f1-fd61180437d9.

16 *Federal Republic of Nigeria* v *Santolina Investment Corporation & Ors* [2007] EWHC 3053 (QB) (03 December 2007) §34. Available at: http://high-court-justice.vlex.co.uk/vid/hc05-co3602-52860369.

17 Kendall Freeman, Recovering Assets Secreted Abroad, paper prepared for Workshop with Bangladesh Anti-Corruption Commission, July 2007, p. 11.

Where violations of financial disclosure laws are serious crimes, public employees confronted with evidence they have broken the law are more likely to cooperate with authorities, admitting to the underlying corruption crime and providing information on the location of the proceeds. In addition, when violations are made serious crimes, convictions for breach are more likely to support requests to other jurisdictions for mutual legal assistance or a freezing or confiscation order.

Depending upon the law where the assets are located and the law of the country seeking return, recovery actions will require either showing a link between the crime committed and the asset sought or that the asset is equal in value to the benefit the offender realised from the crime.[18] Where the corrupt act is the receipt of a bribe, such a showing is relatively straightforward, but for other corruption crimes showing a direct link or quantifying benefit is more problematic.[19] Making forfeiture the penalty for non-disclosure can obviate such evidentiary problems.

Public officials who conceal their assets rarely act alone. It takes the connivance of a friend, relative, lawyer, banker or other complicit party to register property in the name of another or create a corporation where ownership is disguised. In 2009, an appellate court in the United States held that those who knowingly help an individual subject to a financial disclosure law to conceal income or assets are themselves guilty of a serious crime.[20] An express provision in a financial disclosure law making those who abet non-disclosure guilty of a serious crime will provide law enforcement with more leverage to induce cooperation; it can also provide an alternative source for asset recovery when the hidden assets have been dissipated.

18 Theodore S. Greenberg, Linda M. Samuel, Wingate Grant, and Larissa Gray, Stolen Asset Recovery: A Good Practices Guide for Non-Conviction Based Asset Forfeiture, Washington, D.C.: The World Bank, 2009, pp. 13-14.

19 Patrick Conroy and Graeme Hunter, Economic Analysis of Damages under the Foreign Corrupt Practices Act, New York: National Economic Research Associates, May 2011; OECD/World Bank, Identification and Quantification of the Proceeds of Bribery: A Joint OECD-StAR Analysis, Paris: OECD, 2011.

20 *United States* v *Carbo*, 572 F.3d 112, 115 (3d Cir. 2009) ('by assisting the public official to disguise the [asset], he is not merely lobbying, but is engaged in a criminal conspiracy').

The practice of the Unites States Office of Government Ethics, the American agency that administers the federal financial disclosure law, shows how a government agency can make financial disclosure laws a more effective tool for asset recovery. The Office of Government Ethics:

- Offers regular training programs on the law to law enforcement personnel, explaining who must submit disclosure reports and when, how to read them and where they can be located[21]
- Circulates regular updates to the legal community on the ways the courts in their own and related jurisdictions have relied on financial disclosure laws to convict officials of corruption or order the return of stolen assets.[22]

These are modest, low cost initiatives that any anticorruption agency, ethics commission or other body involved in the administration or enforcement of a financial disclosure law can take.

Conclusion

Financial disclosure laws can be important instruments in the asset recovery practitioner's tool kit. They can provide a link in the evidentiary chain needed to establish the underlying offense and if properly drafted can considerably ease the practitioner's task. Both those seeking to recover stolen assets and policymakers seeking to make recovery less burdensome should be alert to the benefits they offer.

21 U.S. Government, Office of Government Ethics, Conflict of Interest Investigations. Available at: www.oge.gov/DisplayTemplates/ModelSub.aspx?id=2147484054.

22 U.S. Government Ethics Office, Conflict of Interest Prosecution Surveys. Available at: www.oge.gov/Topics/Enforcement/Conflict-of-Interest-Prosecution-Surveys.

Emerging trends, good practice

Part 3: Seizure and recovery

L. MUZILA, T. BERGER, M. MATHIAS AND M. MORALES[1]

Illicit enrichment: An emerging tool in the asset recovery process

When a modestly paid public official is suddenly able to take lavish holidays, buy a new sports car or purchase expensive jewellery it raises eyebrows and suspicion. In these circumstances, corruption may be suspected, but it is often frustratingly difficult to prove. To address this issue, the offence of 'Illicit Enrichment' was created, which does not eliminate the burden of proof but rather eases the requirement that the prosecution prove that the assets derive from corrupt behaviour. Instead, the prosecution must only prove that the illicit funds cannot be justified from legitimate sources of income. The public official then has to provide a reasonable and legitimate source of the mysterious newfound wealth, failing to do so means he or she faces prosecution.

Based on the above-mentioned notion that unexplained wealth of a public official may, in fact, be the visible proceeds of corruption, illicit enrichment was identified as a non-mandatory crime in Article 20 of the United Nations Convention against Corruption (UNCAC). The offense is defined in the Convention, when committed intention-

1 The Stolen Asset Recovery Initiative (StAR) is a partnership between the World Bank Group and the United Nations Office on Drugs and Crime (UNODC) that supports international efforts to end safe havens for corrupt funds. StAR works with developing countries and financial centres to prevent the laundering of the proceeds of corruption and to facilitate more systematic and timely return of stolen assets. On the Take: Criminalizing Illicit Enrichment to Fight Corruption is part of the StAR Series, which supports the efforts of StAR and UNODC by providing practitioners with knowledge and policy tools that consolidate international good practice and wide-ranging practical experience on cutting-edge issues related to anticorruption and asset recovery efforts. For more information, visit www.worldbank.org/star.

ally, as a 'significant increase in the assets of a public official that he or she cannot reasonably explain in relation to his or her lawful income'.

The Stolen Asset Recovery Initiative (StAR) of the United Nations and World Bank recently published a study on illicit enrichment in a publication entitled, 'On the Take: Criminalizing Illicit Enrichment to Fight Corruption'. The study is based upon the experiences of the forty-four countries around the world that have enacted illicit enrichment laws.[2] The study analysed how the criminalisation of illicit enrichment works, highlighting both the benefits and challenges, and the paper shed light on its role in the asset recovery process. The study did not seek to recommend or oppose the adoption of particular illicit enrichment provisions. Rather, the aim was to assist jurisdictions that are considering such steps by highlighting key questions that might arise during implementation, including how States define and enforce the offense. Similarly, the study did not endorse nor criticise any practice carried out by States in implementing the criminalisation of illicit enrichment. This paper outlines some of the key findings of the study.

The origins and development of illicit enrichment laws

The crime of illicit enrichment, as it exists today, was initially enacted in Argentina and India in the 1960's to combat unexplained wealth. In the two decades since it was first criminalised, similar provisions were introduced in a number of countries including Brunei Darussalam, Colombia, Ecuador, Egypt, the Dominican Republic, Pakistan and Senegal. By 1990, illicit enrichment was a criminal offence in at least 10 countries, rising to over 20 by 2000 and to 40 jurisdictions in 2010. In some States, such as India, provisions that already existed under the law of evidence were simply criminalised.

Today, illicit enrichment provisions can be found at both the international and domestic levels. Internationally, it was first included in

2 This is the number of jurisdictions that enacted illicit enrichment laws as defined by UNCAC at the time the study was published.

the Inter-American Convention against Corruption (IACAC),[3] adopted by the Organisation of American States in 1996, then in the African Union Convention on Preventing and Combatting Corruption (AUCPCC),[4] approved in 2003, and finally in the UNCAC. Domestically, illicit enrichment can be found in national legislation in most regions of the world, with the notable exceptions of North America and much of Western Europe. The reason for such exceptions is that many of these jurisdictions view illicit enrichment as having implications on human rights and due process protections. Amongst countries choosing not to criminalise illicit enrichment, many have nonetheless enacted alternative means for tackling illicit enrichment by public officials, which involve measures that make it easier to either prosecute corrupt officials or confiscate illicit proceeds. Such legal dispositions usually rely on organised crime provisions, which can sometimes lower or provide for a partial reversal of the burden of proof for the prosecution.[5]

Characteristics of illicit enrichment

Different jurisdictions use various terms and phrases to refer to illicit enrichment, such as 'possession of unexplained property'[6] or 'possession of property disproportionate to known sources of income'.[7] While the terms used to refer to illicit enrichment may be different, there are a number of common minimum elements that form the basis of the offence:

- An illicit enrichment provision will specifically target public officials as persons of interest. Some countries may broaden the scope

3 IACAC, Art. IX.
4 AUCPCC, Art. 8.
5 See Germany, Criminal Code, Section 73d; and France, Article 321(6) of the Penal Code.
6 Lesotho, 1999, Prevention of Corruption and Economic Offences Act no. 5.
7 Pakistan, 1999 National Accountability Ordinance, Article, 9.

of this element by including close family members of a public official.[8]

- There must be a significant increase in assets. Most countries do not define what is meant by 'significant' or 'disproportionate' increase in their legislation, thus leaving it to the determination of the Courts and the prosecution.
- There must be an absence of justification by the public official. This is considered the most controversial element of the offence, as it requires a suspect or accused person to actively participate in the fact-finding process.
- There is a 'period of check' that is the time during which a person can be held liable for having illicitly enriched him/herself. States have adopted three different approaches to determining the period of interest: coinciding with the individual's official term of duty;[9] a limited term after leaving their post;[10] and an open-ended period.[11]
- The enrichment should have taken place intentionally. This inference is drawn from the relevant factual circumstances.

Overall, lessons learnt from States implementing illicit enrichment legislation demonstrate that it is helpful for the legislation to be as specific as possible in defining the elements of the offense, so as to clarify the objectives of the legislators and the respective roles of the court, prosecution and defence when dealing with an illicit enrichment offense. Accordingly, those jurisdictions that consider the reasonable

8 See Paraguay, Law no. 2.523/04, Article 3.

9 See eg El Salvador, Ley Sobre el Enriquecimiento Ilícito de Funcionarios y Empleados Públicos, Título III del Enriquecimiento Ilícito.

10 See eg Penal Code of Panama of 2008, Article 345, states, 'Any public servant who, either personally or through a third party, unduly increases their wealth in relation to the legitimate income obtained during the occupation of their post and for up to five years after having left the post, whose lawful provenance they are unable to show, shall be punished with three to six years of imprisonment'. Translation from OAS (2010g). The original is presented in appendix A.

11 See eg Brunei Darussalam, Prevention of Corruption Act 1982, Article 12, Possession of Unexplained Property. Illicit enrichment is applicable to 'any person, who, being or having been a public officer [. . .] maintains a standard of living above that which is commensurate with his present or past emoluments'.

explanation a defence may wish to specify this in the provision if it is thought to be relevant.

Implementation challenges

Human and constitutional rights concerns

Human rights and constitutional concerns often arise around the subject of criminalising of illicit enrichment. As a result, some State Parties to the UNCAC, the IACAC and the AUCPCC choose not to criminalise the offense in their jurisdictions under the safeguard clauses of these instruments, which allow States subject to the constitutions, laws and the fundamental principles of their systems to determine whether to implement parts of international conventions. The level and reasoning for the objection ranges from jurisdiction to jurisdiction. Some critics have even gone so far as to argue that the offense of illicit enrichment is so flawed that it is 'a remedy that is worse than the ailment' and that the criminalisation of illicit enrichment should be discouraged in an environment with weak governance.[12]

Rule of law is integral and indispensable to good governance, citizens' security, development and human rights. A weaker of rule of law suggests a lower probability of catching a corrupt public agent. Unfortunately, jurisdictions with a pressing need to stamp out corruption often also have a pressing need to strengthen their rule of law.

12 According to Snider and Kidane (2007, 728), it is 'highly doubtful that compromising the fundamental principle of the presumption of innocence in the interest of combating unexplained material gains by government officials is a desirable course. This is particularly true in Africa where, as the African Union Corruption Convention suggests, the crime of corruption is directly linked with the rule of law and good governance. In fact, it directly conflicts with the principles enshrined under recognized universal human rights instruments as well as the African Charter on Human and Peoples' Rights. The implementation of this provision as written in the domestic sphere should not be encouraged, because it might mean prescribing a remedy that is worse than the ailment'.

Some commentators critical of the criminalisation of illicit enrichment also note that prosecutorial discretion, where it is open to abuse, may further add to the concerns. In this respect, a broader understanding of the criminal justice system, its independence from political pressure and its institutional and technical capacity is important when considering whether and how to enact illicit enrichment statutes.

Looking more closely at the specific human and constitutional rights associated with the criminalisation of illicit enrichment, the most oft cited are those associated with the shifting of the burden of proof such as the presumption of innocence and the privilege against self-incrimination. The presumption of innocence requires the State to prove the guilt of an accused and relieves the accused of any burden to prove his or her innocence. The United Nations Human Rights Committee states, 'The burden of proof of the charge is on the prosecution and the accused has the benefit of doubt. No guilt can be presumed until the charge has been proved beyond reasonable doubt [or intimate conviction]'.[13] However, the principle of the presumption of innocence does not exclude legislatures from creating criminal offenses containing a presumption by law as long as the principles of rationality (reasonableness) and proportionality are duly respected. These principles have been applied in order to align the presumption of innocence with an important precedent set by the European Court of Human Rights in *Salabiaku* v *France*.[14]

Similarly, while a fundamental right, there is established precedent that the right against self-incrimination is not absolute. Following

13 United Nations Office of the High Commissioner for Human Rights 1984, 124, para. 7.

14 Salabiaku v France (1988), Application no. 10519/83, Section 28. In its decision, the court outlined its approach to the permissibility of burden-shifting provisions, an approach that can be referred to as the Salabiaku test. The Salabiaku test is based on the recognition that 'presumptions of fact or of law operate in every legal system', but that States must confine presumptions 'within reasonable limits which take into account the importance of what is at stake and maintain the rights of the defence'. Therefore, the court balanced the State's interest in the prosecution with the rights of the accused by keeping presumptions within reasonable limits.

the reasoning in the O'Hallaran[15] case, in assuming a position of trust public officials subject themselves to the legal requirements and the administrative and criminal sanctions that arise from the abuse of that trust. Moreover, where countries have an established income and asset disclosure regime, they also have established the principle that public officials may provide personal information that may be self-incriminating. In this context, providing evidence regarding the sources of income and assets to the court does not appear as a significant additional burden.

States that have prosecuted the offence have learned through their experiences that, with proper legal and institutional safeguards in place, illicit enrichment provisions can be effective and equitable.[16] The challenge for national authorities, therefore, is to ensure that institutions are independent and to be vigilant against potential abuse. In many developing countries, this may require investing in strengthening the capability of prosecutors, the judiciary and law enforcement while ensuring their independence and impartiality.

Operational hurdles

The successful prosecution of corruption is an arduous task in any legal system. Detecting that a corrupt act has taken place is difficult due to the fact that unlike many traditional crimes, such as assault or theft, corruption frequently does not have an obvious victim. Furthermore, corruption offenses, such as bribery, require the demonstration of an offer by the corruptor or acceptance by the official. Similarly, once an offense has been established in a court of law, linking the proceeds to an offense for the purposes of recovering assets can often be a complex endeavour. Efforts to combat corruption are further

15 O'Hallaran and Francis v the United Kingdom, Application nos. 15809/02 and 25624/02 (2007). In O'Hallaran and Francis v the United Kingdom, the accused persons were held liable for refusing to provide records indicating who had been driving a taxi at the time of a criminal violation.

16 Based on feedback received from the surveys used for the StAR publication, On the Take: Criminalizing illicit enrichment to combat corruption (2012). Available at: www.star.worldbank.org.

challenged by the anonymity and fluidity with which assets can be moved, concealed and transferred before effective means can be taken to seize, freeze and return them to their rightful owners. Indeed, the only tangible evidence that a crime has taken place may be the money that changes hands between the corrupt official and his partner in crime, thus the enrichment of the corrupt official becomes the most visible manifestation of corruption.

The criminalisation of illicit enrichment is intended to alleviate some of the aforementioned difficulties in prosecuting a corruption case by requiring the prosecution to simply prove the existence of unexplained wealth. However, there remain significant challenges in investigating and prosecuting cases involving the offence. Perhaps the most significant of these challenges is the collection of evidence. For example, in many countries there are no up to date, searchable databases that can be used to identify assets. The same impediment arises for the identification of bank accounts. The lack of centralised databases or efficient tools to trace assets in many countries often poses an insurmountable hurdle in attaining an overall view of the assets held domestically by a public official.

In addition, financial investigations are particularly difficult in countries where there is a substantial cash economy. In these countries it is not unusual for individuals to hold substantial amounts of cash on hand and for large payments to be made outside of the banking system. For example, in many Middle Eastern and South Asian jurisdictions a number of transactions, including international transfers for trade and migrants' remittances, are channelled through informal *hawala* networks and simply go unrecorded for official purposes. When transactions take place in cash they may be difficult, if not impossible, to trace.

Preparation of an accurate financial profile is further complicated by the use of third parties, front entities and straw men to disguise the ownership of assets. Several countries cite the use of third parties as one of the principle obstacles in pursing prosecutions. Identifying assets held in the name of associates and third parties can be extremely difficult for investigators, especially where evidence is layered through a series of corporate vehicles in multiple jurisdictions.

Experience indicates that the use of illicit enrichment as an offense is most effective when it is implemented as part of a broader anticorruption strategy and where there are systems in place to facilitate the identification of potential cases and generate the information needed to support investigations. Resources need to be put in place at all levels to allow the detection, tracing and preservation of evidence and proceeds of the illicit enrichment. For instance, an effective income and asset disclosure (IAD) system is a valuable support for the investigation and prosecution of illicit enrichment. In countries that have decided to criminalise this offense, consideration should be given to the design of the IAD system and the means by which it interacts with agencies responsible for investigation and prosecution.[17]

International cooperation challenges

Corrupt officials often transfer the proceeds of their crime abroad and hold accounts in foreign jurisdictions so as to evade detection. The movement of assets across borders also creates additional impediments in the asset recovery process. Therefore, international legal cooperation is crucial in illicit enrichment prosecutions, particularly in high profile cases. Although all major international corruption conventions promote enhanced international cooperation in the fight against corruption, the prosecution of illicit enrichment presents specific challenges.

International cooperation challenges specifically related to illicit enrichment include dual criminality, due process and evidentiary concerns. Objections based on dual criminality – the requirement to demonstrate that the crime underlying the request for assistance is criminalised in both the requested and the requesting jurisdictions – can be overcome by adopting a conduct-based approach. This approach simply requires that the requested and requesting States 'trans-

17 Further information on the design and management of IAD systems is presented in the StAR publication, Public Office, Private Interests: Accountability Through Income and Asset Disclosure. See also on PEPs, another StAR publication: Politically Exposed Persons, Preventive Measures for the Banking Sector. Available at: www.star.worldbank.org.

pose the facts (but not the offense) under investigation in the requesting country to the legal system of the requested country and ask whether such facts would be considered illicit if committed there'.[18]

More often than not, the real challenge is lack of understanding and miscommunication. Indeed, experience suggests that jurisdictions requesting international cooperation, particularly mutual legal assistance requests, continue to encounter challenges in obtaining assistance from requested States. However, in many instances these challenges are surmountable. Because many States will render assistance based on the underlying conduct, efforts should be made to ensure that this condition is an offense in the requested jurisdiction. States should look beyond just enrichment and focus on the criminal conduct that generates the wealth prior to making the request.

Conclusion

Assets stolen by corrupt leaders are frequently of considerable magnitude, and their recovery involves an arduous and difficult process. Barriers – both legal and operational – often make the process even more challenging. Illicit enrichment can serve to reduce the potentially burdensome procedural and evidentially requirements associated with other corruption offenses, helping with the identification of illicit funds and triggering of asset recovery efforts.

However, the utility of the illicit enrichment offense in the asset recovery process will depend largely on the broader context of the criminalisation of corruption, the oversight regime for public officials, the specific objectives to be achieved with the offense and the nature of guidance that can be remitted to supporting regulations and administrative instructions. Furthermore, effective, transparent and independent institutions for the administration of justice are essential. Lessons learned by States that have successfully prosecuted illicit

18 Schmid, Jean-Bernard. 2006. 'Off the Beaten Track: Alternatives to Formal Cooperation'. In Denying Safe Haven to the Corrupt and the Proceeds of Corruption: Enhancing Asia-Pacific Cooperation on Mutual Legal Assistance, Extradition, and Return of the Proceeds of Corruption, 25–28.

enrichment in this respect are that, with proper legal and institutional safeguards in place, illicit enrichment provisions can be effective tools that are used fairly. Therefore, the challenge for national authorities is to develop the institutional capacity to assert independence and to be vigilant against potential abuse.

Notwithstanding the numerous challenges outlined above, 'On the Take' reveals the real potential of the offense as a potentially effective tool in fighting corruption and helping in the recovery of stolen assets. Successful illicit enrichment prosecutions, in particular in jurisdictions such as Hong Kong, Argentina and India, that have resulted in the recovery of assets have illustrated the potential usefulness of pursuing the offense through the courts.

Developing countries lose an estimated USD 20-40 billion in total each year to corruption. Well-designed and properly implemented, illicit enrichment can be an important weapon in the battle to combat this global blight and an effective tool in the return of stolen assets.

Charles Monteith

Non-conviction based forfeiture

This chapter is not meant to be a detailed analysis of the law of non-conviction based forfeiture (or civil recovery as it currently applies to England and Wales) but is meant to be more of a general guide to some of the common issues and considerations that might need addressing both by affected individuals and institutions and by countries wishing to implement something similar.

Civil recovery

Civil recovery in England and Wales is a form of non-conviction-based asset forfeiture, which allows for the recovery in civil proceedings before the High Court of property that is, or represents, proceeds obtained through unlawful conduct. Civil recovery is just one way of recovering proceeds of crime. Other ways include recovering them post conviction for criminal matters or taking action in the civil courts for a breach of contract/tort, etc.

Only authorised enforcers can apply for an order that is not a conviction or a sentence. Importantly, the proceedings are against the property itself (in rem) rather than against an individual (in person). On the face of it, the absence of the need to have a suspect or defendant should make the recovery process easier, as the person in possession of the property need not be the person who carried out the unlawful conduct.

These proceedings amount to civil litigation and therefore the civil standard of proof (the balance of probabilities) applies. The court, however, will still require cogent evidence in order to be satisfied that property is on balance more likely to be the proceeds of unlawful conduct than not.

Requirements

To prove that property was obtained through unlawful conduct, it is not necessary to prove the commission of a particular criminal offence by a particular person on a particular occasion. It is sufficient to prove that the property was obtained through offending of a particular type (drug trafficking, fraud, bribery, etc.). This cannot solely be done on the basis that the person holding the property has no identifiable lawful income to warrant their lifestyle. However, the absence of any evidence from the person to explain his or her lifestyle, or the giving of a false explanation, may allow the court to infer that the source of the income was unlawful.

Costs

The cost and duration of civil recovery proceedings varies from case to case depending on the circumstances and complexity of the case. Civil recovery proceedings are often, due to their nature, contested and may in certain circumstances involve protracted litigation. In other cases, however, an order can be obtained quickly and simply when the other party consents to it. Costs awarded normally follow the success or otherwise of the claim. A claim that fails is therefore likely to prove expensive for an enforcing agency. On the other hand, the costs of the recovery investigation can normally be recovered once a civil recovery order has been obtained.

Assessing the likelihood of success is an important consideration for all enforcers, and it may be the main reason why most orders have so far been by consent.

Proceedings

Proceedings normally begin with a civil recovery investigation into what the criminal conduct is (or was), what the conduct generated in terms of recoverable property and whether the property in question is recoverable property or associated property. Investigations will also try to determine the owner and possessor of the property, as well as the property's extent or whereabouts, before obtaining a property freezing order (PFO). A PFO is granted by the High Court to preserve the status quo during the civil recovery investigation often without the knowledge of the possessor or owner. It is then served on the owner/possessor with a requirement to disclose details about the property held, as well as details of the owner/possessor's financial affairs, tax returns, registered income and assets held generally.

'Recoverable' property is property that is or represents property obtained through unlawful conduct and 'associated' property is property, which is not itself recoverable property but is any interest in the recoverable property or any part of it.

This means that if there is reason to believe that a person or persons are holding/controlling property that has been purchased through or is connected with the proceeds of crime or criminal conduct, an application can be made by one of the authorised agencies to freeze and potentially recover that property.

Relevant agencies and results

The agency that is most active against individuals is SOCA (Serious and Organised Crime Agency) shorty to become the National Crime Agency. In most cases involving asset recovery, they will act on a tip off from other law enforcement agencies or tax agencies. For example, such tip offs may refer to suspicious factors such as an individual whose lifestyle is not commensurate with the information provided in their filed tax returns. Specifically, if a person lived a luxurious lifestyle which would clearly require a considerable income to upkeep and if his or her tax returns showed little if any taxable income, a question will be raised by the requisite investigating agency as to the source of the income that funded this lifestyle.

The highest recoveries to date have generally been achieved when enforcers (the Serious Fraud Office) used civil recovery by consent, particularly against corporates.

Some significant civil recovery cases since 2008 (when civil recovery orders became law) include:

- Balfour Beatty plc: GBP 2.25 million (October 2008)
- Macmillan Publishers: GBP 11.264 million (July 2011)
- De Puy: GBP 4.8 million (April 2011)
- M. W. Kellogg: GBP 7 million (February 2011)
- Mabey Engineering (Holdings): GBP 130,000 (January 2012)
- Oxford Publishing Limited (OPL): GBP 1,895,435 (July 2012)
- BAE Systems plc: GBP 500,000 fine/GBP 29.28 million ex gratia payment (December 2010).

The M. W. Kellogg case is of particular interest in that it concerned an innocent parent company that was about to be paid tainted dividends by a US company that had engaged in unlawful conduct. So far, SFO orders have concerned property that is, or is about to be, situated in the United Kingdom and can be recovered from UK incorporated companies. The message for investors is to be wary of where they place their investments and to try to ensure that there are appropriate anticorruption measures in place.

Policy considerations

There has been some controversy over the way the SFO has used civil recovery orders and their connection to possible criminal proceedings. A common objective for all countries is the reduction of crime, which is generally best secured by means of effective criminal investigations and criminal proceedings. Therefore, any country considering designing a civil recovery regime should consider some important policy issues. The benefit of an investigation with a view to prosecution should always be considered by a law enforcement agency faced with suspected criminality. Subjecting offenders to trial and conviction in the criminal courts, and sentencing them in line with the seriousness of their offence, is generally the best and fairest way to serve the public interest and secure public confidence in the system of justice. Conversely, sometimes civil recovery orders have been obtained without clarifying the basis upon which they have been obtained, and this lack of transparency sometimes means that a sense of justice is not conveyed.

Reasons to use civil recovery where a conviction is not feasible:

- The only known criminality is overseas, and there is no extra-territorial jurisdiction to pursue a criminal case in the courts of England and Wales or Northern Ireland.
- There is no identifiable living suspect who is within the jurisdiction or realistically capable of being brought within the jurisdiction.
- Proceeds of crime can be identified but cannot be linked to any individual suspect or offence.
- A law enforcement authority considers that an investigation could not generate sufficient evidence to create a realistic prospect of conviction.
- A criminal investigation has been conducted but the prosecuting authority considers that there is insufficient evidence to create a realistic prospect of conviction.
- A prosecution has been conducted but has not resulted in a conviction.

Particularly, care must be taken to not allow an individual or body corporate to avoid a criminal investigation and prosecution by consenting to the making of a civil recovery order in circumstances where a criminal disposal would be justified.

Reasons to use civil recovery where a conviction is feasible:

- Using non-conviction based powers better meets an urgent need to take action to prevent or stop offending which is causing immediate harm to the public, even though this might limit the availability of evidence for a future prosecution.
- It is not practicable to investigate all of the offenders with a peripheral involvement in the criminality, and a strategic approach must be taken in order to achieve a manageable and successful prosecution.
- Civil recovery represents a better deployment of resources to target someone with significant property, which cannot be explained by legitimate income.

Linked investigations

Criminal and civil/tax proceedings should not be carried on at the same time in relation to the same criminality, save for where criminal proceedings have been stayed by a court or cannot progress (for example, when the defendant has absconded).

Equally, a criminal investigation by a law enforcement authority can be carried out at the same time as a civil recovery and/or tax investigation. Additionally, civil recovery and/or tax proceedings can be instituted where a criminal investigation by a law enforcement authority is being carried out at the same time into unrelated criminality.

Generally, when considering quantum it is best to grant a relevant authority the freedom to agree to accept a reduced sum in satisfaction of a civil recovery claim if it is satisfied that the reduced sum would not damage public confidence and that the sum is still considered a reasonable amount. In determining whether the reduced sum is reasonable, authorities should take into account all the relevant circumstances, including the actual chances of recovering the full amount claimed and the time and public funds likely to be expended in attempting to do so.

Conclusion

Civil recovery is an important new tool for enforcers. Primarily to date, it has been used against companies and individuals residing in the UK who hold criminally obtained assets that are also (or about to be) situated in the UK. At this point in time, however, it is unclear whether the scope of civil recovery covers persons residing outside the UK who possess recoverable property that is also located outside of the UK. In terms of overcoming international barriers to asset recovery, if more States adopted similar civil recovery legislation, it would assist in overcoming both legal issues (not least cross border issues, such as recognition) and practical issues. However, the main obstacle to such an international adoption appears to lie with civil law countries, which may have concerns over criminal matters being dealt with in a civil court.

RONALD VÍQUEZ SOLÍS

Corruption and social damage in Costa Rica

The UN Assembly General acknowledged in December 2000 the importance of having an effective international legal instrument against corruption. This legal instrument was to consider, among other things, international cooperation and the obligations arising from all forms of corruption-related offences. As well as that an open-ended intergovernmental expert working group was convened to examine and prepare a draft mandate for the negotiation of a future legal instrument against corruption. These efforts also examined the issue of illegally transferring assets through money laundering and the return of such assets. Diverting assets from national treasuries threatens the economic, social and political development, especially of developing countries.

Costa Rica has made progress on the asset recovery issue in recent years; importantly it recognises the social damage caused by the commission of offenses involving collective or diffuse interests.

The concept of social damage is not synonymous with asset recovery. The former is the ability to seek redress for damages caused when public interests are harmed. It is a concept that seeks to eliminate the consequences of corruption. Notwithstanding, it has implications in the fight against corruption, but is a novel idea and is still underdeveloped in the Costa Rican legal system.

Costa Rican criminal law allows liability claim resulting from a crime through a civil action for damages. This action is a procedural tool that allows the proposition of economic claims in criminal proceedings in order to establish liability generated as a result of an offense. The goal, in this case, is to obtain a material restitution deriving the object of the crime as well as to repair damages.

Damages and responsibility

It is believed that when there is damage that is the product of human action, there is the expense, damage, injury or loss of legally relevant interests, or individual or supra individual rights. There shall always exist damage when it affects the legal rights of an individual in the enjoyment of property to which the individual is entitled.

In order to be legally compensable, the damage must be certain, real and effective, it must be causing injury to a relevant interest, and it must be brought about by a third party and subsisting. There must be a causal link between the event and the damage. The latter must be the direct and the immediate consequence of a particular behaviour (cause and effect). The causal link is always necessary to determine the existence of the damage and its alleged perpetrator.

Damage has to meet four elements to acquire legal relevance: it must be an injury caused by human behaviour, which in turn must be unlawful, guilty and a causal link must mediate. As a result, the duty to indemnify or compensate emerges. As soon as an individual has suffered an injury that it should not withstand, there is a duty to indemnify, pursuant to the principle of compensation for damages.

According to the legal interests that are affected, these are often classified as material damage, which is the economic or material harm and it includes both disbursements as loss of earnings, and extra-patrimonial or immaterial damages, which are directed at the protection of non-patrimonial amounts that are essential for the person or groups thereof. The latter is also known as moral damage, or the social and emotional part of the moral patrimony – ideal rights – and that may cause material damage.

The diffuse interests – to be discussed below – are inherent to individuals and are also recognised as third generation rights.[1] These interests go beyond the individual holder of the right that may be harmed so as to extend the collective interests that are difficult to determine to other individuals who may otherwise not be enjoined through legal ties.

1 GHERSI, Carlos Alberto. Teoría General de la Reparación de Daños. Buenos Aires, Argentina, Editorial Astrea, 2007.

As indicated, in comparative law there are similar figures to claim compensable harm to such rights, and they are called collective damage or moral damages of collective character. These are understood as those that undermine a protected interest and which affects to a collective victim, ie society in general, not an individual person alone.

Concept of social damage

Our contact with the international community has allowed us to make known this initiative on social damage in various forums, such as: the Mechanism for Follow-Up on the Implementation of the Inter-American Convention against Corruption (MESICIC) of the Organization of American States (OAS), Transparency International, the World Bank, the United Nations (UN) and the Ibero-American Network for International Legal Co-operation (IberRed). The response of different international organisations interested in the subject has been positive, as they feel that it is an innovation that will allow for compensation for damage caused to society as a whole.[2]

The Conference of Ministers of Justice of Ibero-American Countries (COMJIB) in its Latin American conference that was organised in Madrid in September 2011 agreed to take up the Costa Rican proposal of generating a concept of social damage. As a first approach to the conceptualisation of social damage, it was considered that social damage is:

> … the diminishment, impact, undermining, decrease or loss of social welfare (in the context of the right to live in a healthy environment) resulting from an act of corruption which an unreasonable number of individuals suffer from – not the State – by causing a material or immaterial condition to their collective interests and before which there is the duty to repair.

2 MEETINGS: Transparency International, 14th IACC (2010, Thailand); 4th Session of the Conference of the States Parties of the UNCAC (2011, Marrakesh); 19th Meeting of the Committee of Experts of the MESICIC/OAS and 2nd Biennial of the International Alliance for the fight against corruption of the World Bank (2012, Washington, DC); 2nd IberRed Meeting of the Iberoamerican Central Authorities for the UNCAC (2012, Guatemala).

They moreover recommended establishing a model type of legislation.

Approach to the problem and its impact

Corruption is a threat to the stability of society, the establishment and the maintenance of the rule of law, and economic and political progress. To be valid, any solution to this problem must involve not only the recovery of assets derived from corruption but also the effective compensation of the effects of corruption. The recovery of the ill-gotten wealth and social restitution of damage caused by corruption can have a substantial impact in countries recovering from situations of corruption, and it makes it clear that the international community will not tolerate this kind of illegal behaviour.

Corrupt conduct undermines the social development of citizens, it affects their social well-being and, therefore, it harms diffuse interests, that is, interests affecting both the individual and the society of which the individual is part. In short, corruption causes social damage. In response, it is imperative to recognise the right to compensation. To this end, it will be necessary to produce legislation providing at least the following:

- Criminalisation of acts of corruption and of other behaviours that affect collective interests. The former, in addition to complying with international obligations arising from the ratification of the UN Convention against Corruption, meets an assumption of civil responsibility, as the offense is a factual assumption for reparation as a legal consequence from the commission of an offense (subjective responsibility). Furthermore, for reasons of social solidarity, there will be the obligation to repair if damage has been caused by persons under the jurisdiction of the perpetrator (objective responsibility).
- Recognition of the right to claim and the legal obligation to compensate. It is necessary to define the concept and the forms of reparation, including its range of protection (eg, legal and illegal facts and those related to the environment, health, education, development, security, etc.) that affect the community and whose viola-

tion harms the collective or diffuse interests.

- Determination of the authorities, organisations or persons with legal standing to make such applications and ownership for the compensation (theory of diffuse interests and active and passive legal standing – who can claim and against whom?). In terms of legal standing, the law can either determine the subject or widen the scope to allow anyone to protect the collective interests.
- A comprehensive and appropriate evidentiary means that allows for gauging and measuring the different manifestations of the damage caused. The verification of the existence of damage must be unquestioned, and it must eventually be observed by the judge through the different evidentiary means allowed in the legal system, in order to establish the 'truth' or certainty of the facts submitted to a court ruling. It must thus be ensured the widest evidentiary gathering, which is at the core of any legal system. The determination of social harm revolves around two central pillars: the verification of the existence of damage and quantification thereof once its existence is proven. The latter is perhaps the most complex issue to overcome in countries where there is already recognition of the concept of social damage – as it attempts to give a price or monetary value to a damage of immaterial or extra patrimonial nature, which by their characteristics are not economically measurable.
- Mechanisms for fixing and/or determining the economic quantification of collective involvement (the claim for damages) and the rules on attribution of liability. After verifying the existence of damage, it will be necessary to establish the amount for compensation. This aspect sows discord due to the lack of parameters and systems to help determine equally binding criteria for similar cases and, in relation to the amount of damage, to ensure full reparation. Compensation will depend on the model adopted in legislation, which has an impact chiefly in the evidence provided for making such determination. Furthermore, it is desirable to dispose 'on the forms of reparation' due to diverging positions in that regard. Notwithstanding, it will be a decision reserved for the courts. Arbitrary, symbolic or excessive reparations should be avoided. Thus, preference should be given to, in the first instance, the return of the assets to their condition before the damage occurred or, in its absence, to satisfy its value according to the esti-

mation of experts and, if not possible, to allow judges to set its value. Secondly, a determination for the reparation for material and immaterial damage and, finally, compensation for the damage caused should be ensured.

– Final destination and/or use of the sums or amounts recovered for the purposes of achieving an effective social benefit. While it may not always be possible to return things to their status quo ante, the use of such sums or amounts should at least aim to compensate the community, translating the damage caused into social work, seeking to reverse the negative effects of corruption.

Legal basis

Article 41 of the Constitution of the Republic of Costa Rica says:

> Everyone must receive reparation for injuries or damages to himself or his property, or moral interests, through recourse to the laws. Justice must be prompt, enforced, not denied, and in strict accordance with the laws.

This article of our constitution establishes an open clause for the reparation of damage and constitutionally ensures the duty to repair and the right to full compensation, embodying the principle of access to justice, becoming in turn a legal instrument that necessarily ensures the enjoyment and exercise of compensatory right.

Meanwhile, besides this constitutional right, the Article 1045 of the Constitution and the Civil Code establishes the general principle of liability, indicating that anyone that wilfully or negligently causes damage to another has the obligation to repair his damages. Also, the General Law on Public Administration regulates the responsibility of the state. This law recognises the solidarity of responsibility, the guilt *in eligendo* and *in vigilando* and develops other features of liability.

In Costa Rican law, 'social damage' has its genesis in Article 50 of the Constitution, which states:

> [...] Every person has the right to a healthy and ecologically balanced environment, being therefore entitled to denounce any acts that may infringe said right and claim redress for the damage caused. The State guarantees, defends and preserves that right. The Law establishes the appropriate responsibilities and penalties.

The Constitutional Court has recognised that Article 50 regulates the right of all Costa Ricans to live in a healthy environment. It further recognises that the environment should be corruption-free, with social peaceful coexistence, with an optimum welfare and, of course, with good management of public finances. Any violation to any of these contents makes compulsory the need to repair damage, because they are constitutionally guaranteed right.

Living in a corruption-free environment is a diffuse interest of all Costa Ricans. Thus, a guarantee is established to claim damages for affecting collective and individual interests relating to the right to a healthy and ecologically balanced environment.

The protection of shared assets is enshrined in the constitution, and their broad recognition of the Constitutional Court underlines the vital importance of the protection of such socially relevant rights and interests.

Diffuse interests

Diffuse interests are interests whose ownership belongs to groups of persons not formally organised but assembled from a specific social need, a physical characteristic, ethnicity, certain orientation, etc. In general, diffuse interests are those belonging to a plurality of persons, as members of society, linked by claims of enjoyment by each of them. Diffuse interests are part of the same prerogative and have a dual nature, individual or diffuse.

Our Constitutional Court has enumerated various rights that it describes as 'diffuse', such as the environment, cultural heritage, the defence of the territorial integrity and good public expenditure management, among others.[3] Moreover, the Constitutional Court stated that those shared assets transcend the traditionally recognised sphere of diffuse interests, as they relate in principle to issues affecting the national community and not to particular groups therein.

The right to a healthy environment is a broad concept equivalent to the aspiration to improve the living environment of human beings.

3 Decision 8239-01 of the Constitutional Court.

Thus it goes beyond the criteria for environmental preservation and is located within any area in which a person develops, be that in the family, the workplace or the place a person lives. Hence the Constitutional Court claimed that it is a transversal right, which crosses the entire legal system, modelling and reinterpreting its institutes.[4]

A healthy environment is synonymous with social welfare, encompassing the feeling of tangible and intangible satisfaction that is found in people and communities. Living in a healthy environment that is free of corruption and has good management of public funds is in the interest of all citizens.

Diffuse interests concern the existence of life in community. Therefore, the effects on diffuse interests constitute an alteration of welfare conditions that society should enjoy, focusing on the quality of life of citizens.

The set of rules of public order described above provides a framework of protection that guarantees absolute and effective protection of collective rights, and it is within this context that the concept of 'social damage' is framed and understood.

Article 38 of the Code of Criminal Procedure provides that 'the civil action may be brought by the Attorney General of the Republic, in the case of offenses involving collective or diffuse interests'.

This article gives the Attorney General's Office the exclusive power to intervene in criminal proceedings to bring civil action demanding financial compensation for social harm. This social damage is the same as 'collective moral damage' defined by doctrine, where the affected person no longer is a natural or legal person in its individuality, but rather a group or category that collectively and for the same global cause has its rights or interests of vital significance attacked; examples of this can be peace, tranquillity, individual liberty, physical integrity, honour and highest affections.

Although the concept of 'social damage' is in full evolution, Costa Rica has adopted it as a third type of damage, which exceeds the traditional conceptions of material and immaterial damage.

Because it is a harmful behaviour, social damage is perhaps best understood from the negative perspective of corrupt acts committed

4 Decision 2000-00041 of the Constitutional Court.

by public officials that break the faith of citizens in their public servants and in the quality of government services. Corruption also promotes a negative value: the undue advantage as an everyday, tolerated practice. This represents a major problem in modern society, as it causes the deterioration of ethical values, undermines the quality of life for residents and directly affects the effectiveness of the state. While what is meant by social damage is not specifically conceptualised, its meaning can be inferred through its antagonistic concept, 'social welfare'. Social welfare is understood as a set of feelings of satisfaction and intangible assets that produce a number of conditions in people and communities that affect the quality of these people and communities' lives that cannot be reduced only to the level of income. It also includes other important dimensions of human existence, such as health, education, services, infrastructure, housing, security, justice, environment, etc.

When the welfare conditions enjoyed by a society are impaired, the latter affects the 'diffuse interests', which in turn are reflected in the deterioration of the general welfare, thus producing social damage. Under this situation, corruption generates an imbalance in social welfare. Its consequences are social and political instability and the hindering of economic growth. It also produces damage to democracy, because, in the strict sense, democracy is a form of government in which the people take collective decisions through direct or indirect mechanisms that give legitimacy to representatives, and whose aim is to pursue the general welfare of the population in a context of freedom and equality. The illegitimate use of authority, through which a public official or an elected representative attributes to himself or herself extra powers or an undue advantage, is a transgression of democratic legality.

Corruption is therefore a term contrary to democracy, because it violates one of its basic premises that power is subject to the law. Corruption undermines the legitimacy of governments as it conflicts with the corrupt official's interests, the interests of society and the interests of the public administration. This triggers an imbalance between public authority and the state and civil society, which delegitimising government, democratic values and political equality.

It is known that corruption contributes to an increase in poverty, as it postpones the development of peoples, burdens the community with unfair costs, discredits authority and reduces collective confidence in democratic institutions. Public scepticism toward justice is translated, for example, in massive tax evasion. According to the 2001 Nyanga Declaration, corrupt leaders of poor countries, mainly in Africa, have taken between USD 20–40 billion and USD 500 billion in tax evasion,[5] which has the undeniable effect of creating an imbalance in the distribution of wealth and power. In addition, corruption teaches flawed processes that foster a pernicious culture of distorting reality by making illegitimate behaviours appear legitimate when they are not.

Duty to repair

The protection of collective assets and the recognition that they enjoy, as recognised by different regulatory bodies of the international community, are disputed when considering criminal offenses as conducts of reproach. Subject to repression by the state through the threat of punishment, the purpose of criminal law is to discipline or to punish criminal offenses as they attack the most cherished values and principles of a community. For its part, tort is a harmful behaviour not defined by criminal law. Its sanction is imposed on the perpetrator, who has the obligation to repair or to compensate the damage. Its purpose is thus restorative. In Costa Rica, the criminal and civil responsibility are not mutually exclusive, and both can be claimed in a single criminal proceeding.

The commission of a corruption-related offence, apart from the penalty imposed to the person found guilty of it, should also recognise a social damage that must be repaired or properly compensated. It is possible to declare civil liability, even in cases in which no criminal

5 For more information in this subject matter: 'Estudio de alcance mundial sobre la transferencia de fondos de origen ilícito, en especial de los derivados de actos de Corrupción'. Available at: www.unodc.org/pdf/crime/convention_corruption/session_4/12s.pdf, http://siteresources.worldbank.org/NEWS/Resources/Star-rep-full.pdf,

conviction is imposed. This is because the rules on attribution of liability attempt to re-establish the asset harmed by a harmful event, but it is subject to the criteria of guilt, a basic element of criminal liability.

It should not be forgotten that civil liability is atypical and that the duty to compensate is a consequence of the damage, not the crime. Unlawfulness is not an element of civil liability. Even liability without guilt is admissible (liability for legal acts – objective liability). In short, what matters is the existence of damage and its extent.[6]

The assumptions of civil liability differ from those of the criminal one. It is therefore incorrect to speak of civil liability as a criminal offense. The assumption of tort is damage, attributable to the party responsible for an entitlement, which may not necessarily be guilt.

As we have signalled, social damage is equated with the doctrine of 'collective moral damage', where the affected person is no longer a natural or legal person in its individuality, but rather a group or category that. For the same global cause, the group is collectively attacked in its rights or interests of vital significance, such as peace, tranquillity, individual liberty, physical integrity, honour and highest affections.

Collective moral damages can be understood as the decrease of mental and spiritual tranquillity that the community suffers as a whole, equivalent to damages to non-patrimonial collective interests caused by damages against an asset determined to be of common or collective nature. It consists of the harm to the asset itself, regardless of the patrimonial impact it may have, and bases itself on the fact that harm has been caused to a collective asset in its own existence or extent. The 'ownership' in the claim for damages could never be indi-

6 Cf. Rivero Sánchez, Juan Marcos. Responsabilidad Civil, op. cit., pp.68–71. This is the approach that has been held by the Court of Cassation in many of its decisions, especially after vote 481-98 (Llobet Rodríguez, Javier. El proceso penal en la jurisprudencia. San José, Editorial Jurídica Continental, T. I, 2001, pp. 201–202). On this matter, Juan Marcos Rivero Sánchez states: 'The fact that the act is not typical (in the sense of being expressly provided in law as a postulation for liability), does not necessarily lead to the conclusion that there is no liability, since, by definition, extracontractual civil responsibility is governed by the principle of lack of type' (Cf. Rivero Sánchez, Juan Marcos. Responsabilidad civil, p. 56). Agrega luego: 'From the perspective of civil law, in order for the duty to indemnify arise, it is important that a damage to a person who does not have to withstand it occurs' (Rivero Sánchez, Juan Marcos, op. cit., p. 62).

vidual (unjust enrichment) but rather exclusively collective or of the group, whereby the state is the supreme representative of the community.

The definition established by the COMJIB seems appropriate as it considers that social damage is 'the diminishment, impact, undermining, decrease or loss of social welfare (in the context of the right to live in a healthy environment) resulting from an act of corruption which an unreasonable number of individuals suffers from – not the State – by causing a material or immaterial condition to their collective interests and before which there is the duty to repair'.

Consequences in the application of the principle

The direct consequences of recognition of the concept of social damage are:

- Strengthening the social and democratic rule of law, by issuing judgments that recognize the concept of social damage and the duty of redress.
- Positioning, at the judicial level, the social damage caused by corruption and other behaviours that affect collective or diffuse interests as a result of judgements that declare and recognise or validate it.
- Acceptance with the objectives and contents established in international treaties on combating corruption.

The concept of social damage is a useful tool to curb the commission of corrupt practices in the corporate world, for three reasons:

- It validates the application of the procedural rule governing the liability of companies (jointly and severally liable with the perpetrators of the offense).
- It reduces the conception of impunity, as cases where private companies are sentenced to cancel important sums of money on account of the social damage caused (it highlights the need to overcome the aphorism 'societas delinquere non potest').

- It produces a deterrent effect in that the negative effects of corruption are perceived by businesses or corporations sentenced to cancel monies in respect of social damage, such as the reputational risk for the legal person, which is reflected in the reduction in its income, resignation of valuable staff and loss of credibility. It also affects their patrimony, due to the payment of compensation and the negative impact in its share prices.

If companies are part of the problem, they must also be part of the solution. In many cases it would be wrong to blame only corrupt public officials. It should not be forgotten that, at least in bribery transactions, for every corrupt public official there is a private corruptor, be it an individual or a company.

Proposed action

After presenting the legal and practical peculiarities of the concept of social damage and its various impacts, we look at the dimension of the concept itself. It should therefore be recognised first that corruption causes social damage, to then give the latter the extent necessary to enable a comprehensive treatment that contributes to effective compensation and quantification of the effects of corruption, and to identify and determine the subjects with legal standing to claim and redress. It is important to consider the possibility of developing a model type law to the effect that the principle of social damage is incorporated and recognised in international conventions. Perhaps the biggest challenge will be to legislate internally in each country around the theme that social damage is caused by corruption and the correlative duty to repair or compensate for it.

As noted, it is important to emphasise that the concept of social damage is not synonymous with asset recovery. Social damage is a tool that seeks to eliminate the consequences of corruption, both in their remuneration and compensation effects, as well as in its deterrent effect. These contribute to its preventive character and ensures entities and persons, which have been harmed as a result of an act of corruption, the right to take legal action against those responsible for that harm and obtain pecuniary compensation.

It is essential to create common awareness and to join forces. Archbishop Oscar Rodriguez Maradiaga claimed that the corruption of truth and the corruption of power are not always seen. Closing one's eyes to corruption is a mechanism used by people who believe they are honest, but who are actually ignoring injustice. The statue of Justice is blindfolded, however, injustice also closes her eyes. In times of crisis it is necessary that Justice remove her blindfold in order to look the perpetrators in the eye. It is necessary for Justice to see.

OSCAR SOLORZANO AND PEDRO GOMES PEREIRA

The Swiss plea-bargaining practice and asset recovery: The Alstom case

Negotiated resolutions agreements (NRA) concluded in the context of plea-bargaining procedures are efficient legal tools in complex cases of foreign bribery involving multinational enterprises (MNE). The positive effects of their implementation in terms of enforcing anti-bribery regulations can be seen in the large number of convictions, particularly in the Organisation for Economic Co-operation and Development (OECD) countries.[1]

Plea-bargaining procedures do not by definition allow for victim participation. Hence, jurisdictions have been solving foreign corruption cases mostly between national enforcement authorities and offenders. However, upon closer inspection there may not be legal or moral justification for a jurisdiction to enforce anti-bribery regulations in a transnational context thereby excluding from the proceedings the jurisdictions affected by the acts of corruption. It is particularly questionable when large amounts of monies are confiscated as a result of such enforcement and when the affected States are likely to assert claims arising from the harm they have suffered.

The lack of interest of law enforcement authorities in enforcing anti-bribery regulations may be partly explained by the fact that enforcing them is perceived to be an internal matter. Consequently, the focus is placed on domestic anti-bribery laws. Restorative justice promoting compensation for foreign victims is thus not perceived as a

1 The Comparative Table of Enforcement Data collected from the 39 Parties at the OECD Anti-Bribery Convention shows only one criminal conviction in Switzerland (2012) as opposed to, for instance, the 29 plea agreements in the US (+ 48DPAs/NPAs agreements), 10 in Italy, including plea agreements, and 21 in Germany (+67 agreed sanctions). Available at: www.oecd.org/daf/anti bribery/WorkingGrouponBribery_2012EnforcementData.pdf (13.6.13).

priority. In fact, the general assumption that corruption is a victimless crime is stronger in such cases than, for instance, in a case relating to a politically exposed person (PEP) who looted public funds. As a result, this may, from a standpoint of asset repatriation, prove detrimental to the commitments with the international community.

The NRA concluded with Alstom in Switzerland, which is perceived by many to be an important milestone in the fight against corruption, provides an opportunity to explore the position of foreign victim States within plea-bargaining procedures.

This chapter, taking into consideration the Swiss legal framework, will attempt to: [i] review the procedural rights of the foreign affected jurisdiction in comparison to a similar situation within an ordinary criminal proceeding; [ii] discuss the compatibility of the outcome of NRAs with the obligation of asset repatriation; and [iii] strive to create a common understanding of existing legal avenues available to jurisdictions seeking compensation while stressing practical and procedural impediments the jurisdictions may encounter in their endeavour.

Swiss plea-bargaining in foreign bribery cases: A new issue

General remarks

Swiss enforcement authorities have long advocated for the adoption of innovative legal tools to fight offences related to economic crime, particularly cross-border corruption where difficulties linked to a lack of evidence are commonplace. Traditionally, however, policymakers have been reticent to adopt such instruments. Their objections relate to insufficient protection of the procedural rights of the accused and those of victims of the criminal offences.[2]

2 Kuhn A., La procédure pénale suisse selon le CPP unifié, RDS (128) 2009 II, p. 125–184, 165 et seq.; Bommer F., Abgekürztes Verfahren und Plea Bargaining im Vergleich, RDS (128) 2009 II, p. 5–124; Schwarzenegger C., Kommentar zur schweizerischen Strafprozessordung (StPO), Zurich 2010, Art. 358 N 1 et seq.;

It was not until the entry into force of the federal Code of Criminal Procedure (SCCP) in 2011[3] that ground-breaking legal tools to fight economic crime were introduced in Switzerland.[4] The first Swiss NRA regarding foreign bribery was concluded with two companies of the Alstom Group. While still unique, the use of this procedure in complex cross-border cases of foreign bribery is likely to become a trend in Switzerland.[5]

Summary punishment order (SPO)

The SPO is a procedural mechanism whereby the prosecution and the accused seek to settle the case. This implies a 'decision of procedure' that allows the accused, who accepts responsibility for the offence in the preliminary proceedings,[6] to avoid a trial by accepting an 'offer' made by the prosecution.

Kuhn A. / Perrier C., Quelques points problématiques du Code de procédure pénale suisse, in Jusletter, 22 septembre 2008; Breguet A., La procédure simplifiée dans le CPP: un réel progrès?, in Jusletter, 16 march 2009; Schmid N., Handbuch des schweizerischen Strafprozessrecht, Zurich 2009, p. 628 et seq.

3 Swiss Federal Code of Procedure of 5 October 2007, SR 312.0. These mechanisms were available in some cantons before the entry into force of the SCCP, cf. The Swiss Federal Council's Message on the unification of Criminal Procedural Law, of 21 December 2005, FF 2006 1057, p. 1279 (Hereinafter: Message).

4 Art. 352 SCCP. In practice, however, despite this fact, the SPO has been extensively used in some cantons before the entry into force of the SCCP; cf. Dubs H., Strafbefehl – Möglichkeiten und Grenzen eines vereinfachten Strafverfahrens, in Mélanges Rehberg, p. 141.

5 See Federal Prosecutor's Office, Annual Report (2011), p. 23.

6 The preliminary proceedings are the pre-tribunal phase of the Swiss criminal procedure. It is conducted by the Prosecutor's Office and other investigative bodies (police). At the end of the preliminary proceedings, the prosecutor pronounces whether he or she will go forward with indictment (if there is enough evidence to continue the criminal prosecution) or whether the prosecution will abandon the preliminary proceedings (Art. 319 SCCP). While carrying out the investigation, the prosecutor may conclude a case out-of-court (SPO) if, besides the acceptance of the facts by the accused, the prosecutor considers a 'minor' penalty may be appropriate to conclude the case, namely [a] a fine; [b] a monetary penalty of no more than 180 daily penalty units; [c] community service of no more than 720 hours; [d] a custodial sentence of no more than 6 months (Art. 352 SCCP).

The accused has the right to oppose the offer made by the prosecution. Under these circumstances, the case is transferred to a regular court. Therefore, unless a valid rejection is filed, the SPO becomes definitive and has the same effects of an enforceable judgment.[7]

This procedure is implemented out-of-court without the jurisdictional control of a court, and it relies on the need to accelerate the criminal proceeding regarding minor offences.[8] Unlike administrative or civil out-of-court agreements, the SPO has a criminal law nature. Because of this, serious concerns have been raised with regard to its compatibility with the procedural rights granted to victims in criminal trials. While the SPO stems from the logic of procedural efficiency, its compatibility with the jurisprudence of the ECtHR[9] and other international instruments granting victim's rights within criminal proceedings is doubtful.[10]

In the context of cross-border corruption involving MNEs and foreign pubic officials, the competence for the investigation and the prosecution of the case belongs to the Federal Prosecutors' Office (FPO).[11] Therefore, the federal prosecutor alone is competent to make the 'offer' to the bribe-giver company.

In addition to the deficiencies regarding the procedural rights of the accused, the SPO raises several questions vis-à-vis the procedural rights of the victims of the corruption-related offences, particularly regarding the possibility to assert civil claims within criminal proceedings. Ordinary criminal proceedings provide for relatively large pro-

7 Art. 354 sec. 3 SCCP; See also, the Federal Tribunal Decision (FTD) 92 IV 161.

8 Message (note 3), p. 1272.

9 Counsel of Europe, European Convention on Human Rights and Fundamental Freedoms of 1950, RS 0.101.

10 See art. 5 § 1(a) and 6 § 1 of the ECHR requiring a competent and independent tribunal to rule in criminal proceedings. However, due to the fact that the accused has the legal right to reject the SPO, the jurisprudence of the Federal Tribunal (FTD 112 Ia 290 c. 5d) and part of the Swiss doctrine admits its compatibility with the jurisprudence of the European court of Human Rights (ECtHR), see for instance: Donatsch A., Der Strafbefehl sowie ähnliche Verfahrenserledigungen mit Einsprachemöglichkeit, insbesondere aus dem Gesichtswinkel von Art. 6 EMRK, ZStrR 112 (1994), p. 322 et seq.; Piquerez G., Traité de procédure pénale Suisse, N 1152. For further details, see Commentaire Romand du Code de procedure Pénale (Hereinafter: CR CPP-Author) CR CPP-Gilleron/Killias, art. 352 CPP N 22 et seq.

11 See art. 24 SCCP; FTD 130 IV 68, p. 71.

cedural rights to victims,[12] who can declare their intention to participate as private claimants[13] in order to seek compensation. In the SPO, however, victim rights are severely limited since the accused and the prosecution alone are admitted to the proceedings.

Unlike ordinary proceedings,[14] victims do not have a right to be heard during the proceedings leading to the conclusion of a NRA.[15] Thus, victims are not able to, for example, actively participate in procedural acts, make submissions regarding civil claims to the director of proceedings and access the record of the proceedings.[16]

Unlike the accused, victims of bribery are not granted the right to oppose to the SPO. They also do not have the right to appeal, as the SPO is not a judgement but a 'decision of procedure'. The reasons put forward for this is that a SPO does not lead to an acquittal of the accused[17] and that a refusal of the victim's civil claims would result in transferring them to the civil judge.[18] For foreign victims, transferring claims arising from the criminal offense to a civil judge would further result in a denial of justice or procedural unfairness, especially as a consequence of the opaque mechanisms implemented by the SPO. The right of the victim to lodge an opposition would therefore ensure the control of the FPO's activity and better ensure individual rights of the

12 See art. 104 et seq. SCCP.

13 See infra IV.2 (p.14).

14 See art. 107 SCCP.

15 This procedural shortcoming exists also vis-à-vis the accused, because, in general, the prosecutor acts proprio motu without any kind of participation. Nevertheless, it is generally admitted that this violation can be subsequently 'healed' since, as a consequence of the opposition to the SPO, the case is transferred to a regular tribunal.

16 See art. 109 Sec. 1 SCCP. However, the latter can be limited in order to preserve the rights of the offender given the nature of the victim (i.e. the State) whose powers to act against the offenders are more extensive than any other ordinary private claimant. As a consequence, the State must follow MLA procedures to fully access the information related to the case.

17 CR CPP-Gilleron/Killias, art. 353 CPP N 5.

18 Art. 353 sec. 2 SCCP. See also CR CPP-Gillieron/Killias, art. 352 CPP N 28. This wouldn't be the case within the ordinary criminal proceeding whereby the judge must, in principle, rule on the civil claims of the victim.

participants.[19] It should be maintained as long as the victim can justify a legal interest[20] to the modification of the SPO.[21]

A case concluded under the SPO procedure, by definition, leads to a verdict without contradictory debates. In this sense, public scrutiny of the administration of justice is unlikely. Similarly, the SPO procedure provides that a communication to the parties must be made insofar as they have the right to appeal the decision before a criminal court.[22] Therefore, apart from the prosecution, only the accused is entitled to receive such a communication. As a result, the SPO procedure would be unknown to any 'affected person' and the victim herself, unless a complaint by the victim initiated the FPO investigation.

The obligation to prosecute is mitigated by the principle of opportunity whereby the prosecutor, using discretionary powers, determines whether or not to initiate a prosecution.[23] This exception is closely related to the protection of the rights of victims in ordinary proceedings,[24] particularly those linked to the compensation of damages.[25] In the context of the SPO this protection is weakened due to the fact that victims' participation is either limited or non-existent. The SPO must thus be regarded as an exception to the exception to the general rule[26] that may result in severe transgressions of the public interest regarding

19 Schmid N., StPO Praxiskommentar, StGB 354 N 6; CR CPP-Gillieron/Killias, art. 354 CPP N 3 et seq.

20 For an example regarding the victim's right to lodge an opposition in the former law at the cantonal level, cf. FTD 131 IV 145. After the entry into force of the SCCP, the FT has ruled out that a private claimant can lodge an opposition based on art. 354 (b) 'other concerned persons' of the SPO. In this case, the private claimant was allowed to appeal the SPO since the prosecutor's characterisation of the underlying offence had an impact on the victim's civil claims, cf. FTD 6B_79/2012 of 13 August 2012.

21 Schmid N., Schweizerische Strafprozessordnung, Praxiskommentar, N 6 Art. 354 StPO; Jeanneret Y., L'ordonnance pénale et la procédure simplifiée selon le CPP, in Procédure pénale suisse, Neuchâtel 2010, p. 94–95; BSK StPO-Riklin, art. 354 StPO N 6 and 11; Schwarzenegger C., Kommentar zur StPO, in Donatsch/Hansjakob/Lieber (éd.), N 5 ad art. 354 StPO.

22 Art. 353 sec. 3 SCCP.

23 Art. 8 sec. 1 SCCP; art. 52 SCC.

24 Art. 8 sec. 2 SCCP.

25 CR CPP-Roth, art. 8 CPP N 20; art. 53 (b) SCC.

26 Message (note 3), p. 1107.

the prosecution of criminal offenses, leading to the 'privatisation' of the criminal action.[27]

The SPO in practice: The Alstom case

This case illustrates what has been said in the previous section regarding the SPO. In this section, a description of the facts leading to the SPO will be given along with succinct comments regarding the outcome of the case in light of the principle of asset repatriation. Finally, we will table some ideas concerning the procedural avenues that may be open to foreign victim States seeking compensation.

Alstom Network Schweiz AG[28]

The FPO's investigation in this case established that bribes had been paid through intermediaries to foreign public officials on behalf of the Alstom Group for the attribution of contracts in Latvia, Tunisia and Malaysia. In this corruption scheme Alstom Network Schweiz AG, the Swiss branch of the group, was responsible for transferring the funds used to make the unlawful payments.

In November 2011, only a few months after the SCCP entered into force, the FPO concluded the case through a SPO[29] carried out in summary proceedings. Under the terms of the agreement the company admitted to all the allegations and the FPO agreed not to bring charges against the company.

27 Schmid N., Schweizerische Strafprozessordnung, Praxiskommentar, N 5 Art. 8 StPO.

28 Alstom Network Schweiz AG is an intra-group compliance services provider whose purpose was to ensure that third-party intermediaries used by various European Alstom affiliates conformed to internal compliance rules and to transfer payments to these third-party intermediaries via its bank accounts.

29 Available at: www.star.worldbank.org/corruption-cases/sites/corruptioncases/files/Alstom_Summary_Punishment_Order_Nov_22_2011.pdf. (EAII.04.0325-LEN).

Alstom Network Schweiz AG was found guilty of corporate criminal liability (article 102 section 2 SCC) and bribery of foreign public officials (article 322^{septies} SCC). The FPO considered, in fact, that the company failed to take all necessary and reasonable organisational precautions to prevent bribery of foreign public officials. As a result, the Swiss subsidiary was ordered to pay a fine of CHF 2.5 million and a compensatory claim[30] of CHF 36.4 million that was estimated on the basis of the operating profit margin generated during the relevant periods for the three projects (Latvia, Tunisia and Malaysia).[31]

Alstom SA

The investigation initiated against the French-based parent company shows the multijurisdictional anticorruption enforcement climate facing companies with a global presence.[32] Acknowledging that the parent company had great control over its subsidiary, Swiss authorities sentenced the French-based parent company on charges of corporate criminal liability (article 102 SCC) and bribery of foreign public officials (article 322^{septies} SCC), because they considered that Alstom SA had failed to take sufficient action to prevent the bribery of foreign officials within the Swiss branch's business operations. Applying the territorial principle of ubiquity,[33] according to which the lack of organisation of Alstom SA had produced a result in Switzerland, the Swiss authorities deemed to have jurisdiction over the matter.[34] The Swiss

30 See art. 71 sec. 1 of the Swiss criminal code (SCC) of 21 December 1937, SR 311.0: 'If the assets subject to forfeiture are no longer available, the court may uphold a claim for compensation by the State in respect of a sum of equivalent value […]'.

31 EAII.04.0325-LEN § 19, p. 9.

32 For more details, see Federal Prosecutor's Office, Annual Report (2012), p. 19.

33 Art. 8 sec. 1 SCC: 'A felony or misdemeanour shall be considered to be committed at the place where the person concerned commits it or unlawfully omits to act, and at the place where the offence has taken effect'. For a detailed assessment of this provision in cases related to cross boarder corruption, cf. Cassani U., Grenzüberschreitende Korruption – Internationale Zuständigkeit der schweizerischen Strafjustiz, Europa Institut Zürich, Vol. 110, 2010.

34 For further details on this issue, see Lenz S/ Mäder W., Grenzüberschreitende Korruption: Die Anwendbarkeit des schweizerischen Unternehmensstrafrechts aus Sicht der Praktiker, forumpoenale 1/2013, p. 33 et seq.

FPO's approach appeared to reflect that the French-based parent company, because of its control over the group, was liable for the acts of the Swiss branch of the company and had failed to take sufficient action to prevent bribery of foreign officials.

Applying its discretionary powers,[35] the FPO ordered the abandonment of the proceedings since the French-based parent company had made every reasonable effort to right the wrong it caused.[36] This encompassed: [i] reinforcing the compliance function within Alstom Group; [ii] training of staff; [iii] obtaining an independent certification of Alstom Group's internal controls and procedures; [iv] punishing personnel implicated in the corruption offenses; [v] disbursing on a voluntary basis USD 1 million to the International Committee of the Red Cross (ICRC) for its projects in the countries whose officials were bribed.

Unlike the Alstom Network Schweiz AG case, this case was not settled through a SPO procedure. Moreover, neither a fine nor a disgorgement of profits was ordered to be paid. The NRA granting the abandonment of the proceedings took place solely under the assumption that the company had reasonably repaired the damage it had caused. It is noteworthy that the USD 1 million was paid on a voluntary basis.

Principle of repatriation of assets

General remarks

Switzerland is the leading jurisdiction when it comes to the restitution of corruption-related assets. In fact, Switzerland has returned far more money to affected jurisdictions than any other financial centre,

35 See supra II.2.
36 Cf. art. 319 SCCP *cum* art. 53 SCC.

amounting to a total of CHF 1.7 billion. This is, according to the World Bank's statistics, half of all the assets recovered globally.[37]

It appears that Swiss authorities draw a clear line between foreign bribery against companies and other forms of corruption when it comes to the application of enforcement strategies. While in other corruption cases foreign affected jurisdictions enjoy large procedural rights with a view to recover ill-gotten assets, in the SPO against Alstom the foreign jurisdiction was left out since the enforcement method follows a domestic-centred logic. Still, some domestic laws, particularly article 322^{septies} SCC, also protect the foreign administration and are intended to overcome the shortfalls within criminal proceedings foreign States may encounter.[38]

The question arises as how to protect the patrimonial interests of victims in summary proceedings such as the SPO, especially when large sums of money are confiscated as a result of the enforcement of such legislations. To date it appears that the political will with regard to the restitution of proceeds or instrumentalities confiscated is ambiguous and seemingly no general debate has been drawn to this issue.

One might wonder whether there is a valid justification to bridge a disparity in treatment of bribery and other types corruption with regard to asset repatriation. A prima facie analysis suggests that the United Nations Convention against Corruption (UNCAC) does not make such a distinction. The offence of active bribery of foreign public officials is a mandatory offence under UNCAC.[39] Hence, the obligation of repatriation may exist if the conditions required in article 57(3)(b) UNCAC are met – including: [i] if the proceeds recovered are originated in an offense covered by the Convention; [ii] if the confiscation has been made according to relevant provisions of the UNCAC; [iii] if the victim country can demonstrate prior ownership or alternatively a damage.

37 Swiss policy on the restitution of illicit assets: myths and facts, Speech by Ambassador Valentin Zellweger, Head of the Directorate of Public International Law Federal Department of Foreign Affairs, Geneva Press Club, 5 May 2010, p. 2.

38 Jositsch D., Das Schweizerische Korruptionsstrafrecht, p. 403; Perrin B., La répression de la corruption d'agents publics étrangers, p. 97.

39 UNCAC Legislative Guide, p. 66 et seq. (art. 16 UNCAC).

The compensatory claim of CHF 36.4 million ordered in the Alstom case is a form of confiscation[40] used to forfeit proceeds or other instrumentalities resulting from an offense when the proceeds are no longer available.[41] The FPO most likely applied the Federal Tribunal (FT) case law ruling that the benefits obtained by the active briber company can be confiscated as long as a link, even indirect but adequate, is established between the offence and the derived benefits.[42]

Article 57(3)(b) UNCAC states that the confiscation must be carried out in the context of mutual legal assistance (pursuant to a request under article 55 UNCAC).[43] In the context of foreign bribery, this requirement seems to point out the situation whereby a 'passive' briber (the foreign public official) deposits the bribe received in a financial institution of the recipient State.

Two things must be said in this regard. UNCAC is far-reaching with regards to asset repatriation, and it encourages State Parties to overcome procedural impediments to achieve the fundamental principle of repatriation.[44] In addition, in the context of SPO, the stringent application of this requirement seems contrary to the principle of proportionality, especially given the fact that MLA requests under article 55 UNCAC presupposes that the affected jurisdiction knows that assets resulting from corruption offenses against its interests are likely to be confiscated. As it has been shown, the SPO procedure is particularly opaque in this regard.

40 Art. 69 to 73 SCC.

41 This procedure allows the forfeit of proceeds and instrumentalities related to a criminal behaviour by operating an abstract calculation. Like the other types of confiscation in the SCC, it demands the prosecution authorities take into account the restitution of the confiscated assets to the affected persons of the offense (art. 73 SCC) and is directed against all the patrimony of the wrongdoer.

42 FTD 137 IV 79, c. 3.2, p. 81; see also Perrin B., La répression de la corruption d'agents publics étrangers, p. 272 et seq.; Jositsch D., (note 38), p. 425; Bertossa B., Confiscation et corruption (in toto).

43 See art. 57 § 3 (b). It is worth noting that the obligation of restitution under UNCAC was conceive primarily to be applied in the context of embezzlement of public funds, where this type of cooperation is likely to be indispensable.

44 The restitution of the assets could also be made by means of the procedure implemented in article 57 § 3 (c) UNCAC (all other cases), according to which the State enforcing anti-bribery regulations and forfeiting the proceeds must give priority consideration to, among others, compensate the victims of the crime.

Without going into too much detail about the specific approaches an affected jurisdiction may undertake to prove damages, suffice it to say that focus is placed on existing avenues so the affected jurisdictions may play a part in the proceedings with a view to seeking compensation.

Is bribery likely to cause damage to a foreign jurisdiction?

Under Swiss law, the object of protection of corruption offenses is the citizens' trust in the objectivity and impartiality of the activity of the administration.[45] This is commonly understood as a collective object of protection.[46] In recent case law, however, the Federal Criminal Court (FCC)[47] has deemed that a State can suffer damages as a result of the commission of acts of corruption by its public officials.[48]

When it comes to bribery perpetrated by companies, however, the situation remains uncertain. In an obiter dictum of its 2013 decision,[49] the FCC envisaged that States can suffer damages as a result of the offense of active bribery perpetrated by companies, but it ultimately let the question go unanswered.[50] The decision to admit Tunisia as a private claimant within the ordinary criminal proceedings seems to consider that the offenses having taken place in the context of kleptocratic regimes are likely to be disjointed.[51] On one hand, what happened in Tunisia in the context of the so-called 'Arab Spring' seems enough to consider an alleged damage to the State. In the same factual background, however, the FCC suggests that there would be good grounds for doubting that the corruption offense involving the Tunisi-

45 FTD 117 IV, c. 4a p. 288.
46 Jositsch D., (note 38), p. 403.
47 Federal Criminal Court Decision (FCCD) of 20 March 2012 (BB.2011.130) (Tunisia); FCCD of 30 April 2012 (BB.2011.107) (Egypt).
48 FCCD of 18 September 2008 and 18 May 2009 (Brazil) and (note 47). Following this interpretation, the Federal Criminal Court has 'expanded' the object of protection of the legal provision in order to encompass the patrimonial and individual interest of the affected State.
49 FCCD of 22 January 2013 (BB. 2012.101).
50 *Ibid.* c. 2.3.b.
51 Which supposes the perpetration of all kind of offenses including foreign bribery, cf. *Ibid.* c. 2.2.

an public official and the company (Alstom) can justify a claim of the State for damages. This hesitant approach does not take into account the fact that money laundering and foreign bribery investigations regarding Tunisian public officials, for which the Tunisian republic was granted status of private claimant to prove its damage, was, at least to some extent, initiated following discovery of the underlying facts of the Alstom case in 2009.[52]

In summary, even if it may appear impracticable to some, the States affected by the acts of corruption perpetrated by MNEs and involving their public officials should be granted the possibility to prove damages within domestic summary proceedings enforcing anti-bribery laws in the recipient countries. From this perspective, the SCCP provides three different but closely related notions that may allow affected jurisdictions to participate in the proceedings with the goal of seeking compensation, namely [a] the victim (strictu sensu),[53] [b] the person suffering harm[54] and [c] the private claimant.[55] Whereas the victim is always a natural person,[56] natural or legal persons suffering harm and the private claimant are closely related – the latter being a procedural option to assert civil claims.

The category of persons suffering harm refers to a person whose legally protected individual rights have been violated as a consequence of the commission of an offence. Hence, a prerequisite is that the specific provision, in the case of foreign bribery article 322^{septies} SCC, aims to protect the rights of the affected jurisdiction. As we have seen, this is no longer an impediment under Swiss law.[57]

A private claimant is a person suffering harm who expressly declares[58] the intention to participate in the criminal proceedings as a criminal or civil claimant.[59] The granting of this status opens an effective avenue for affected foreign States to assert civil claims within

52 FPO's office procedure (ref. SV.11.0007, 19 January 2011).
53 Art. 116 SCCP.
54 Art. 115 SCCP.
55 Art. 118–121 SCCP.
56 CR CPP-Guy-Ecabert, art. 116 CPP N 6.
57 See supra IV.2.
58 CPP CR-Jeandin/Matz, art. 119 N 9.
59 Art. 118 SCCP; Message (note 3), p. 1150.

Swiss domestic proceedings. For this to happen the foreign State has the obligation to demonstrate that the corruption offense has caused patrimonial damage and that a causal link between the offense and the damage exists. It is worth noting that the recognition of the private claimant status is a preliminary decision that does not rule out on the merit of the case. Therefore, the damage and the causal link have to be proven only in principle (in all likelihood).[60]

In the context of money laundering of embezzled public funds, the FCC has frequently granted the status of private claimant to foreign States in order to prove their damages within the Swiss criminal proceedings. Here, the laundered assets must originate from a criminal offense against the jurisdiction in question.[61] This is particularly the case in acts of corruption having a direct impact in the financial interest of the State.[62] Although this approach is regularly and widely used in the context of other cross-border corruption offenses, it will ultimately be a question of whether or not Swiss authorities create mechanisms of participation for affected States within criminal SPO procedures, subsequently developing a consistent approach with regards to Switzerland's international commitments towards asset repatriation.

Conclusions and the path forward

Switzerland has no interest in harbouring assets of criminal origin within its borders. Subsequently, it has been seeking more proactive and innovative solutions to ensure that proceeds and instrumentalities of crime are restituted to their rightful owners. By leading the efforts in the restitution of assets, Switzerland has also created more possibilities for restraining assets for future repatriation.

When the talk turns to bribery involving MNEs, however, the assessment of the first case appears ambivalent to say the least. Although it would, perhaps, be inappropriate to refer to the involvement

60 FTD 6B_908/2009 c. 2.3.2 (3 Novembre 2010 ; FCCD of 20 mars 2012, c. 2.3.1.

61 FTD 129 IV 322 c. 2.2.4.

62 FTD 6B_908/2009 c. 2.3.2 (3 Novembre 2010).

of victim States in these proceedings as the asset recovery process strictu sensu, the outcome in terms of retributive justice vis-à-vis victim jurisdiction must be considered equivalent. The UNCAC foresees specific avenues for this to happen, and it provides for several solutions to overcome the procedural impediments that may arise in these cases. In this sense, if the international community has as a whole agreed that corruption is not a victimless crime, then jurisdictions that have been victim of foreign bribery should be given both legal standing and the opportunity to present the harm they suffered in any proceedings. In fact, compensating victims must be a constant concern of crime policy, on par with the penal treatment of offenders.

Questions remain on how the harm should be evaluated. The conceptual approach intended to do so is identical whether we face a case involving the supply or the demand side of bribery. As we have shown, the possibility to present and evaluate the harm victim States have suffered is fully operational for the latter. We believe that there is not a valid justification to operate such a distinction, especially since the duty of asset repatriation does not include such a distinction under the UNCAC. Despite this, we are fully aware of the paradigm shift it may require and the legal barriers practitioners are likely to encounter to achieve this goal. In this sense, Switzerland's experiences in the last 30 years in relation to the asset recovery process have shown a need to think outside the box, so that innovation and dynamism pave the way for an appropriate resolution of cases relating to the restitution of assets and the compensation of victims of corruption-related offenses.

NURIA GARCÍA SANZ AND MANUEL OLLÉ SESÉ [1]

Political corruption and human rights in Equatorial Guinea

Equatorial Guinea is among the major oil producing countries in Sub-Saharan Africa, and it has the consequent economic growth. But despite the income generated from the exploitation of this resource, over half the population lives in extreme poverty and without access to drinking water. A high percentage of children suffer from malnutrition, and public spending on education and health care are very low. In contrast, President Theodore Obiang is one of the wealthiest heads of state in the world.

This situation is possible because in Equatorial Guinea President Theodore Obiang and members of his government control the most valuable resources in the country. The president has holdings that including majority stakes in construction, oil, natural gas and communication companies. His eldest son, Theodore Nguema Obiang, controls the exploration and exports of wood, and the president's brother controls the country's security services. From the beginning of the exploration for oil and gas, foreign American companies and their subsidiaries have acted as partners of President Obiang and the companies he controls. There is therefore a clear conflict between the pub-

1 The Asociación Pró Derechos Humanos de España (ADPHE) would like to thank the Basel Institute for Governance for the invitation to write for such an interesting publication. It is a great opportunity to share our experience on Equatorial Guinea with other experts involved in this publication and all its readers. In this article we discuss the political corruption in Equatorial Guinea, and the criminal investigation being carried out by a Spanish court for money laundering arising from corruption in that country.
Hopefully, citizens from Equatorial Guinea will soon see the triumph of democracy and respect for human rights and fundamental freedoms prevail over oppression and inequality.

lic interest and the personal business interests of the members of the governing elite.

Not only do the members of the government hoard the proceeds from natural resources, but Equatorial Guinea also charges extremely low (between 13–20 percent) fees to oil and gas corporations for the rights to explore the country's natural resources. In countries with similar conditions as Equatorial Guinea, oil and gas corporations pay fees of between 45–90 percent. Because members of government are shareholders in these corporations, they are the main beneficiaries of the low fees for foreign oil contracts in production sharing.

Moreover, there is no external control over the actions of the government, which further contributes to the appropriation of natural resources by the rulers and consequently harms the citizens and violates their human rights.

Between 1995 and 2004 the government of Equatorial Guinea opened over 50 bank accounts at Riggs Bank in Washington, DC. These were not only institutional accounts but also personal accounts for government officials and their families. By 2003 they were the main clients of the bank, with a turnover amounting to an estimated USD 700 million.

The Permanent Subcommittee on Investigations of the US Senate investigated these bank accounts and issued a report on 15 July 2004. It found that Riggs Bank had opened accounts in the name of the president of Equatorial Guinea, his wife and other relatives, all of whom had deposited over USD 13 million in cash with few questions asked. Additionally, Riggs Bank helped the president and his eldest son create shell companies, including an entertainment company that eventually had a balance of more than USD 12 million. In short, the US Senate investigation revealed information that questioned the legality of the origin of the funds deposited in the Obiang bank accounts.

Among the institutional accounts held at Riggs Bank, one belonged to the Treasury of Equatorial Guinea. In this account, US oil companies deposited payments for the exploration of crude oil in the country. But in this and in other accounts of the State of Equatorial Guinea, the oil companies also deposited funds for services that held no relation to the oil industry, such as money for scholarships for students from Equatorial Guinea to study in the United States or payments for expenses of diplomatic property. The companies also made payments to the personal accounts of members of the government.

The US Senate discovered that Riggs Bank had authorised wire transfers in excess of USD 35 million from the account belonging to the Treasury of Equatorial Guinea to the accounts of two companies in Spain and Luxembourg. Because of bank secrecy provisions in the laws of these two countries, the financial institutions that handled the funds refused to provide information regarding the beneficial ownership of the companies that had received the funds. Later, President Obiang also refused to provide this information. He stated merely that the signatories of the accounts had duly authorized the transfers. The Subcommittee on Investigations of the US Senate expressed it had reason to believe that at least one of the two companies could be wholly or partially owned by the president of Equatorial Guinea.

The US Senate concluded that Riggs Bank ignored indications that the president and other senior officials of the government of Equatorial Guinea were managing funds obtained through corrupt practices abroad. The bank allowed suspicious transactions to be carried out and did not inform the competent authorities. Riggs Bank could not explain its actions, and it finally closed the accounts of Equatorial Guinea in 2004.

The negligence of Riggs Bank in the management of the funds from Equatorial Guinea was evident again in 2006 when the manager of the Equatorial Guinean accounts was found guilty and convicted of bank fraud and money laundering (US Judgment against Simon P. Kareri, Case No.05-0212-01).

Between June 2000 and December 2003, Riggs Bank transferred from the Equatorial Guinean accounts to an account in Madrid a total of USD 26.5 million. Although neither the bank in Madrid nor President Obiang provided information on the company receiving the funds, it was soon discovered to be a company with headquarters in Panama that had been incorporated in 1998 and whose purpose was the provision of shipping services. One of the representatives of this company had a longstanding relationship with the government of Equatorial Guinea as a former diplomat to the country.

The Money Laundering Prevention Service of the Bank of Spain (Servicio de Prevención de Blanqueo de Capitales or SEPBLAC) investigated these transactions in 2003 and concluded that a fraction of the USD 26.5 million had been transferred to the provision of shipping services. Consequently, there were large amounts of funds transferred that held no relation to the purpose of that shipping company. In other cases, the reason for the transaction could not be determined. Also, the Panamanian company did not develop any kind of commercial activity in Spain. The main purpose of the bank account in Spain therefore was to receive the public funds of Equatorial Guinea and transfer them to a plurality of companies in numerous countries. Moreover, the Panamanian company transferred the public funds as a favour to some high-ranking government officials of Equatorial Guinea. Therefore, the receipt of Equatorial Guinean public funds in Spain and their transfer abroad was done to divert the money through a shell company. As noted, the US Senate considered this company to be either owned by the president of Equatorial Guinea or to be under his control.

Meanwhile, in 2004 the New York District Attorney's Office began an investigation after SEPBLAC provided banking information on certain senior government officials from Equatorial Guinea as well as on individuals and companies related to those government officials.

Due to the fact that the information discovered by the US Senate could have resulted in the crime of money laundering in Spain, the Special Prosecutor's Office for the Repression of Economic Crimes Related to Corruption in Spain also opened an investigation in October 2004.

SEPBLAC continued to investigate the activity in Spain of the Panamanian company that received funds from Riggs Bank and found that as of 2005 their agents had formed new companies in Panama, for which bank accounts were also opened in Spain. Reproducing the operations of their predecessor, these new Panamanian companies also received funds from accounts in France belonging to Equatorial Guinea that were then used for the acquisition of property in Spain.

Although SEPBLAC concluded that the movements of this capital in Spain were highly suspicious, the anticorruption special prosecutor closed the investigation in July 2007, because there was no record of the funds originating from a previous offence.

The Open Society Justice Initiative (an organisation that promotes justice for society) was working on an investigation of corruption in the extraction of oil and gas in Equatorial Guinea. It was keen to take legal action in countries, including Spain and Luxembourg, to which monies stemming from corruption in Equatorial Guinea could have been laundered.

With the support of this organisation, the Human Rights Association of Spain (Asociación Pro Derechos Humanos de España or APDHE) filed before a Spanish court a criminal complaint for an alleged money laundering offence in October 2008. The popular action is foreseen in Article 125 of the Spanish Constitution, and it provides legal standing to any citizen or legal person – normally associations, NGOs and other public or private institutions. As an association, APDHE held a direct and legitimate interest in filing this complaint, as the organisation's mission is to 'defend human rights in all its forms and in all places, ensuring the fulfilment of those already proclaimed and fostering the recognition and guarantee of those not yet recognised'. While in Spain the Popular Action can intervene in criminal proceedings without the indictment of the prosecutor, the support of APDHE was fundamental to advance the investigation not only because of its staff specialised in economic crime investigations but also because the investigating magistrate is more receptive if the proceedings requested through the Popular Action have the support of the prosecutor.

With respect to jurisdiction, according to the United Nations Convention against Corruption and the European Convention on Laundering, Search, Seizure and Confiscation of the Products of Money, Spanish domestic legislation establishes the jurisdiction of its courts to investigate money laundering offences committed in Spain, although the predicate offense to money laundering may have been perpetrated abroad.

This criminal complaint sought to prove that the funds received from Riggs Bank in Spain were channelled through a special purpose vehicle and that those funds were used to acquire property in different Spanish provinces. The criminal action was directed against senior government officials of Equatorial Guinea, excluding the president because he enjoys immunity.

Because the properties related to the alleged money laundering offence were located in different regions of Spain, the complaint was filed with the Spanish Audiencia Nacional. However, the court was declined its jurisdiction in favour of a court in the Canary Islands on the grounds that the jurisdiction should be determined by the place where the company that received the funds had opened its bank account. Although a branch in Madrid received the transfers, it was decided that a court in Las Palmas in Gran Canaria was competent, because it was where the company had originally opened its account.

Regarding the predicate offence to money laundering, it was understood that its origin was the misappropriation of funds in Equatorial Guinea by such practices as requiring payments to the country's rulers from oil companies for the rights to explore crude oil and demanding bribes from multinational enterprises to members of government for the same purpose.

But what transcended the criminal proceedings was the continuous and systematic violation of the economic and social rights of the Equatorial Guinean people, which was a direct consequence of the excessive corruption in the country.

Upon acceptance of the criminal complaint, the Special Prosecutor against Corruption and the Judicial Police Unit with expertise in economic crimes began making inquiries. They looked into the 2004 criminal investigation, and they conducted a comprehensive analysis of the bank account belonging to the company that received the funds from Riggs Bank, which had been open since 1998. The accounts for companies that were opened later by the people involved in the original company were also analysed, and it was discovered that these companies were receiving funds in Spain without ever developing economic activities in the country. Moreover, the investigation determined that representatives from the company who received funds from Riggs Bank had acquired substantial properties in Spain. In parallel, senior government officials from Equatorial Guinea are under investigation for laundering monies into the Spanish territory.

It is well know that a major challenge in advancing criminal proceedings pertaining to money laundering is verifying the predicate offence. Although Spanish law does not require a prior conviction for the predicate offence, it is necessary to demonstrate unlawful activity through circumstantial evidence.

Therefore, in addition to proposing measures in order to determine money laundering took place, APDHE has been providing the special prosecutor with relevant information about the predicate offence to the money laundering in Spain. The coordination between investigators from other countries – in whose courts there are also proceedings related to money laundering from corruption in Equatorial Guinea – has been key, especially those from France and the United States. In addition to these efforts, APDHE has been maintaining contact with potential witnesses on the corruption practices in Equatorial Guinea.

APDHE has extensive experience as a popular complainant in cases of serious crimes against humanity, including cases dealing with genocide and torture. However, economic crime investigations require knowledge of very specific subjects, such as company and business law and accounting. Although it is a complex task to determine the investigative steps that should be practiced in cases like the one involving the officials of Equatorial Guinea, APDHE is playing a relevant role in the promotion and advancement of the procedure before the court.

To obtain the legal knowledge that is required by the investigation of such crimes, lawyers from APDHE are researching the legal regulations on corruption and money laundering as well as Spanish jurisprudence in such cases. This analysis allows APDHE to acquire an overview of the key aspects of organised economic crime, such as proof of the predicate offence to money laundering, restitution of the misappropriated funds to the public administration or the seizure and confiscation of proceeds of crime. Moreover, in Spain corruption is becoming a major concern for Spanish citizens because of serious corruption-related scandals involving members and high-ranking officials of all political parties.

Another fundamental element in court cases that defend public interests is attracting enough media coverage. As illustrated, the citizens of Equatorial Guinea are the ones ultimately affected by the alleged money laundering committed in Spain, because corruption undermined their basic rights. Despite the serious violations of human rights in Equatorial Guinea, the major media outlets in Spain do not cover the events in the former Spanish colony perhaps due to the cordial relationship between the two countries. Therefore, civil society organisations must seek alternative channels to disseminate information about the widespread corruption in the country, the systematic practice of arbitrary arrests, the mistreatment and persecution of political opponents and other things. By attaining international support for the human rights defenders, it favours both the visibility of the complaints and protects the citizens of Equatorial Guinea from the harassment to which they are often subjected.

Returning stolen assets

Boni de Moraes Soares

Early restitution of assets: The Nicolau dos Santos case

In 1992 Nicolau dos Santos Neto, a former Labour Judge from Brazil, was the President of the Labour Regional Court of the Second Region in São Paulo (TRT-SP). In the same year, he conducted a public tender in order to build a new courthouse for the city's first instance courts. In 1993, a contract was signed with the winner of the public bid, the company *Incal Incorporações S.A*,

Because of suspicious activities related to the construction process, in February 1999 several criminal and civil proceedings were launched against the people involved in the building of the courthouse, including Nicolau dos Santos Neto. During the investigations law enforcement officials discovered that dos Santos had transferred stolen assets overseas, mainly to the United States and Switzerland. An official audit of March 1999 concluded that BRL 169 million (approximately USD 85 million[1]) had been diverted from its legal purposes.[2]

One of the biggest corruption and money laundering scandals in Brazilian history emerged from the 1992 public tender, and 21 years later the final judicial convictions against the wrongdoers are still mostly pending.

The lack of a final conviction would have caused Brazil to lose millions of dollars already frozen, because a final judgment is the

1 Amounts in this essay were converted to US dollars using the exchange rate of 1.0 US dollar = 2.0 Brazilian real.

2 MR Machado, Judicial system and corruption in Brazil: A TRT/SP case study (in Portuguese), *Revista Jurídica da Presidência*, vol. 14, no. 103, Brasília, June-September 2012, pp. 273-304, p. 282. Available at: www4.planalto.gov.br/revistajuridica/copy_of_vol-14-n-102-fev-mai-2012/menu-vertical/apresentacao/rjp-103-integral.pdf.

traditional requirement every State needs when seeking the repatriation of stolen assets. However, despite the unfavourable circumstances, Brazil was able to bring back approximately USD 7 million by means of a decision from the Swiss Federal Court in August 2012.

Although it is 21 years after the incident, legally speaking we should call this case an early restitution of assets, because there was no final conviction in Brazil at the time of the Swiss ruling.

This essay addresses some of the questions raised from this successful experience. How was Brazil able to surpass the absence of a final conviction to repatriate the stolen assets? How can this experience lead States to seek more restitution of assets overseas? How could States use the experiences of early restitution of assets to envisage the deficiencies of the mechanisms of mutual legal assistance?

Brazil's role in bringing back stolen assets from abroad

In 1999, in response to reports published by the Brazilian press, Santander Bank in Geneva informed the Geneva Attorney General about the existence of bank accounts belonging to Nicolau dos Santos Neto and his wife.

Based on the information it received, the Geneva Attorney General began an investigation into money laundering and subsequently froze the funds deposited into Nicolau dos Santos' account. The Geneva Attorney General determined that Santander Bank had presented all the documentation it had on the account.[3]

In order to prove the illegal origin of the assets belonging to dos Santos and his wife, Swiss authorities sent Brazil a request for mutual legal assistance to obtain evidence and documents related to the case.

3 It is worth mentioning that according to the Swiss Federal Law on Money Laundering of 1997 a financial intermediary must immediately file a report with the Money Laundering Reporting Office of Switzerland if he or she knows or has reasonable grounds to suspect that assets involved in the business relationship are connected to a criminal organization or a crime of money laundering (article 9, 1).

In January 2000, Brazil responded to the Swiss request and sent documents that pointed to the unlawfulness of the assets and consequently requested that the Swiss authorities freeze the dos Santos bank account.

The work intensified when, in August 2000, the Brazilian Ministry of Justice created a task force responsible for guiding the various initiatives of the Brazilian State in its search for the assets misappropriated by the criminal organisation in the construction of the São Paulo Labour Courthouse.

As a result of the investigations conducted in Brazil, Brazilian authorities decided to send mutual legal assistance requests in criminal matters to other jurisdictions, including the Bahamas, Spain, the United States, France, Lebanon and Uruguay. The assistance requests were sent between 2000 and 2008 and sought information on Nicolau dos Santos' eventual property abroad, mainly real estate and bank accounts. The assistance requests began the process for future freezing requests and repatriation of the assets.

The confirmation that dos Santos owned assets in the United States and Switzerland led the Brazilian government to adopt a different strategy in these countries. Besides sending the aforementioned assistance requests, Brazil started legal procedures in US and Swiss courts to prove it had been victim to the illegal acts carried out by Nicolau dos Santos. Victim status would allow Brazil the repatriation of the property acquired by dos Santos as a result of criminal practices carried out during the courthouse construction process.

In September 2000, the Federative Republic of Brazil started a legal process in the Eleventh Judicial Circuit Court of Florida in the United States to prove that an apartment with an appraised value of about USD 700,000 had been bought by dos Santos with illegally diverted resources. In August 2001, the US judge recognised Brazil's right, and in mid-2002, the assets derived from the sale of the apartment were deposited in a Brazilian government bank account.

In 2001, after evaluating the asset recovery probabilities through the mutual legal assistance mechanisms and especially in light of the difficulties in obtaining a final conviction against Nicolau dos Santos in Brazil, the Brazilian authorities decided that the Federative Republic of Brazil should collaborate with the Swiss authorities and enter the Swiss criminal procedure as a civil party.

Later in 2001, the Brazilian Attorney General of the Union followed the instructions of the Brazilian authorities and enlisted a Swiss law firm to legally represent the Federative Republic of Brazil in the Geneva courts.

After being accepted as civil party by the courts in Geneva, the Federative Republic of Brazil was able to intensely collaborate with the Swiss authorities in their criminal proceedings. Brazil made use of the powers invested in its Swiss legal representatives under Swiss law to consult the process, to request investigative measures, including for other bank accounts allegedly belonging to Nicolau dos Santos, and to produce statements from the employees of Santander Bank in order to assess their responsibilities in the case.

The Swiss authorities obtained in 2008 a judicial order to freeze the assets of dos Santos, which remained active after some appeals and up to the final judgment by the Federal Court, the highest court in Switzerland, in August 2012.[4]

The Swiss Federal authorities discovered that between 1991 and 1994 dos Santos and his wife made 18 deposits in their Swiss bank accounts totalling USD 6.8 million. The deposits, according to the Swiss courts, derived from embezzlement practices during dos Santos' involvement in the construction process of the São Paulo Labour Courthouse. The Swiss Federal Court also ordered Nicolau dos Santos and his wife to pay the Brazilian government USD 2.2 million in compensation for the illegal resources they obtained and withdrew from their Swiss bank accounts before the restraining order went into effect.

In Brazil, meanwhile, the first judicial conviction came in 2002. In the scope of three criminal proceedings, Nicolau dos Santos was convicted of the crimes of money laundering, embezzlement, fraudulent larceny, passive bribery, capital flight and crime against the fiscal system. Four years later, the Federal Regional Court of the 3rd Region

4 Swiss Federal Court, Criminal Law Chamber, 6B_688/2011, Judgment of 21 August 2012 (in French). Available at: www.bger.ch/fr/index/juridiction/jurisdiction-inherit-template/jurisdiction-recht/jurisdiction-recht-urteile2000.htm.

sentenced dos Santos to more than 48 years in prison and a fine of BRL 1.2 million (approximately USD 600,000).

In May 2012, the Superior Court of Justice confirmed the sentences. On 3 April 2013, only a day before the criminal proceedings became time-barred, the Federal Supreme Court denied the appeal against the charges of money laundering, rendering the sentence final.[5] The other crimes are still waiting a final conviction.

Lessons learned

The mechanisms of mutual legal assistance are and, hopefully, always will be the primary avenue to be explored by countries involved in an international fraud case for recovering stolen assets. The advantages of the mechanisms are well known to the international community, and their disadvantages should not discourage the mechanisms' utilisation. Rather, they should serve as motivation to enhance their effectiveness. After all, obligations established under mutual legal assistance treaties should be taken seriously, as they could lead a State that breaches them to face the jurisdiction of an international court.[6]

However, the Nicolau dos Santos case and other international fraud cases have demonstrated that a double way strategy of pursuing requests for mutual legal assistance and legal actions in the courts of the requested country can be crucial.

Among the successful international recovery of stolen assets cases in Brazilian history, several have combined requests for mutual legal assistance with legal actions in the courts of the requested country. This strategy was used in the Jorgina de Freitas case, in which Brazil in 2003 recovered from the United States approximately USD

5 M. Oliveira, STF confirms the first final conviction against Nicolau dos Santos Neto (in Portuguese), G1, 2 April 2013. Available at: www.g1.globo.com/sao-paulo/noticia/2013/04/stf-confirma-primeira-condenacao-definitiva-de-nicolau-dos-santos-neto.html.

6 J Grote, Case Concerning Certain Questions of Mutual Assistance in Criminal Matters (Djibouti vs. France), *Max Planck Encyclopedia of Public International Law*, 2011. Available at: www.mpepil.com.

11 million,[7] in the Banestado case, when in 2012 Brazil recovered from the United States USD 1 million,[8] and also in the Nicolau dos Santos case, in which Brazil recovered from the United States USD 700,000.[9]

The same strategy is currently being used in other important cases, such as the Paulo Maluf case. In this case, the Brazilian authorities are in a favourable position to recover more than USD 28 million from the island of Jersey.[10]

The double way strategy was also applied in other notable international fraud cases. Nigeria successfully used a combination of requesting mutual legal assistance and lodging criminal and civil complaints for money laundering in jurisdictions where assets of the former General Sani Abacha and his allies had been identified.[11] The Philippines adopted the same combined strategy to recover USD 681 million from the former President Ferdinand Marcos, his family members and servants.[12] Peru succeeded in using this combination of tools in several jurisdictions to recover assets from Vladimiro Montesinos, an important advisor to former President Alberto Fujimori,[13]

7 W. Silveira, Repatriation of assets will take years (in Portuguese), *Folha de S. Paulo*, 9 August 2000. Available at: www1.folha.uol.com.br/fsp/brasil/fc090820 0008.htm.

8 MJ and AGU recover R$ 2,2 million from USA (in Portuguese), *JusBrasil*, 29 August 2012. Available at: mj.jusbrasil.com.br/noticias/100044615/mj-e-agu-recuperam-r-2-2-milhoes-desviados-para-os-eua.

9 Dos Santos' property in Miami is now owned by the Union (in Portuguese), *Consultor Jurídico*, 28 August 2001. Available at: www.conjur.com.br/2001-ago-28/agu_recupera_imovel_juiz_nicolau_miami.

10 T Herdy, Jersey's court denies appeal from companies of Maluf's family (in Portuguese), *O Globo*, 11 April 2013. Available at: www.oglobo.globo.com/pais /justica-de-jersey-rejeita-recursos-das-empresas-da-familia-de-maluf-8092323.

11 This double way strategy allowed the Government of Nigeria to freeze about USD 2 billion in 10 jurisdictions, of which to date USD 1.2 billion has been recovered. Cf. E Monfrini, 'The Abacha case' in M Pieth (ed.), *Recovering Stolen Assets,* Bern, 2008, p. 41.

12 S Salvioni, 'Recovering the proceeds of corruption: Ferdinand Marcos of the Philippines' in M Pieth (ed.), *Recovering Stolen Assets,* Bern, 2008, p. 82.

13 G Jorge, 'The Peruvian efforts to recover proceeds from Montesinos's criminal network of corruption' in M Pieth (ed.), *Recovering Stolen Assets,* Bern, 2008, p. 120.

The importance of mutual legal assistance is recognised by the most comprehensive treaty dealing with mechanisms to recover stolen assets, the United Nations Convention against Corruption (UNCAC). UNCAC establishes the 'measures for direct recovery of property', which state that each State Party shall adopt the necessary measures to permit another State Party to present a civil action, or any other type of claim, in its courts to establish title to or ownership of property acquired through the commission of a corrupt act.[14] The legal claims also entitle the courts of the recipient State to order that the wrongdoers pay compensation or damages to the State that has been harmed by criminal offences.[15]

Additionally, it is worth noting that a civil claim initiated by a State in another jurisdiction can charge not only the corrupt public official but also his family and associates, companies incorporated to launder the proceeds of crime, banks, lawyers, financial advisers and other professionals involved in the criminal organisation.[16]

In international asset recovery, the prominence of civil claims derives from the several advantages they provide. The burden of proof in civil claims is usually lower than in criminal cases. While the criminal burden requires proof 'beyond reasonable doubt', usually 'a balance of probabilities' fulfils the burden of proof in civil claims. Civil claims also allow the authorities of the involved countries closer and faster cooperation, which is vital to providing further allegations and evidence in the courts of the recipient State. Another, and possibly the biggest, advantage is that the absence of a final conviction in the requesting State does not prevent the recovery of assets from the foreign jurisdiction. By concluding judicial proceedings in its own jurisdiction, the recipient State can send stolen assets back to the victim country.

There are also disadvantages associated with launching civil claims in the recipient State. The most prohibitive of which is cost. Judicial representation for the claimant State by local lawyers is usual-

14 Article 53, 1, (a) and (c).

15 Article 53, 1, (b).

16 T Daniel & J Maton, 'Civil proceedings to recover corruptly acquired assets of public officials', in M Pieth (ed.), *Recovering Stolen Assets,* Bern, 2008, p. 246.

ly very expensive. Additionally challenging are the complex legal procedures required in some financial centres for obtaining a restraining order to freeze the stolen assets – something crucial to guaranteeing the effectiveness of a final judgment. Usually mutual legal assistance requests are more likely to seek restraining orders.

Applying this double way strategy in the Nicolau dos Santos case was vital in obtaining the final judgment that recognised the funds in Geneva as rightfully belonging to Brazil. The positive outcome of the case would not have been possible without the legal actions conducted in Switzerland.

Furthermore, it should be noted that one of the most important events in the Nicolau dos Santos case took place when Santander Bank sent the Attorney General of Geneva the suspicious transactions report. The Brazilian authorities would not have known that dos Santos had transferred money to the Santander bank account without the report, and the report would not have been sent to the Swiss authorities without the important role played by the Brazilian press. Comprehensive coverage by several Brazilian media groups at the beginning of the case served to internationally expose Nicolau dos Santos as a political exposed person (PEP). Consequently, the Brazilian media was essential in raising the necessary awareness of the public and private parties involved in the case, which ultimately led the Brazilian authorities to recover millions of dollars in embezzled assets.

What's next? Perspectives for more efficiency in recovering stolen assets

In the field of mutual legal assistance, some improvements could be made to allow countries to more effectively request and provide cooperation.

It is important to encourage media vehicles to cover more intensely transnational fraud cases. In the case of Nicolau dos Santos, the Brazilian media prompted Santander Bank to notify the Geneva Attorney General of suspicious transactions. This type of indirect and even unintentional contribution to investigations by the press was also an important part of cases involving Angola, the Republic of Congo and Kenya as victim countries.[17]

It is also necessary to develop more expeditious legal procedures in the victim State, so that a mutual legal assistance request can function properly as the basis for the repatriation of assets. It is widely known that the biggest weakness of the mechanisms of mutual legal assistance in criminal matters is the slowness at which the procedures operate. The lengthy process is mainly the result of the complex procedures and the appeals allowed under law, which ultimately result in the lack of a timely final conviction in the State of origin. Generally, when a final conviction is pending in the courts of the origin State, the recipient State is unable to send back the embezzled funds.

When a final conviction in the victim State seems improbable a double way strategy can better promote the interests of the victim State. Therefore, some measures should be adopted to improve the ability of the victim State to pursue legal action in the requested State.

In order to minimise the prohibitive costs associated with legal procedures, some initiatives should be considered. As already suggested, a sort of 'revolving fund' could be available to victim States interested in conducting legal procedures overseas.[18] Developing countries could also explore contemporary mechanisms of private investment in high-risk legal actions, something that is increasing in financial centres.[19] Lastly, law firms specialising in international fraud cases that are interested in representing developing countries in forfeiture actions should work on an outcome-based approach. With this approach, the developing country could afford the expenses incurred by the law firm and also pay an amount of legal fees established in advance. This amount of legal fees would fairly reflect a balance between the expertise delivered by the attorneys-at-law and the frustrat-

17 M Pieth, 'Recovering stolen assets – a new issue' in M Pieth (ed.), *Recovering Stolen Assets,* Bern, 2008, p. 10.

18 E Joly, 'Preface: repatriation of assets' in M Pieth (ed.), *Recovering Stolen Assets,* Bern, 2008, p. x.

19 MS Kenney, Access to Restorative Justice for the Victims of Fraud – The Finance of Complex Fraud Recovery. Available at: www.icc-ccs.org/home/publications/viewdownload/3/14-access-to-restorative-justice-for-the-victims-offraud-the-finance-of-complex-fraud-recovery-investigations-and-litigation.

ed expectations of the victim State in case of a negative outcome in the proceedings – that is, non-recovery of assets. A positive outcome – that is, partial or total repatriation of the assets targeted – would allow the law firm to collect a second instalment of legal fees comprising a percentage of the assets recovered by its client and taking into consideration the risks inherent to this type of lawsuit.

For a successful double way strategy it is also essential that the national authorities work together closely. Prosecutors, police officers, agents from the financial intelligence unit and the central authority for mutual legal assistance should work in the closest possible way to improve their chances of success. A task force for the most complex cases is strongly recommended.

Recipient States should ensure that their law provides grounds of jurisdiction on both criminal and civil forfeiture proceedings, in line with article 53 of UNCAC. Authorities in the victim State must be certain they can use legal actions in the requested State, because it is rare that national legislation grants jurisdiction based solely on the fact that it is where stolen assets are located. Usually jurisdiction is granted only if it is the place where the fraud was committed or if it is the State of nationality for either the victim or the offender. Wider grounds for jurisdiction are already in place in Switzerland and, hopefully, similar grounds for jurisdiction will be adopted in other important financial centres.

In addition to establishing broader grounds for jurisdiction, the law should allow for lower standards of proof for the plaintiff or even the reverse burden of proof for the perpetrators. In some cases, it is likely impossible to prove that a certain amount of money derived from specific illicit practices. In these cases, law enforcement officials should be allowed to prove not the traditional standard of proof 'beyond a reasonable doubt' but a lower standard of proof, such as the 'balance of probabilities', which is common in civil procedures. Even more complex cases should impose a reverse burden of proof on the perpetrators based on contemporary concepts of criminal offense, such as the 'illicit enrichment' as prescribed by article 20 of UNCAC or in the case of the perpetrators belonging to a criminal organisation, as defined by article 72 of the Swiss Penal Code.[20]

Effective mechanisms of cooperation with whistle-blowers and asset holders are other important tools in this area. People who want to avoid prosecution or even mitigate their punishment can dully cooperate with law enforcement officials when the law provides such benefits.

Cases of early restitution of assets should work to inspire future positive outcomes in other international fraud cases, but more importantly they should function specially to raise awareness about the urgency of enhancing mechanisms of mutual legal assistance. Exploring legal actions in the jurisdiction of the recipient country should be considered an exceptional tool. Mutual legal assistance is and always should be the conventional way to recover stolen assets overseas. We hope the success reached in the Nicolau dos Santos case can prove this point.

20 According to the article 72 of the Swiss Penal Code, a judge shall order the confiscation of assets belonging to persons qualified as a criminal organization, unless they can prove the lack of connection between such assets and the criminal activities.

IGNASIO MALIZANI JIMU

Asset recovery and the civil society in perspective: Nigeria, Peru, the Philippines and Kazakhstan cases considered

Asset recovery is one of the major themes in development funding, due in part to awareness of the enormous resources lost annually by developing countries to corruption. Corruption is generally considered the abuse of public office for private gain.[1] Abuse of public office includes accepting, soliciting or extorting and offering bribes to circumvent public policies and legitimate processes. Other forms include patronage and nepotism, theft and diversion of state assets and revenues.[2] Often proceeds are transferred from one jurisdiction to another to disguise the true nature of the source. Combined estimates suggest that proceeds of corruption, tax evasion and other criminal activities amount to between USD 1 trillion and USD 1.6 trillion per year. In Africa over USD 148 billion or about 25 percent of gross domestic product (GDP) is lost to corruption.[3] Bribes received by public officials in all developing countries and countries in transition amount to between USD 20 billion and USD 40 billion per year, which is between 20 and 40 percent of official development assistance (ODA).[3]

Big corruption actors are often politically exposed persons (PEPs). The process of recovering assets stolen by PEPs is often complicated and requires the involvement of different players, for example law enforcement agencies, law firms, financial institutions and civil society organisations (CSOs). By definition civil society refers to or-

1 The World Bank (1997) Helping Countries Combat Corruption, available at: www1.worldbank.org/publicsector/anticorrupt/corruptn/corrptn.pdf.

2 Akçay, S. (2006) *Corruption and Human Development*, 26 CATO J. 33. Available at: www.cato.org/pubs/journal/cj26n1/cj26n1-2.pdf.

3 The World Bank and United Nations Office on Drugs and Crime, Fact Sheet on Stolen Asset Recovery. Available at: www.unodc.org/pdf/Star_FactSheet.pdf.

ganised activity not associated with major institutional systems, such as government and administration, education and health delivery, business and industry, security and organised religion. In practice civil society may include faith-based organisations, cooperatives, trade unions, professional associations, non-governmental organizations (NGOs), academic institutions, community and youth groups. NGOs form a small segment of CSOs, but they are the face of CSOs in developing countries. Civil society plays a critical role in the democratic process by promoting transparency and accountability[4] and human rights. Civil society organisations are also known for raising awareness of acts, claims and cases of corruption. They have even helped to pass domestic legislation necessary for the implementation of the United Nations Convention against Corruption (UNCAC) provisions. This paper explores the challenges of civil society as a watchdog in monitoring stolen assets once they have been repatriated. While I am aware of the broad nature of the civil society, my reflections are in fact biased towards NGOs.

Attention is on the utilisation of proceeds repatriated from the loot of Sani Abacha of Nigeria, Vladimiro Montesinos of Peru and Ferdinand Marcos of the Philippines. The amounts involved are large in relation to the national budgets of the concerned countries. Marcos stole between 1.5 and 4.5 percent of the annual GDP of the Philippines, while Abacha looted between 1.5 and 3.7 percent of the Peruvian GDP.[5] These three cases represent scenarios in which repatriated funds passed through national budgets. The fourth case in Kazakhstan provides the overview of a scenario in which recovered assets did not pass through government machinery, but rather that of an independent not-for-profit organisation, the BOTA Foundation.

4 Ghaus-Pasha, A. (2004) 'The role of civil society organisations in governance', 6th Global Forum on Reinventing Government, Towards Participatory and Transparent Governance, 24–27 May 2005, Seoul, Republic of Korea.

5 The World Bank (2007) *Stolen Asset Recovery (StAR) Initiative: Challenges, Opportunities and Action Plan*, Washington, D.C.: The International Bank for ReconstruZction and Development/The World Bank.
Available at: www.unodc.org/pdf/ Star_Report.pdf.

The Abacha loot in Nigeria

Sani Abacha was president of Nigeria from 1993 to 1998. Investigations carried out after his death revealed that he looted between USD 3–5 billion of public money.[6] Proceeds were laundered through banks and front companies in Nigeria, the United Kingdom, Switzerland, Luxembourg, Liechtenstein, Jersey and the Bahamas. A decree made on 26 May 1999 by General Abubakar (Decree No. 53) facilitated the recovery of USD 800 million in cash and assets.[7,8] Focus, however, is on USD 505.5 million, known as the 'Abacha loot', hidden in Swiss banks until its successful repatriation between late 2005 and early 2006.

Following long negotiations, Nigeria and Switzerland agreed that the Abacha loot should go into pro-poor projects under the watchful eye of a third party, which was later identified as the World Bank. The review of the utilisation of the recovered resources was supposed to be part of an on going program to improve public finance management. The Swiss government provided through the World Bank a grant of about USD 280,000 to co-finance the Public Expenditure Management and Financial Accountability Review (PEMFAR), which was initiated as a means of executing reforms in budget spending with regard to Nigeria's national economic empowerment development strategy (NEEDS) priorities in education, health and basic infrastructure (power, roads and water). Out of a total sum repatriated from Switzerland the allocations were to go into power (USD 168.5 million), works (USD 144.5 million), health (USD 84.1 million), education (USD 60.1 million) and water resources (USD 48.2 million).[9,10]

6 The World Bank (2007), see fn 5.

7 Daniel, T. and Maton, J. (2008) 'Recovering the proceeds of corruption: general Sani Abacha- a nation's thief', Pieth, M. (ed.) Recovering Stolen Assets, Bern: Peter Lang. pp. 64–78.

8 Monfrini, E. (2008) 'The Abacha case', Pieth, M. (ed.) *Recovering Stolen Assets*, Bern: Peter Lang. pp. 41- 61.

9 Okonjo-Iweala, N and Osafo-Kwaako, P. (2008) *The Role of Civil Society Organizations in Supporting Fiscal Transparency in African Countries Some Lessons from Nigeria,* Centre for the Study of the Economies of Africa, CSEA Policy Brief PB/08/001, available at: http://cseaafrica.org/publications/CSEAPolicy

The World Bank mobilised Integrity, a Nigerian civil society organisation, to prepare and administer field-monitoring surveys of the selected projects.[11] Integrity, together with other local civil society organisations, reviewed 51 projects.[12] A total of 168 people were interviewed, including contractors, local government officials and potential project beneficiaries. The participation of civil society organisations came as n afterthought following pressure from both the Swiss NGO coalition and the Nigerian Network on Stolen Assets (NNSA).[13]

The greatest challenge encountered was related to the appropriation and tracking of funds in the national budget. Follow-ups showed that between 2004 and 2005 there was a substantial increase in allocations to various spending agencies, but due to incomplete utilisation of appropriated funds in 2004 some spending was actually undertaken as part of the 2005 capital budget.[14] There wcrc several instances in which spending agencies used the Abacha loot either to defray outstanding arrears or to make partial payments for on going multi-year projects. There were also several cases in which projects that had been completed prior to the repatriation of the funds were subsequently paid for using the returned assets. In some cases, projects were still incomplete at the time of the survey although part of the projects' costs had been paid.[14] Many projects implemented using the Abacha

Brief%20PB0 8001.pdf.

10 The World Bank and Federal Ministry of Finance (Nigeria) (2006) Utilization of Repatriated Abacha Loot: Results of the field monitoring exercise, Report Prepared by the World Bank with Cooperation from the Federal Ministry of Finance, December 2006 Abuja. Available at: http://siteresources.worldbank.org/INTNIGERIA/Resources/Abacha_Funds_Monitoring_1221.pdf.

11 The World Bank (2007), see fn 5.

12 Okonjo-Iweala, N and Osafo-Kwaako, P. (2008), see fn 9.

13 Simon Hirsbrunner 'Stolen Asset Recovery: Swiss experience', Economics of Corruption Training in Passau, 4–10 October 2008. Available at www.wiwi.uni passau.de/fileadmin/dokumente/lehrstuehle/lambsdorff/Economics_of_Corruption_2008/Poster_EOC2008_simon.pdf.

14 The World Bank and Federal Ministry of Finance (Nigeria) (2006), see fn 10.

loot were not of good quality.[15] Others lagged behind schedule or were virtually abandoned.[15] Furthermore, a comprehensive physical inspection was not possible, because a complete list of the projects funded by the repatriated funds was not available.[16]

The case of Vladimiro Montesinos

Vladimiro Montesinos was head of Peru's secret service and advisor to President Alberto Fujimori between 1990 and 2000. In 2000 secret videos were televised showing Montesinos bribing the opposition. The scandal caused him to flee Peru, but it also discredited the government and President Fujimori, who resigned as a consequence. Subsequent investigations revealed multi-million dollar dealings in illegal activities, including extortion of high profile entrepreneurs, embezzlement, graft, dealings in the arms trade and drug trafficking.[17] The actual amount of money accumulated by Montesinos is not known, but it is estimated that during Fujimori's rule close to USD 2 billion was stolen. Bribes were facilitated by legal provisions that allowed secrecy in the bidding process for military hardware on the grounds of 'national security'. Montesinos and his cronies used shell companies to launder the proceeds. Since his conviction the government of Peru has recovered over USD 185 million,[18] including USD 33 million returned by the Cayman Islands in August 2001, USD 77.5 million returned by Switzerland in August 2002 and USD 20 million returned by the United States in January 2004.[19] The remaining balance possibly came

15 Report by Ugolor, D., Nwafor, A. and Nardine, J.H. on behalf of the Nigerian Network on Stolen Assets, 'Shadow Report on the PEMFAR Monitoring Exercise' (Pages 57–58). Available at www.evb.ch/cm_data/Report_Abacha.pdf.

16 Ugolor, D., Nwafor, A. and Nardine, J.H. (2006), Shadow Report on the PEMFAR Monitoring Exercise, Nigerian Network on Stolen Assets (NNSA), available at: http:// www. evb.ch/cm_data/Report_Abacha.pdf.

17 Jorge, G. (2008) 'The Peruvian efforts to recover proceeds from Montesinos' criminal network of corruption', Pieth, M. (ed.) Recovering Stolen Assets, Bern: Peter Lang. pp. 111–132.

18 The World Bank and UN Office on Drugs and Crime, see fn 3.

19 The World Bank (2007), see fn 5.

from Luxembourg, Mexico, Panama, Trinidad and Tobago or Uruguay where Montesinos and his associates also had bank accounts.[20]

The government of Peru created by emergency decree 122-2001 of 27 October 2001 the *Fondo Especial de Administracion del Dinero Obtenido Ilicitamente en perjuicio del Estado* (FEDADOI) (Special Fund of Management of Illegally Obtained Money Against Interests of the State).[21] Repatriated assets were channelled into this special fund managed by a board of five members appointed from different government ministries. Although guidelines and detailed procedures were defined to ensure the transparent use of the recovered assets, money in the fund has so far ended up supplementing the budgets of institutions that have a member on the board.[22] Spending has often adhered to standard budgetary procedures, but since the spending items are not clearly set out in advance, questionable spending allocations have been a norm. For example, the Interior Ministry received over USD 9 million in 2004 for the payment of vacations for both active and retired police personnel for the 1995 and 1996 fiscal years.[22]

The case of Ferdinand Marcos in the Philippines

Ferdinand Marcos was president of the Philippines from 1965 to 1986. He relinquished power during the 'people power revolution' on allegations of corruption. Marcos and members of his family siphoned off between USD 5 billion and USD 10 billion using various methods including taking over large private enterprises, creating state-owned monopolies in important sectors of the economy, awarding government loans to private individuals acting as fronts or cronies, directly

20 Basel Institute on Governance/International Centre on Asset Recovery 'Efforts to Recover Assets Looted by Vladimir Montesinos of Peru'. Available at: www.assetrecovery.org/kc/resources/org.apache.wicket.Application/repo?nid=1aafec73-a345-11dc-bf1b-335d0754ba85.

21 Decreto de Urgencia Nº 122-2001. Available at: www.minjus.gob.pe/normatividad/decretos/ds001-2002-jus.pdf.

22 The World Bank (2007), see fn 5.

raiding the public treasury and government financial institutions, soliciting kickbacks and commissions from firms and diverting foreign aid and other forms of international assistance.[22] The proceeds of the crimes were laundered through shell corporations, which invested the money in real estate in the United States, or by way of deposits in various domestic and offshore banks under pseudonyms, unnumbered accounts or accounts with code names.

After a long legal process the Philippines received USD 624 million in February 2004 from the Swiss government, which was deposited in the Philippines Treasury.[22] While the funds were in the escrow account in the Philippine National Bank, the Swiss authorities, through the Canton of Zurich Attorney General, had control over the investments that could be made from the account.[23] Later the funds were transferred to an off-budget fund known as the 'Agrarian Reform Fund'. In October 2006 the Commission on Audit reported that a significant portion of the recovered funds were used to finance excessive and unnecessary expenses. These expenses were unlikely to benefit the agrarian reform beneficiaries, for example some of the money was spent on items unrelated to priority projects or on procuring items at inflated prices.[24]

The Department of Land Reform (DLR) reportedly appropriated about USD 57 million to pay cash advances to the Land Bank of the Philippines and USD 46.5 million for office operations of the Comprehensive Agrarian Reform Program (CARP).[25] Moreover, USD 10.4 million was withdrawn by request of the Department of Agriculture to support the hybrid rice program, ostensibly because the majority of the farmers participating in hybrid rice technology were also beneficiaries of agrarian reform. The Department of Agriculture spent the USD 10.4 million on 217,000 bags of hybrid rice distributed to differ-

23 Freeman, K. (2004) 'Repatriation of looted state assets: some case studies and UN Convention against Corruption', Available at: www.ipocafrica.org/cases/assestsrecovery/commentaryandopinions/DanielJun04.pdf.

24 The World Bank (2007), see fn 5.

25 House of Representatives (Philippines), 'Full accounting of recovered Marcos money sought', The committee of oversight of September 5, 2005. Vol. 13, number 69. Available at: www.congress.gov.ph/committees/commnews/commnews_det.php?newsid=420.

ent regions in the country. However, the Director of Agriculture could not give a definite number of agrarian reform beneficiaries who received the hybrid rice. Another questionable expenditure was the USD 33.8 million used to survey land that cost only USD 21.1 million to acquire.[25] The recovered assets illegally obtained by former President Marcos were mixed with the general fund, making it difficult to render a full accounting of it. Additionally, in March 2006 a press release from the Senate President of the Philippines alluded to massive corruption in the acquisition of liquid fertilizer for farmers using the repatriated funds. Staff at the Department of Agriculture and some lawmakers perpetrated the corruption sometime between 2004 and 2006.[26]

The Kazakhstan case: BOTA Foundation

A 1999 case involving a US citizen investigated under the US Foreign Corrupt Practices Act uncovered corrupt payments to Kazakh officials amounting to USD 84 million that was paid into a Swiss bank.[27] The details of the case correspond with US investigations of James H. Giffen, a New York banker indicted in 2003 on charges of making more than USD 78 million in unlawful payments to two senior Kazakh officials. Giffen allegedly made the payments in the 1990s on behalf of US oil companies, including Mobil Oil Corp, to obtain concessions to exploit oil resources. The BOTA (meaning young camel in Kazak) is an independent not-for-profit foundation established in May 2008[28] following the 2007 trilateral agreement between the governments of the Republic of Kazakhstan, the United States of America

26 Press Release by the Philippine Senate President and Liberal Party head Franklin M. Drilon titled 'Drilon surprised over Nograles reaction on COA report' (28 March 2006). Available at: www.senate.gov.ph/press_release/2006/ 0328_drilon1.asp.

27 Alima Bissenova in an article titled 'Swiss to hand over $ 84 million in blocked assets to Kazakhstan', Ref. Available at: www.cacianalyst.org/?q= taxonomy/term/4&page=5.

28 IREX 'The BOTA Foundation'. Available at: http://irex.org/programs/bota/index.asp.

and the Swiss Confederation to channel the recovered funds into projects that benefit disadvantaged children in Kazakhstan. The foundation began its child welfare programs in September 2009. Although it was initially dependent on the original USD 84 million, BOTA also worked to mobilise additional funding from individuals, corporations and government sources.[29]

The Board of Trustees of the BOTA Foundation consists of seven members: five Kazakh specialists and one representative from the governments of the United States of America (the US Ambassador in Kazakhstan) and the Swiss Confederation (Pietro Veglio).[30] The five Kazakh Board members were nominated and vetted by the governments, and their services are not salaried though they receive 'reasonable costs of reimbursement for expenditures incurred in connection with the carrying out of their functions'.[31] The BOTA Foundation's salaries for local staff are approximately 80 percent of those of similar international and domestic organisations, such as affiliates of the United Nations, United States Agency for International Development and local foundations employing staff with international development experience and qualifications. Furthermore, the BOTA Foundation intends to spend 85 percent of its funding on direct program expenses including the Conditional Cash Transfer (CCT) Program, the Social Services Program (SSP) and the Tuition Assistance Program (TAP).[32] The CCT Program enables poor households access to services that improve children's development and welfare by promoting increased access to knowledge and improved practices in the areas of maternal and child health, pre-primary school attendance and increased home-based care for children with disabilities. The SSP seeks to provide grants and technical assistance to community-based groups and non-

29 Available at: http://botafoundation.org.kz/index.html?id=68.

30 Stefan Howald, 'Money from corrupt deals for Kazakh children', Finanzplatz Informationen 3/2008. Available at: www.aktionfinanzplatz.ch/pdf/en/AFP_Kazakh_0908.pdf. Also reported in The World Bank's News Release No. 2008/07/KZ (Kazakhstan BOTA Foundation Established). Available at: http://siteresources.worldbank.org/INTKAZAKHSTAN/News%20and%20Events/21790077/Bota_Establishment_June08_eng.pdf.

31 Available at: http://botafoundation.org.kz/index.html?id=68.

32 IREX 'The BOTA Foundation'. See fn 28.

governmental welfare services providers. The TAP provides post-secondary education scholarships to young people who would otherwise lack the resources. For the 2009–2010 academic year alone, up to 100 students were earmarked for support.

Lessons from the three cases

Asset recovery is a vital means of fighting corruption and promoting development in developing countries. As shown by increased allocations to pro-poor sectors in Nigeria following the repatriation of USD 505 million from Switzerland, the fight against corruption and the fight against poverty are complementary. However, using recovered assets to fund anti-poverty projects and to promote development requires better oversight mechanisms involving the civil society. Where there are no such mechanisms, as was the case in the repatriation of assets stolen by Montesinos in Peru and Marcos in the Philippines, recovered assets end up financing activities that are not pro-poor and in some cases they may be corruptly repossessed by those entrusted with their management. Yet, having oversight mechanisms is not an end in itself. There is need for continuous monitoring by the civil society. Appropriation of the Abacha loot into the Nigerian national budget created difficulties in following-up on the flow of funds as well as in building commitment for careful utilisation by government field staff and the public. The actual implementation of the projects funded by the Abacha loot was affected by problems of inefficiency, lack of good faith and corruption.

Consensus is emerging that while corruption erodes economic development, repatriation of illegally acquired money and assets to the countries of origin promotes development.[33] The total amount of public money embezzled by Abacha, Montesinos and Marcos is far greater than what the concerned governments have been able to recoup. For Nigeria alone large sums of money remain frozen in other countries, of which close to USD 1.3 billion is presumably held in Luxembourg

33 Okonjo-Iweala, N and Osafo-Kwaako, P. (2008), see fn 9.

and Liechtenstein.[34] The same situation applies in the case of funds stolen by the Marcos family. Once the hurdles to recovery are overcome the greatest challenge will be how to ensure that the returned monies are used properly and efficiently[35] towards achieving development targets, for example the Millennium Development Goals (MDGs) set out by the United Nations.[36] On the part of developing countries, recovering proceeds from corruption is sometimes complicated by politicians' and officials' immunity from prosecution in corruption related offences.[37] While on the part of developed countries that serve as financial centres for stolen money, the challenge is meeting legal standards before stolen funds can be repatriated. It took Nigeria and Peru close to five years to achieve positive results, while in the case of the Philippines it took about 20 years. These facts point to the need to improve systems to identify funds acquired illicitly, to facilitate the authorities' power to freeze and confiscate stolen assets and to create instruments to hand back funds to the countries from which they were looted. Appropriate forms of collaboration involving civil society groups in both developing countries and developed countries are needed to facilitate the process and to ensure that repatriated funds are well managed. As noted above, the civil society in Nigeria in partnership with their Swiss counterparts campaigned for a speedy repatriation of looted funds and later played oversight in the utilisation of the funds.[38]

Discussions leading to the establishment of the BOTA Foundation were conducted in a bureaucratic, opaque and non-transparent style and with minimal and selective involvement of the Kazakh civil

34 UNCAC Team (2007) Asset Recovery – A Breakthrough by the UN Convention against Corruption (UNCAC), September 2007. Available at: www.gtz.de/de/dokumente/en-gtz-asset-recovery-2007.pdf.

35 Lugon-Moulin, A. (2008) 'Asset recovery: concrete challenges for development assistance', Pieth, M. (ed.) Recovering Stolen Assets, Bern: Peter Lang. pp. 297–308.

36 Veglio, P. and Siegenthaler, P. (2008) 'Monitoring the restitution of looted states assets: the role of multilateral development banks (MDBs)', Pieth, M. (ed.) *Recovering Stolen Assets*, Bern: Peter Lang. pp. 316–329.

37 Turner, B (2004), see fn 33.

38 Okonjo-Iweala, N and Osafo-Kwaako, P. (2008), see fn 9.

society. Kazakh officials implicated in the alleged corruption are no longer liable to investigation and prosecution. Moreover, there are flaws in terms of how to assess the implementation of the aims of the BOTA Foundation by NGOs that are part of a professionalised service industry.[39] Initial Kazakh members of the BOTA Board were hand-picked. Then the BOTA Foundation was mandated to competitively hire a reputable international organisation to provide initial management, technical design and the delivery of its programs. Under the supervision of the World Bank, the Board of Trustees selected the International Research & Exchanges Board (IREX) to manage the foundation for four years, with Save the Children as a subcontracting consultant.[40] IREX and Save the Children staff includes six international specialists hired for a period four years after which they will be replaced by Kazakh specialists. Channelling recovered stolen assets to developing countries through independent foundations, as the case of the BOTA Foundation in Kazakhstan illustrates, is an experiment that might shape future efforts.

The ideal situation is one in which governments receiving stolen funds have effective accounting mechanisms for all budgeted activities, regardless of the source of the funds. Even with such a high level of efficiency there would still be need for broad-based participation within which the civil society can have a role to play, including that of championing asset recovery. The challenge is that the civil society, and NGOs in particular, are neither accountable nor transparent to direct democratic control. In many developing countries information about civil society – its number, size, area of activity, sources of revenue and the policy framework within which it operates – is not available in any systematic way.[41] While this may be true what matters most is the capacity of civil society to represent interests that are otherwise unrepresented or ignored. In the case of asset recovery civil society may, besides playing watchdog and whistle-blower, encourage respect for legitimate institutions and processes.

39 Stefan Howald, see fn 30.

40 Available at: http://botafoundation.org.kz/index.html?id=68.

41 Ghaus-Pasha, A. (2004) 'The role of civil society organisations in governance', 6th Global Forum on Reinventing Government, Towards Participatory and Transparent Governance, 24–27 May 2005, Seoul, Republic of Korea.

KODJO ATTISSO AND GRETTA FENNER ZINKERNAGEL

Past experience with agreements for the disposal of confiscated assets

Introduction

The General rule on the disposal of recovered assets

In general, a victim country initiates different forms of proceedings in a foreign jurisdiction to recover its stolen assets (through mutual legal assistance [MLA], civil action, etc.). Conversely, in certain cases, a foreign jurisdiction can initiate its own domestic proceedings to recover the assets stolen from another country and laundered in its jurisdiction. Once the proceedings are successfully completed and unlawful assets are confiscated, the question of their restitution arises.

The manner of conducting restitution was one of most contentious issues during the negotiations in the United Nations Convention against Corruption (UNCAC), and it remains extremely delicate. While there was universal agreement that funds should be returned – a major advance over prevailing practice – a common approach to how they should be returned has yet to emerge.

In principle, UNCAC foresees that confiscated assets are returned to their prior legitimate owner. In the case of corruption and misappropriation of State funds, this legitimate owner would be the requesting State, after taking into account the rights of bona fide third parties[1] and possibly the deduction of expenses incurred by the foreign jurisdiction.[2] This approach departs from earlier international treaties under

1 Cf. Article 57 para 1 and 2 UNCAC.
2 Cf. Article 57 (4) UNCAC.

which the confiscating State has ownership of the proceeds.[3] The returned assets thus become property of the recovering country. Most of the time these funds are used to compensate for direct or indirect damages caused by the offence (social projects, corruption prevention programmes, etc.).

However, there are usually no clear or well-developed provisions for the valuation and disposal of the returned assets. In addition, the capacity for the transparent and effective management of the returned funds may be limited in the recovering country.[4] UNCAC for this reason foresees that, where appropriate, countries involved may conclude agreements on a case-by-case basis for the final disposal of confiscated property.[5]

The restitution of looted assets under agreement: Why?

It is well known from past cases that the recovery of assets from foreign jurisdictions is a long, protracted and hazardous endeavour.[6] In earlier cases, it has taken anywhere between five and 20 years to recover and repatriate stolen assets from foreign jurisdictions.[7]

However, and despite the considerable time and resources usually required to recover and repatriate stolen assets, the return and ultimate disposal of confiscated assets is of practical importance. In particular, it is widely recognised that the recovery of stolen assets could provide essential resources for the financing of public services and investments in infrastructure and other programs aimed at social and economic development. In addition, the recovery of stolen assets is seen

3 Legislative Guide for the Implementation of the UNCAC, United Nations 2006, p. 233.
4 Corruption: A Glossary of International Standards in Criminal law, OECD 2008, p. 47.
5 Cf. Article 57 (4) UNCAC.
6 Global crime, illicit funds and nowhere to hide: the World Bank and the United Nations build a global recovery mechanism to fight corruption and the misappropriation of assets, 8 April 2013 by Jiang Wei.
7 See 'Selected case studies', later in this chapter.

as a deterrent to corruption as it fundamentally undermines the key incentive for corruption.

On the other hand, there are legitimate concerns regarding repatriating the confiscated assets to countries where corruption levels remain high and governance is weak. Indeed, this may give rise to fears that the returned assets could be poorly managed or simply embezzled again. To overcome this dilemma, and to prevent or address such a predicament, practical and legislative solutions have been drawn up.

The legal and policy framework on the disposal of returned assets

Before the adoption of UNCAC, there was no policy or international legal framework guiding the disposal and monitoring of repatriated assets.[8] As a result, there were no globally accepted rules to follow when repatriating confiscated assets to requesting countries. Even after the adoption of UNCAC, global practice regarding the disposal of repatriated assets remains unclear. This creates challenges for both returning and receiving States,[9] but also an opportunity to be creative.

Agreement on the disposal of assets under UNCAC: Article 57 (5)

Apart from Article 57 (1) and (2) of UNCAC, Article 57 (5) provides guidance on the modalities for returning stolen assets:

> Where appropriate, States Parties may also give special consideration to concluding agreements or mutually acceptable arrangements, on a case-by-case basis, for the final disposal of confiscated property.

This article is the compromise between two positions that emerged during the negotiations of UNCAC. Developing countries argued for

8 Cf. Planning for the return of stolen assets to Nigeria, UK policy outline, HMG Asset Return Working Group, December 2011.
9 Ibid.

the non-conditional return of stolen assets, identifying themselves as the 'victims' and the countries having hosted the stolen assets in their financial systems as complicit in the original theft. On the other hand, developed countries, usually donors, were concerned about such unconditional return. They were in particular keen to ensure that adequate safeguards were put in place to ensure funds would not be stolen twice. They argued strongly for clauses that would require returned assets to be put to productive, development oriented purposes and that the assets be disposed of transparently. They considered this consistent with the overall statement of purpose in UNCAC's Preamble that highlights the negative impact of corruption on development and the intent of UNCAC to repair the damages done by corruption. This position also seems supported by statements in the UNCAC Legislative Guide in relation to Article 57, which notes that the provisions in this article will 'contribute greatly to the reparation of harm and reconstruction efforts in victim States […]'.[10] However, beyond that statement in the Legislative Guide no further guidance is provided to help clarify the intent of this article; the Technical Guide makes no statement on this provision at all.

Because Article 57 (5) of UNCAC does not provide clear guidance in relation to the final disposal of confiscated assets and because each case is different in relation to the origin of funds, no global standard has emerged in relation to the modalities for the return of stolen assets. We thus suggest looking at past practice and at domestic legislation on the disposal of stolen assets to draw lessons for a potential future policy framework guiding countries in the implementation of Article 57 (5) UNCAC. For this, we will in particular focus on Swiss legislation and practice, due to the particularly proactive and innovative role that Switzerland has played in the past decade or so in recovering and returning stolen assets.

10 Cf. Legislative Guide for the implementation the United Nations Convention Against Corruption, p. 233.

Swiss legislation and practices

The Restitution of Illicit Assets Act (RIAA 2011) recently codified the Swiss practice.[11] This codification follows the practice established by Switzerland over a few years in connection with some of the cases illustrated later in this chapter, though it should be noted that whilst being an important legal basis, the law has limited scope. It applies only in the case where the requesting country qualifies as a failed State.

The most important feature of RIAA in relation to asset recovery is Article 8, which provides that Switzerland will return confiscated assets with the objectives to improve the living conditions of the population in the country of origin and to strengthen the rule of law in that country, while making efforts to combat the impunity of criminals.[12] According to this law, Switzerland and the government of the requesting State determine jointly the final disposal through an agreement.[13] This agreement determines the nature of the programmes of public interest to be financed by the returned assets, the way in which these assets are to be used, the parties involved in the restitution effort, and checks and monitoring mechanisms over the use of the returned assets.[14] Where no such agreement can be reached, Switzerland can unilaterally determine the process of restitution.[15]

RIAA has not yet been tested. Additionally, the Swiss Federal Council in May 2013 opened a consultation procedure on the draft of a new federal act on the freezing and restitution of potentates' assets.[16]

11 The Federal Act on the Restitution of Assets of Politically Exposed Persons obtained by Unlawful Means (RIAA), as the full title of this act reads, entered into force on 1st February 2011.

12 Art. 8 RIAA: The restitution of forfeited assets has the following objectives:
a) to improve living conditions for the people in the country of origin;
b) to reinforce the rule of law in the country of origin and to prevent serious crimes from being committed with impunity.

13 However, an agreement is not an essential condition for restitution (article 9 para. 2 RIAA).

14 Article 9 (3 a–d) RIAA.

15 Article 9 (5) RIAA.

16 Federal Department of Foreign Affairs, 22.05.2013. Available at www.admin.ch/aktuell/00089/index.html?lang=en&msg-id=48933.

Regardless, as we will see in the following section, this legislation and the new draft law correspond to a large degree to past practice by Switzerland. The following cases will, however, also show that even when such practice is established, each case is distinct and no 'one-size-fits-all' solution exists.

Selected case studies

Peru: National monitoring

Overview of the case

The restitution to Peru concerned assets frozen in Switzerland and in the US misappropriated by the former head of Peruvian secret service and presidential advisor, Vladimiro Montesinos Torres,[17] and related people.

In Switzerland, a total of USD 113 million was frozen on two different grounds: part based on the Swiss domestic money laundering prosecution and another part upon the Peruvian authorities' mutual legal assistance request. The restitution by Switzerland to Peru was based primarily on a ruling from the Public Prosecutor's Office of the Canton of Zurich in money laundering proceedings against Vladimiro Montesinos. In 2002, the Public Prosecutor's Office ordered the restitution to Peru of around USD 77.5 million.[18] With the consent of the persons concerned, a further tranche was returned the same year. In addition, in October 2006 Switzerland returned to Peru a further USD

17 Vladimiro Lenin Montesinos Torres was the right hand man of President Alberto Fujimori of Peru, whose presidency lasted from 28 July 1990 to 17 November 2000. Montesinos was officially head of Peru's secret service (Servicio de Inteligencia Nacional SIN) and de facto presidential advisor and national security advisor.

18 In total, Peru has recovered around US 185 million. In addition to the assets returned by Switzerland, USD 33 million from Cayman Islands in 2001, USD 20 million from the United States in 2004 and the balances from other jurisdictions were returned.

11.5 million that originated from accounts held by one of Montesinos' associates.[19]

In the US, USD 20 million was frozen and ultimately repatriated to Peru in 2004.[20]

The disposal of the assets

In 2001, Peru established a special national fund for the administration of forfeited corruption proceeds (FEDADOI)[21] with a view to ensuring the appropriate and transparent management of the proceeds of corruption recovered by the country. While money from the fund went through normal budgetary channels, not Congress but the FEDADOI board, composed of representatives from five government agencies involved in fighting corruption, determined the allocation of these funds.[22]

This mechanism was used to return the Montesinos' assets from Switzerland to Peru. As such, this restitution did not give rise to an agreement whereby the returning State was involved in the determination or monitoring of the final use of the assets.[23] Instead, a national mechanism was used. Nonetheless, the two concerned States agreed on the use of this mechanism prior to the assets being returned.

In the case of the restitution of the Montesinos assets that were confiscated in the US, an agreement between the US and Peru preced-

19 Available at www.bj.admin.ch/content/bj/en/home/dokumentation/medieninformationen/2002/2002-08-20.html.

20 Stolen Asset Recovery (StAR) Initiative: Challenges, Opportunities, and Action Plan, p. 20; Cf. also: Acuerdo Entre el Gobierno de la Republica del Peru y El Gobierno de Los Estados Unidos de America Sobre Transferencia de Activos Decomisados, 21 January 2004.

21 Fondo Special de Administracion del Dinero Obtenido Illicitamente en perjuicio del Estado (FEDADOI): Decreto de Urgencia No 122-2001 (27 October 2001).

22 Cf. Ignacio Jimu, Managing Proceeds of Asset Recovery: The Case of Nigeria, Peru, the Philippines and Kazakhstan.

23 Cf. P. Veglio and P. Siegenthaler, Monitoring the restitution of looted state assets: the role of Multilateral Development Banks, in Recovering Stolen Assets Mark Pieth (ed.), pp. 324–325.

ed the return, whereby it was determined that Peru would invest the returned assets in anti-corruption efforts.[24]

Lessons learned

The establishment of a national mechanism for monitoring the return of stolen assets is generally considered a good practice in line with the principles of ownership and alignment of the Paris Declaration and the Accra Agenda.

Unfortunately, some questionable spending allocations of the funds repatriated to Peru were found.[25] According to reports, it seems items of expenditure were not clearly set out in advance and the funds were used to supplement the annual fiscal budget of agencies that had a member on the FEDADOI board. Other monies were used to finance leisure activities for the police.[26]

Consequently, the arrangement with Peru does not seem to have yielded only satisfactory results. Perhaps, better transparency and oversight of the allocation of assets could have been achieved with a different, possibly multi-stakeholder composition of the FEDADOI board, hence creating more checks and balances.

24 Acuerdo Entre el Gobierno de la Republica del Peru y El Gobierno de Los Estados Unidos de America Sobre Transferencia de Activos Decomisados, 21 January 2004.

25 Cf. the factsheet on 'Asset Recovery – a Breakthrough by the UN Convention against Corruption (UNCAC)' published by the Deutsche Gesellschaft für Technische Zusammenarbeit (GTZ) GmbH, Division State and Democracy in June 2007. Available at: www.giz.de/Themen/en/dokumente/en-gtz-asset-recovery-case-of-montesions-2007.pdf.

26 Ibid.

Nigeria: External ex-post monitoring

Overview of the case

In total, approximately USD 1.2 billion of 'Abacha assets'[27] have been repatriated to the Federal Republic of Nigeria from a number of jurisdictions, including Belgium, Jersey, Luxembourg, Switzerland and the UK. In Switzerland, the Swiss Federal Supreme Court on 7 February 2005 decided to return USD 700 million that had previously been frozen in Switzerland in the context of MLA, domestic criminal proceedings for money laundering and criminal organisation. Out of these USD 700 million, USD 500 million were returned as a result of judicial rulings in Switzerland; USD 200 million were returned based on the consent of the 'owners' of those assets.[28] The court determined that the majority of the Abacha assets frozen in Switzerland were of evident criminal origin (money laundering, fraud and taking part in a criminal organisation).[29] The decision allowed the funds to be handed back to Nigeria successively even though the latter had not issued any forfeiture order. The Swiss Federal Council subsequently determined detailed terms under which the assets were to be restituted.

The disposal of the assets

The USD 700 million were restituted into the Nigerian central budget, based on an agreement on restitution modalities signed in 2005 by

27 General Sani Abacha was the military dictator of Nigeria from 17 November 1993 to 8 June 1998. Nigeria had long been plagued by corruption, but under his rule these practices became blatant and omnipresent. Funds were removed in cash from the central bank, sometimes by truckload, and taken out of the country by members of the Abacha family and their associates. Moreover, inflated public contracts were systematically rewarded to the members of this group. It was only after the end of the dictatorship that the full extend of the practice and the modus operandi were revealed to the general public.

28 Cf. Swiss Federal Council Dispatch 28 April 2010 concerning_Restitution_Illicit_Assets_Act, pp. 39–40.

29 Federal Office of Justice, Press Release, 16 February 2005. Available at: www.ejpd.admin.ch/ejpd/en/home/dokumentation/mi/2005/ref_2005-02-16.html. See the Swiss Federal Supreme Court judgment ATF 131 II 169, 7 February 2005, published leading cases.

Switzerland, Nigeria and the World Bank. Under this agreement, the World Bank was mandated to review the Nigerian budgetary process. Nigeria agreed to use the repatriated funds for specific projects designed to alleviate poverty and to undertake a comprehensive Public Expenditure Management and Financial Accountability Review (PEMFAR). Following pressure from both Swiss and Nigerian civil society organisations (CSOs), efforts were made to ensure civil society participation in this endeavour.[30]

Lessons learned

The direct return of assets into a country's central budget is the preferred modality from the viewpoint of a number of requesting countries as voiced in different international forums. However, and depending on the quality and capacity of the concerned country's administration, it also offers very limited assurance that the returned assets are used according to good practice in public financial management. Indeed in development cooperation, direct budget support is only provided under certain very strict criteria.

The agreement between Nigeria, Switzerland and the World Bank, and in particular the provisions on the review of the Nigerian budgetary process and the PEMFAR, sought to deal with some of these challenges. Regardless, a number of problems arose during the monitoring of the returned assets. Notably, while the Abacha assets were repatriated to the Nigerian treasury in 2005 and 2006, spending of these funds had already begun as part of the 2004 budget. There were also cases in which spending was allocated to projects that had been completed prior to 2004. Consequently, the monitoring and other control mechanisms were implemented largely ex post facto.

The findings of the World Bank review were also mixed. They showed that implementation for all projects had commenced and that most had been completed. However, the quality and impact of projects varied greatly across sectors and significant weaknesses in budget accounting and reporting were identified.

30 See supra notes 25 and 26.

The difficulties experienced show that appropriate budget coding for tracking the use of resources is crucial to demonstrate the developmental impact of asset recovery and to make sure that a maximal part of the population profits from the restitution.[31] They further show that ex post facto monitoring mechanisms are of limited use and that systems should be set-up to enable a continuous monitoring, which also encompasses the stage during which a country may decide on the allocation of funds, the allocation of contracts related to the expenditure of funds, etc.

Kazakhstan: Trilateral monitoring

Overview of the case

The restitution of Kazakh assets took place within the context of a criminal investigation initiated by the Geneva judicial authorities on suspicions of money laundering. These measures were related to a request for assistance from the US in the context of a bribery investigation. In fact, US authorities suspected that funds paid by US citizens into certain Swiss bank accounts were bribes paid by American oil companies to Kazakh officials in exchange for obtaining operating or prospecting rights for oil in Kazakhstan.[32] In 2011, the proceedings led to the confiscation in Switzerland of USD 48 million;[33] these funds had been frozen in accounts in Geneva in the framework of international mutual assistance proceedings involving the US (approx. USD 84 million), as well as proceedings in Geneva (approx. USD 60 million).[34]

Unlike, for example, in the Abacha case, in this case the confiscated assets do not constitute funds that were stolen from Kazakhstan. Instead they originated as bribes paid by a US investor to Kazakh

31 Ibid.

32 Available at: www.star.worldbank.org/corruption-cases/node/18528.

33 Swiss Federal Department of Foreign Affairs. Available at: www.news.admin.ch/message/index.html?lang=en&msg-id=47337.

34 See supra note 32.

officials. Because the ownership of the assets is more complex, it has consequences on the modalities for the restitution of the funds.

The agreement on the disposal of the assets

Given that the confiscated assets related to legal proceedings in Switzerland and in the US, the two countries sought to find a common solution for their repatriation. Discussions between Switzerland, the US and Kazakhstan started in 2003 and aimed to identify a restitution mechanism that would guarantee that the returned assets would be used appropriately.[35]

In 2007, Switzerland, the US, Kazakhstan and the World Bank signed agreements regarding the restitution of USD 84 million of funds through the 'BOTA Kazakh Child and Youth Development Foundation' (BOTA) for projects that benefit the Kazakh population, notably in the domains of youth development and energy efficiency.[36] BOTA's board of trustees is composed of five local Kazakh citizens and one representative each from the governments of the US and Switzerland; its duty is to monitor the expenditure of the money. The foundation is administered by an international NGO set-up by the concerned parties, which operates independently of the Kazakh authorities. The frozen assets are to be transferred in tranches to this foundation and deployed by it under the supervision of a consortium of two internationally recognised institutions (IREX Washington and Save the Children) and with the advice of the World Bank.

Lessons learned

The restitution of the Kazakh assets is an example of trilateral monitoring involving requested countries and the requesting country (though the monitoring does not involve the government in the case of Kazakhstan, as the Kazakh representatives on the BOTA board must

35 Swiss Federal Department of Foreign Affairs. Available at: www.admin.ch/aktuell/00089/index.html?lang=en&msg-id=47337.

36 These are the Conditional Cash Transfer (CCT) program that provides regular cash transfers to poor households, the Tuition Assistance Program (TAP) that disburses grants for higher education and the Social Services Program (SSP) that offers funds to local NGOs to support vulnerable groups.

be independent) and an uninvolved third party, the World Bank. Apart from this tripartite arrangement, the most striking difference of this arrangement to others is that the agreements explicitly prescribe that BOTA has to remain independent from the Kazakh government. BOTA further cannot fund any activity of this government, its ministries or national public institutions.

As compared to other examples, the BOTA monitoring model addresses concerns regarding timeliness (ex ante rather than ex post) and independence of the oversight. The high quality of the oversight provided by the World Bank has been recognised by all parties involved in the Kazakh restitution. The qualitative evaluation of the BOTA programme conducted over the last two years by Oxford Policy Management (OPM) at the request of the concerned parties also confirmed that the implementation of the program across all activities was highly effective for the beneficiaries.[37]

On the other hand, it was found that the administrative costs of the arrangement are extremely high and may end up amounting to one third of the total funds returned to Kazakhstan. This is mainly because entirely new programs and organisations had to be set-up due to the prohibition to fund any (pre-existing) activities of the Kazakh government. During the first two years, up to seven foreign specialists managed the most important aspects of the implementation of the BOTA program. However, since then, the administrative costs have been substantially reduced by the progressive replacement of all foreign specialists by Kazakh managers.

Secondly, while the assets seem to have been spent on highly valuable projects, the question of the sustainability of their impact remains open. Once all assets of the BOTA Foundation have been spent – a little over half the funds remain – no mechanism exists to maintain the foundation's operations. Discussions are ongoing between parties on the future financial sustainability of BOTA. Of course, this project is still ongoing and only the final evaluation of the restitution effort will allow for definite conclusions.

37 See Evaluation of the BOTA Foundation's programmes, Kazahstan, Summary notes 1, 2, 3, Oxford Policy Management, February 2013.

Angola: Monitoring by a bilateral development agency

Overview of the case

The repatriation of assets to Angola by Switzerland relates to two separate cases. In the first case, Switzerland confiscated assets as part of a domestic criminal investigation in Geneva in April 2002, which related to the diversion of Angolan oil revenues supposedly destined to repay the country's debt with Russia. While proceedings were suspended in 2004 after the investigation found no irregularities, a total of USD 21 million held in accounts in the names of four high-ranking Angolan public officials remained frozen as the concerned individuals had not disputed that the money actually belonged to the Angolan State.[38]

In the second case, the backdrop to the restitution were the judicial proceedings conducted by judicial authorities in Geneva regarding alleged money laundering, which at the end of 2008 led to the confiscation of USD 43 million to be restituted to Angola.[39]

The agreement on the disposal of the assets

In the first case, the Swiss and Angolan authorities in 2005 signed an agreement determining that the assets were to be used for social and humanitarian purposes and that the Swiss Agency for Development Cooperation (SDC) should administer the fund and provide support to the programme. The assets were to be held in an account with the Swiss National Bank, on which Angola was named as the beneficial owner but only SDC was authorised to initiate the withdrawal of funds.

The funds were used to finance two projects in the area of mine clearance and agricultural development. Interestingly, at the request of the Angolan government the funds dedicated to the mine clearance

38 Cf. Swiss Federal Council Dispatch 28 April 2010 concerning_Restitution_Illicit_Assets_Act, pp. 39–40. Available at: www.star.worldbank.org/corruption-cases/node/18461.

39 Cf. Press Release of Federal Department of Foreign Affairs, 17.12.2013. Available at: www.news.admin.ch/message/index.html?lang=en&msg-id=47233.

component were used to finance an existing contract for the removal of mines between the country and the Swiss company RUAG.

As for the second restitution case, in 2012 Switzerland and Angola signed another agreement over the repatriation of about USD 43 million. According to information released, the funds will again be administered by SDC as per the earlier arrangement, and they will benefit similar purposes.

Lessons learned

The arrangements between Switzerland and Angola represent particularly close involvement of the requesting country in the restitution and the disposal of confiscated assets. When the two concerned countries have an ongoing relationship in development cooperation, this can be a useful and sustainable arrangement. It is important, as was the case with the Angola restitution, that when assets are channelled back to requesting countries through aid programmes the principles of the Paris Declaration and the Accra Agenda for Action are respected. Notably ownership, alignment and mutual accountability are important principles in this context.

Some Swiss NGOs criticised the use of part of the confiscated assets for a contract with the Swiss company RUAG, as it was perceived as not transparent and reminiscent of the old tied aid principles. Given that this arrangement was chosen at the request of the Angolan government, however, it would seem an adequate choice. This case illustrates some of the risks associated with channelling funds back through bilateral aid programmes, as the requested State may be exposed to potential criticism.

Conclusions

Opinions diverge on the question of the modalities of the restitution and the disposal of returned assets.

Proponents of returning assets based on mutual agreements argue that when corruption remains an issue of great concern in the victim country, making specific arrangements for the disposal of returned assets is the only way to ensure credibility and transparency in the process.

Those reluctant to any such arrangement contend that the unilateral imposition of measures regarding the monitoring of funds is a violation of UNCAC.[40] It may also be that the international legal framework and the technical and political difficulties inherent in public financial management make the monitoring of the use of funds a difficult challenge.[41]

There are two crucial points that everybody seems to agree upon: first, that stolen assets should be returned, and second, that they should not flow back into the pool of criminal financial capital.

UNCAC provides some guidance but this guidance remains vague; different parties disagree on how to interpret it. In the absence of clearer, internationally accepted guidance, it is in the interest of both requesting and requested States for the debate on the arrangements of the disposal and monitoring of repatriated assets to move beyond the contingent issue of 'conditionality'. Instead, a pragmatic approach with the principle aim of ensuring transparency and thus securing the sound use of the returned assets should be taken.

Victim countries enjoy sovereignty and should be able to decide for themselves how to use the recovered stolen assets. However, sovereignty has to be accompanied by a responsibility. Thus, recipient countries must demonstrate their commitment to transparency and accountability and to making sure that the recovered assets are used for the benefit of their population.

A perusal of the case studies in this chapter shows that the appropriate mechanism of restitution strongly depends on the specific situation. Elements that shape particular situations include: the nature of the crime from which the assets have derived (bribery in the case of Kazakhstan or corruption or misuse of function in the case of Nigeria), the origin of the confiscation order (legal proceedings in the request-

40 Stolen Asset Recovery (StAR) Initiative: Challenges, Opportunities, and Action Plan, p. 24.

41 Ibid.

ing or in the requested State) and the capacity of the requested State to ensure a transparent and purposeful disposal of assets.

In States with well-functioning institutions, recovered funds could be integrated in the general budget and their use monitored through a domestic audit mechanism or an external third party, such as the World Bank or a multi-stakeholder arrangement as determined by the recipient countries. On the other hand, in countries with weak or virtually absent public institutions ('fragile or failing States'), it could be more appropriate and effective to conclude an agreement on the disposal and monitoring of the returned assets in line with the country's own development plans through, for example, a bilateral or multinational development agency.

Swiss legislation and practice offers some insight into feasible solutions and the potential pitfalls of some arrangements. The Swiss experience also shows that an amicable solution normally can be found, which usually produces the best results. We are only at the beginning of a constructive debate on this matter. Therefore, more dialogue and more studies into different past restitution arrangements and best practices could assist in building consensus around this issue.

Gretta Fenner Zinkernagel, Charles Monteith, Pedro Gomes Pereira

Conclusion

Ten years have passed since the adoption of the United Nations Convention against Corruption (UNCAC). Despite previous important and noteworthy regional and sectorial efforts to tackle corruption, UNCAC was the first global standard for preventing and combating corruption-related offences. Moreover, it was the first international instrument to bring forth an international standard for the recovery of assets (Chapter V). The international community has applauded the instrument as a whole, as evidenced by its rapid ratification by almost all UN Member States within a very short period of time. Chapter V has been welcomed as particularly innovative; however, its mere existence has also led to high expectations.

As this book has shown, the efforts to prosecute international corruption and money laundering cases and to successfully recover stolen assets have made considerable progress over the last five years. However, not all challenges have been overcome and, apart from a handful of cases, little money has effectively been recovered, especially in international cases. This has led to frustrations among citizens at large, as in the Egypt-Mubarak case, as well as among concerned authorities in requesting and requested States.

On the other hand, we have seen a clear increase in action: cases under investigation with assets at stake have increased exponentially. Ten years ago, there were fewer than 60 foreign bribery offenses under investigation, with the vast majority of them conducted by the US (which, in these cases alone, recovered over USD 5 billion of assets and disgorged profits).[1] Today there are over 500 ongoing investiga-

1 US Department of Justice, and Security and Exchange Commission websites.

tions being conducted by over 50 different countries.[2] By way of example, since 2008 the Serious Fraud Office of the UK has recovered nearly USD 150 million of assets,[3] with the UK as a whole freezing over USD 150 million in 2011–12.[4] Germany too has recovered millions and other countries, like South Korea and Hungary, are quickly scaling up their investigations in spite of all the difficulties they encounter.

Despite these positive developments, the asset recovery process remains complex. It requires the communication and the coordination of multiple interests from the public and private sectors, on the one hand within jurisdictions and on the other hand between jurisdictions. The process transcends different national strategies and policies, ranging from the anti-corruption to the anti-money laundering efforts of each jurisdiction in addition to the applicable international norms and standards. Not only must these interests, policies and strategies interrelate and intertwine in the context of the asset recovery process, but also all must be done in respect of, and through the interaction of different legal traditions and the legal tools within them to prevent and combat corruption-related offences and other serious crimes.

Moreover, as a legal process, the asset recovery process must abide by and respect due process requirements of the jurisdictions involved. Beyond the legal and formal institutional issues above, it has also been noted repeatedly throughout this publication that both domestically and internationally informal institutions and politico-economic considerations play an important role.

There is a consensus that the existing international norms and standards applicable to the asset recovery process suffice, however, challenges remain as to their implementation in practice, be it because of lack of capacity, lack of political will or hurdles to swift cooperation domestically and internationally.

2 320 ongoing investigations cited in the OECD Anti Bribery Working Group Annual Report 2013 from 24 member countries, the remainder from other countries. The OECD report mentions 222 individuals and 90 legal persons being sanctioned. Available at: www.OECD.org.

3 Available at: www. SFO.gov.uk. (News items since 2008.)

4 Available at: www. SOCA.gov.uk.

This being said, cases in recent years have seen new legal practices and tools emerge that have been useful in certain circumstances. For example, the growth of non-conviction based forfeiture (or 'civil recovery') involving the civil courts with civil burdens of proof and civil penalties is a relatively new tool that has helped to recover proceeds of crime, particularly in the UK (and its equivalent of disgorgement of illegal profits in the US). Forfeiture has emerged since in many civil law jurisdictions as well, such as Colombia and Peru, among others.

While not a mandatory provision under UNCAC, illicit enrichment offences target public officials who have large, inexplicable increases in assets. Compulsory disclosure of public official's assets (backed by a criminal offence of failing to declare them) allows for the monitoring of the wealth of public officials and thus is an important tool in preventing and combating corruption-related offences.

Other factors that have proved to be essential in the asset recovery process are proactivity and speed. These concern both authorities from the countries of origin and from the jurisdictions where the alleged stolen assets are hidden. To this end, existing national and local legal frameworks should be used to their full extent, and agencies should look beyond past practices to bring new solutions to the old challenges.

Increasing dynamism and proactivity in the asset recovery process, however, requires a sound knowledge of the process and what it entails. The Basel Institute on Governance established in 2006 its International Centre for Asset Recovery (ICAR), which has been assisting jurisdictions around the world in strengthening their capacities to recover stolen assets. This is done through tailored training, reviewing legal and institutional capacities, and facilitating reform processes. ICAR also offers case specific consultancy and support to law enforcement, prosecution and specialised anti-corruption agencies. Since inception, it has helped over 20 countries in the asset recovery process. Similarly, the United Nations Office on Drugs and Crime and the World Bank jointly established in 2007 the Stolen Asset Recovery (StAR) Initiative, which provides training and capacity building, policy analysis and knowledge building, and assistance to countries in the recovery of stolen assets.

Accessing relevant information quickly is the key building block for all asset recovery investigations. Building trust and enabling communication and dialogue have been most effective when first done through informal channels. Here, specialised networks, such as the Camden Assets Recovery Inter-Agency Network[5] (CARIN) or similar networks in Southern Africa (Asset Recovery Initiative for Southern Africa ARINSA) or in the Americas (*Red de Recuperación de Activos* or Asset Recovery Network – RRAG), are but some of the regional networks currently in existence that assist local authorities in informally coordinating their asset recovery efforts beyond national borders.

Complementary actions include not only those undertaken by national authorities with their foreign counterparts but also those that strengthen public-private partnerships between jurisdictions. Important information communicated from the private sector to national authorities, through suspicious activity reports, is paramount to the success of the asset recovery process.

The role of effective financial intelligence units (FIUs) is also critical for the identification of new trends and money laundering risks and in providing appropriate feedback and follow-up mechanisms between the financial institutions. Increased membership of the Egmont Group, which provides vital coordination between FIUs, by non-EU countries is another encouraging sign of international support for assessing and sharing relevant financial information. Finally, clear, consistent policies issued by regulatory bodies allow the financial industry to be better equipped in assisting others within the asset recovery process.

The Arab Spring has once again initiated the discussion on freezing, seizing and repatriating stolen assets attributed to politically exposed persons (PEPs), their relatives and close business associates. Over USD 1 billion of Arab Spring PEP assets have been successfully frozen, which would not have happened so quickly 10 years ago. The

5 CARIN is an informal network of practitioners who are experts in identifying, tracing, freezing and confiscating proceeds and instrumentalities of crime. It includes national contact points from both law enforcement and prosecution to ensure that all stages of the asset recovery process are covered.

process of confiscating and repatriating those assets still has some way to go, but nonetheless the fact that some countries (and the EU) acted with commendable speed to identify and preserve assets in question represents a new way forward.

Financial and non-financial banking institutions are also obliged by international standards and under the national and international anti-money laundering framework to conduct enhanced due diligence with PEPs. Continuous efforts to increase the sophistication of this practice, whilst also recognising the limits of what banks can do in this regard, will contribute to enabling the swift and consistent freezing of suspicious PEP assets.

The non-financial industry has also not been immune to recent developments. Indeed an exponential increase in foreign bribery law enforcement action has led to the rapid growth of anti-bribery and corruption initiatives within the private sector. The emergence of legislation on proceeds of crime and strengthened anti-money laundering laws has given a strong impetus for this; most recently the UK Bribery Act has incentivised effective anti-bribery and corruption procedures. The confiscation of tainted dividends from an innocent holding company via civil recovery in the UK has made corporates sit-up and take notice, as did the record fine imposed by US and German courts on Siemens. These developments are important in the context of asset recovery, because almost all (legal and illegal) asset movements are done on the backs of companies. Thus, the role of the private sector in preventing and detecting such illicit flows of funds is not to be underestimated.

There is still much to be done, particularly in reducing the number of safe places in the world to hide stolen assets. A great deal has already happened as many so called tax havens have introduced their own anti-money laundering and anti-bribery and corruption regimes and are now routinely cooperating with other enforcers. However, all countries need proceeds of crime legislation (and they need it to include legal persons) in order to deal effectively with unlawfully generated assets. Countries without the equivalent spend far too much time proving and arguing over the loss or damage suffered as a result of acquisitive crime.

Where there is opportunity, however, assets will continue to disappear. Countries are naturally slow to react to changes in criminal behaviour and the concealing of assets. Therefore, much more needs to be done in the potentially tricky area of information and intelligence exchange, not only in regard to cases but also in regard to patterns and trends in asset movements and asset hiding. Data protection issues have been streamlined across EU members, but improvements are needed in non-EU countries to provide the necessary assurance on information handling and security issues. Otherwise, sensitive information cannot be shared. In addition, countries need to improve the accuracy, completeness and transparency of their domestic sources of information, for example in their land and company registries.

Political immunities are also a concern. While they are initially seen as a prerogative, undue checks and balances and privileged jurisdiction may hamper the effectiveness of an investigation or a prosecution for corruption-related offences.

Another challenge for the private and public sector alike is determining beneficial ownership. Being able to identify the person who is in fact behind a corporate vehicle or company, or who actually owns land and other valuable resources, is difficult. This allows criminals to hide the true nature and origin of proceeds of crime arising from corruption-relate offences.

There remain issues over interpretation, for example in proving the origin of assets suspected to be laundered. Although most countries now have anti-money laundering laws that follow an international standard in terms of the different ways money laundering can be committed, there is no consensus on the nature of and extent to which money laundering offences have to be traced back to a predicate offence. In England and Wales, for example, prosecutors can rely on an 'irresistible presumption' that assets must have been generated through unlawful conduct, whilst just specifying the type of unlawful conduct concerned. In other countries, prosecutors must go further and establish a more direct link to an actual predicate offence.

Such concerns mean that increasingly some countries are using illicit enrichment or failure to declare assets legislations. But while it may be a criminal offense in some countries to fail to declare assets, of whatever origin they may be, a failure to declare assets does not automatically mean that the assets concerned were generated through unlawful activity. Moreover, as many countries do not criminalise a failure to declare assets or illegal enrichment, there are inevitable issues concerning reciprocity and requests for mutual legal assistance.

There have been issues in the UK regarding a lack of transparency as to why civil recovery orders are used instead of conventional prosecution. Recent guidance from the Attorney General[6] outlining some policy issues and concerns has helped to provide some clarity, and it will be of considerable use to those countries considering introducing a civil recovery regime.

The sheer number of interested parties involved, the cross border issues, together with the need for rapid informal communication and consequent building of trust means that authorities dealing with asset recovery cases have to consider strategy building in each case. An investigation/case strategy must be put in place to help navigate the issues discussed above, as well as local ones. No one can achieve anything on his or her own and this is particularly true of asset recovery, which requires tremendous coordination between the requesting and requested countries. Informal and formal mechanisms of communication and coordination need to be established at the earliest opportunity and set out in the strategy. With so many different players involved, agreement needs to be reached regarding who does what and when. Too often this is completely missing from case strategies.

We have highlighted some of the recent challenges as well as some of the recent trends. We have found that many countries now have sufficient capacity and the right laws and regulations backed by good anti-corruption and anti-money laundering enforcers who are armed with the right powers. There has been growth in transparency and accountability. There has also been growth in non-governmental and civil society anti-corruption awareness, as illustrated by the street protests during the Arab Spring – a recurring and very prominent theme of which was the stealing of those in power from those without power. All in all many of the lessons learnt in the last 10 years have

6 Asset Recovery Powers for Prosecutors: Guidance and Background Note. Available at: www.gov.uk.

helped overcome or mitigate some of the challenges associated with asset recovery.

At the same time challenges remain. Notably, we are still in the middle of a paradigm shift that is leading us away from the traditional approach to preventing and combating crime with its primarily domestic focus towards a much more interconnected, international, more complex, but ultimately more effective approach. At least equally difficult, as hinted at earlier, is that politico-economic factors will continue to interfere with the sincere efforts of asset recovery practitioners around the world.

As such, there remains much work to be done, not only in making legislations more comprehensive and enabling and building capacities to use them but also in breaking down political barriers, domestically and internationally, to recovering stolen assets. Armed with the right tools and a resolute determination, countries can increasingly expect to overcome future asset recovery issues with some confidence.